W9-BSB-239

The Church in the British Era

JOHN S. MOIR

The Church in the British Era

From the British Conquest to Confederation

Volume Two of *A History of the Christian Church In Canada.* General Editor: John Webster Grant

McGRAW-HILL RYERSON LIMITED

Toronto Montreal New York London
Sydney Johannesburg Mexico Panama Düsseldorf
Singapore Rio de Janeiro Kuala Lumpur New Delhi

THE CHURCH IN THE BRITISH ERA

Volume Two of A HISTORY OF THE CHRISTIAN CHURCH IN CANADA

ISBN 0-07-092959-9

Library of Congress Catalog Card Number 73-37321

1 2 3 4 5 6 7 8 9 THB-72 0 9 8 7 6 5 4 3 2

Printed and bound in Canada

To the Memory of H. H. (Nick) Walsh
Teacher, Scholar, Friend

Foreword by the General Editor

The publication of these volumes is a direct result of the initiative and persistent prodding of the late Dr. Lorne Pierce. Dr. Pierce had determined many years in advance that The Ryerson Press, of which he was Editor-in-Chief, could most fittingly contribute to Canada's centenary celebrations by sponsoring a definitive study of the place of the Christian Church in her history. His hope, now brought to fruition, was that a team of church historians should collaborate on a three-volume work. Dr. Pierce foresaw not only the need but the difficulty of such an undertaking. There were a number of specialized studies, and a few denominational histories, but source material was scattered and the necessary community of scholars was lacking. Instead of admitting defeat he set out, typically, to create the conditions under which an inclusive history could be written. He stimulated the collection and organization of archival material, especially within his own communion, The United Church of Canada. He played a leading part in the formation in 1959 of the interdenominational Canadian Society of Church History, within whose membership he hoped to find his authors. He published a number of studies upon which a larger work could be based, notably Dr. Walsh's *The Christian Church in Canada* (Ryerson, 1956).

The team of writers took shape during early meetings of the Canadian Society of Church History, and the story most naturally lent itself to division into periods of French, British and Canadian dominance. Assignments were soon made: the French era to Professor H. H. Walsh, the British Era to Professor John S. Moir, and the Canadian Era to myself.

The work now being offered is the most comprehensive account of the history of the church in Canada that has yet been written. In the main it is based on past studies, but these have been extensively supplemented by original research. We hope that readers will find it both useful and enjoyable, and that students will find in it suggestions for areas of future research.

Each author has been left free to interpret the evidence in his own way, and it is only to be expected that some differences in viewpoint will be evident. Nevertheless, the project has been a team effort. There has been constant mutual consultation and criticism, and all the writers have accepted two general assumptions about the nature of their task.

One of these assumptions, embodied in the reference of the title to "the Christian Church" rather than to churches, is that this history should be ecumenical in both range and sympathy. Such a commitment does not imply an ironing out or even a playing down of the controversial elements in the story. It does involve a recognition that the history of each communion is part of the history of all communions. This assumption is not easy to maintain in dealing with periods when Canadians tended to regard their various denominations as, in effect, so many separate religions, but without it the story loses any vital link with the common source and common destiny that are integral to the existence of the Christian Church.

The other assumption is that the Canadian locale should be taken seriously. Once again writers are bound to no particular estimate of the significance of the existence of Canada as a nation but only to an awareness of the setting within which the church has lived and worked. This assumption is no easier than the other, for much of Canadian church history has seemed to consist of little more than the importation of European and American forms and folkways. Inevitably, however, the Canadian environment has affected the churches and in turn been affected by them, with results that have sometimes received inadequate recognition from both religious and secular historians. The writers of these volumes concern themselves not only with the institutional development and the devotional life of the church, but also with its public witness and especially with its relation to the development of the Canadian character.

The time at which the present project comes to fruition is in many ways fortunate. On the one hand, the recent spectacular broadening of dialogue among members of various branches of the Christian Church is beginning to make an ecumenical perspective more natural for all of us. On the other, the growing interest in church history evident in many university departments is initiating a dialogue with secular historians that promises to be equally rewarding. This work will amply justify itself if it leads to a quickening of interest that will result in the filling of some of the many gaps in our knowledge and understanding that still remain.

Each writer will undoubtedly wish to acknowledge some particular debts. I am grateful to Dr. Moir for his constant willingness to give and receive criticism graciously, to The Ryerson Press for conceiving the project, and to McGraw-Hill of Canada for adopting it. I should especially like to record my indebtedness to the late Dr. Walsh for the constant inspiration of his enthusiasm and the stimulus of his creative mind, as well as my deep regret that he did not live to see the completion of our work. It has been our collective wish that this series may be a worthy memorial to Dr. Lorne Pierce, scholar, churchman and Canadian.

JOHN WEBSTER GRANT

Preface

Since the appearance in 1967 of H. H. Walsh's *The Church in the French Era* our friend "Nick" Walsh has died and events have conspired to delay the publication of the remaining two volumes in the series. For me at least the additional time has meant an opportunity to deepen my own knowledge of the period being surveyed. Unlike either of its companion volumes the subject matter of this one lacks any overriding theme or unifying factor which can draw its parts into a cohesive whole. During the century under discussion the British colonies in North America lived separate lives, cherished different traditions, and in a host of ways manifested a strong sense of their own distinctive provincial identity. No adequate system of communications or transportation existed to foster common interests before Confederation, and Confederation itself was an imposed and artificial unity rather than one that grew from any pre-existing feeling of nationhood. Nova Scotians or Upper Canadians might be fiercely loyal to their own colony and to the empire, with little awareness that they were neighbours in British North America. The same condition of isolation was true of the Christian churches in two ways. Heirs to almost two thousand years of Christian tradition, the churches in British North America existed not only as separate bodies which at best sent fraternal greetings annually to units of the same denomination in the sister colonies, but they lived in spiritual and sometimes even physical separation from other churches in their own province.

To attempt to sketch the history of such diverse geographical, organizational and ideological elements over the course of one hundred years must inevitably produce a patchwork in which the reader will seek in vain for certain familiar incidents, personalities or trends which the author has regretfully but arbitrarily excluded because of the physical limits of the book. The only palliative for this subjective approach may be the select bibliography which the author hopes will satisfy his critics while stimulating the general reader. Although responsibility for the contents of this volume is mine alone, I must express my thanks for moral support and critical advice to my colleagues, H. H. Walsh and John Webster Grant, to the Canada Council and Carleton University for a year's leave of absence from teaching duties which permitted me to cover most of the basic research, and to Carleton University and Scarborough College, University of Toronto, for stenographic assistance. My research was facilitated by the kindness and cooperation which I invariably received at numerous archives and libraries, and my personal indebtedness for aid and helpful suggestions extends to such a vast circle as to preclude paying those persons the individual acknowledgments that I know they deserve.

JOHN S. MOIR

The Church in the British Era

ONE

Transatlantic Heritage

The British conquest of New France in 1759 gave promise of a continental empire in North America, stretching from the Atlantic to the Pacific and from the Gulf of Mexico to Hudson Bay. The famous Proclamation of 1763 spelled out clearly the official policy for the imperial future—English law, English political institutions and England's religion would now be extended to the newly acquired territories to create a unified pattern of life throughout the vast region. Already in the 1750s immigration and the resettlement of the Acadians of Nova Scotia had begun the process of Anglification in that colony taken from the French in 1713, and now the intention was to model Canada, the former French colony on the St. Lawrence, after Nova Scotia and the other thirteen English colonies.

In this new North American empire the place of the Christian churches had been determined over the previous century and a half. Not religious unity in the European tradition, but religious diversity, had become the pattern in the older colonies where a veritable kaleidoscope of denominations was firmly entrenched, a few as official state churches and the rest as tolerated religions. Their very diversity reflected the troubled religious history of western Europe since the Reformation, and although the local needs of the North American environment had shaped them to a greater or lesser degree in forms different from their European parent churches, whether Protestant or Catholic, still the dominant influence in their growth in the New World remained their transatlantic heritage of eighteen centuries of Christianity.

RELIGION IN THE AGE OF REASON

The scientific revolution of the seventeenth century, personified by Descartes and Newton, had led men of the eighteenth century to distrust tradition and to reject authority unless verified by the experimental method. The new science appeared at first to prove God's wisdom and power as reflected in the created universe, but to the eighteenth century philosophers God became impersonal—a great architect or mechanic, at most a Supreme Being, who, having set the machine-universe in harmonious and orderly motion, neither could nor would interfere with the natural laws that governed its operation. God was Reason, and Reason soon became God.[1] The century of the Enlightenment that opened on this seemingly harmless note of optimism—natural laws could point man the way to perfection in this world—closed, however, on a note of deepest scepticism as David Hume cast doubt on the very existence of the Grand Geometrician of the Universe.

Enlightenment philosophy may have been English in origin but it was Frenchmen such as Voltaire who popularized the new and destructive mood of scepticism.[2] In France the scathing attacks of the *philosophes* on the organized church were met by a repressive and unbending orthodoxy rather than by any reasoned rebuttal. In England the restrained arguments of the deists were received first with a disarming openness and then were countered by three intellectual giants—William Law, the mystic who influenced John Wesley's religious thought; Bishop Berkeley, father of the science of psychology; and the foremost theologian in this antitheological age, Samuel Butler, whose *Analogy of Religion* (1736) turned the weapon of reason against the deists themselves by emphasizing the reasonable probability of religion.

Rationalism—the cold philosophy—was displayed to all as a poor substitute for the love of a self-sacrificing God, but the cult of Reason nevertheless left its mark on human history. Both the American and French Revolutions testify to its influence, yet in the end religion survived because the orthodox faith of the masses remained unaffected. On the transatlantic branches of the Christian churches the Age of Reason had an even slighter effect. In New France the Roman Catholic Church was virtually untouched by the Enlightenment at the time of the British Conquest in 1760; and in the next generation the very victory of Reason in the American and French revolutions produced a political and religious reaction among the churches in the remaining British colonies in America that fostered a return to orthodox Christian beliefs. From the Conquest to Confederation the greatest theological influences in British North America were Butler's *Analogy*, William Paley's popular *Evidences of Christianity* and the Catholic writings of Jacques Bossuet; for each of these men in his own way had heralded the age of renewed faith, the nineteenth century.

Just as the Christian churches in colonial North America mirrored the thought, worship and government of their mother churches across the Atlantic, so too their architecture, music and religious art reflected this overseas dependence. The Age of Enlightenment witnessed religious laxity and indifference in Europe, yet paradoxically it was an age of unparalleled cultural achievements in religious life. Baroque architecture, art and music which emphasized light and space were in revolutionary contrast to the sombre majesty of Gothic forms. The new architectural style, at its best in such fine examples as the colonnade of St. Peter's in Rome, was modified in England first by Christopher Wren, whose classic parish churches rising from the ashes of London's great fire were in turn the model for such graceful churches as James Gibbs's St. Martin's-in-the-fields. In North America Gibbs's churches were widely imitated in the eighteenth century, though usually on a smaller scale and with wood replacing stone construction, and ornamentation reduced and simplified.

The decoration of church interiors with painting and sculpture was alien to the Reformation tradition, and North American Protestants have been more uncompromising in this matter than Europeans. The Roman Catholic Church, however, continued to patronize the visual arts. In New France excellent woodcarving for church decoration was an established tradition long before the British Conquest, while to embellish parish churches further local Canadian painters produced competent but hardly masterful canvases depicting religious themes.

If church architecture was the first glory of that age, church music was certainly the second. The Enlightenment produced Handel and Mozart in Europe, and Henry Purcell and William Boyce in England. Religious oratorios and anthems were the popular musical forms wherein choir and organ could display their virtuosity, although in North America sheet music and instruments were expensive and few people had sufficient musical training to play or enjoy the baroque music of contemporary Europe. Colonial congregations, forced to rely on music of a simple form which the laity could master, emphasized congregational singing as a central part of the worship service, and so reinforced its traditional role among such bodies as the Presbyterians who viewed instrumental music as one of the Devil's works.

While the churches in North America were obvious extensions—theologically, liturgically and organizationally—of the Christian communions of western Europe, differences inevitably developed in the process of their growth in the New World environment, and those differences go far to explain the difficulty of finding a unifying theme for their history in the British era of Canadian history. All the churches shared a common heritage of Christianity and western European civilization, and all were operating within the political structure of the British Empire. Except for moments of general crisis, however, each denomination showed little awareness of its neighbours, and less ecumenical spirit. The hallmark of religious life was strident denominationalism; yet even individual denominations were divided and isolated into regional organizations by the undeniable fact that great distances and local loyalties inhibited communication between the colonies until the very eve of Confederation.

The growth of the Christian Church and of the denominations can best be understood by examining specific regions—the Maritimes, united by the sea but divided by patriotism towards one's own colony; the two Canadas, Upper and Lower, linked by the St. Lawrence River but isolated by language and to a lesser degree by religion; and the West, half a continent inhabited by a few thousand natives, fur traders and a sprinkling of settlers, cut off from the eastern colonies by the barrier of the Canadian Shield. Like the colonies, the churches in the British era developed in isolation one from the other and even from members of their own persuasion in other places.

The churches in British North America constantly faced the same challenge as the settlers—to meet, conquer or compromise with the presence of an emerging frontier society. The frontier, however, and all that that word implied—rude living conditions, isolated settlements, the struggle for a subsistence and the dearth of civilizing forces—was a spatial, not a temporal concept. The frontier moved forward erratically across the face of British North America, and behind it fine churches, good schools, transportation facilities, social amenities and cultural activities appeared in each area at different times. The frontier admittedly influenced aspects of Canadian life in the British era, but it could never supplant the centuries-old transatlantic heritage that settlers brought with them.

THE BRITISH RELIGIOUS HERITAGE

Older historians have described the English religious scene in the eighteenth century as being in a dark age of spiritual decline. This estimate not only ignores the tremendous impact of John Wesley's Methodist revival but it does less than justice to the national Church of England itself.[3] In that age of poverty, hardship, immorality and injustice there were incompetent clergy who held multiple offices and failed to fulfill their spiritual duties, but such men were the exception rather than the rule. More serious were the problems of the great discrepancy between the lavish incomes of the bishops and the meagre salaries of parish clergy, and of the too intimate connection of state and church. A bishop's salary might be reckoned in thousands of pounds when the average wage of a vicar or curate was under £50, but the clerical profession was still so attractive that the supply of ministers was always greater than the demand.

Since the church was controlled through political patronage like any other branch of government, promotion depended on one's politics and the assistance of a political friend. Bishops were expected to be ardent workers for the Whigs, the political party that monopolized power for half of the eighteenth century. To silence supporters of the exiled House of Stuart and ensure at least passive support from the lesser clergy, Convocation—the parliament of the church—had been suppressed by the government in 1717. Thereafter for one hundred and thirty-three years the Church of England had no governing body of its own and its spiritual functions were often subordinated to political purposes. One result of this Erastian or state control of the national church had been government's consistent refusal to establish bishops in the American colonies where the church might have been employed as an agent to promote loyalty. When a sustained but belated effort was made to create a colonial church establishment, after 1760, the American colonists reacted in violent hostility against this supposed double threat to their political and religious liberties. The so-called "episcopal plot" played no small part in promoting the American revolution against English institutions.[4]

Following, as it did, the civil war and political chaos of the seventeenth century, the Age of Enlightenment in England was undoubtedly an era of stability and material progress, and the Church of England was no worse than the secular society in which it lived. Anglicanism could still claim virtually the whole five million population of the nation as its members. Only one person in twenty-five was a nonconformist or dissenting member of a tolerated Protestant church, less than one in a hundred belonged in the Roman Catholic fold. Nonconformity as a religious faith existed legally in England, but Congregationalists, Presbyterians, Baptists and any other non-Anglican Protestants were politically second-class citizens, while the status of Roman Catholics was even lower. The Corporation and Test Acts, passed in 1661 and 1673, practically excluded all non-Anglicans from Parliament, the armed forces, universities, courts and municipal offices by requiring them to take the sacrament of the Lord's Supper according to the Anglican rite and to make a declaration against transubstantiation. Although in the cynically tolerant atmosphere of the eighteenth century Protestant nonconformists frequently evaded these regulations with the approval of the government, the statutes were rigorously enforced against Roman Catholics and remained officially the law of the land until the 1820s.

The most momentous religious development in eighteenth-century England was unquestionably the rise of Methodism.[5] John Wesley, born in 1703 to a pious Anglican minister's family, had associated during his university days at Oxford with the small group whose regularity of devotional practices earned them the nickname of Methodists. During a brief and unhappy ministry in Georgia, John Wesley was influenced by his contact with the pietistic Moravian brethren. Soon after his return to London he experienced, in 1738, a religious conversion. Thereafter Wesley's attempts to bring sinners to repentance by preaching led to his exclusion from many pulpits of the established church and to physical attacks by enraged defenders of the religious status quo. Wesley's reply to opposition was to copy, however reluctantly, the example of his Oxford acquaintance George Whitefield, the Calvinistic evangelist, by preaching out-of-doors to the spiritually destitute multitudes of miners and factory hands in areas where the Church of England failed to provide new churches for the expanding population. With his *Discipline*, published in 1743, Wesley began the close organization which became the foundation of the future Methodist Church. Local classes were served by itinerant preachers (usually unordained) who travelled a circuit of preaching stations within a given area.

Although Wesley insisted that he and his Methodist societies were part of the national church, his gathering of the first conference of Methodist workers—mostly Anglican laymen—in 1744 was a step towards separation from the Church of England. For a long while he refused to ordain his own clergy but the necessity of providing an ordained ministry for an independent Methodist body in the United States after the Revolution completed the institutional separation of Methodism from Anglicanism.

Doctrinally the Methodists remained one with the Arminian Church of England—"God willeth all men to be saved" was Wesley's reply to Calvinism. The essential difference of the new Anglican sect was the religious fervour of its members which marked them as "fanatics" and "enthusiasts" in the minds of their "reasonable" and comfortable contemporaries. The secret of Methodism's growth really lay in the conditions of an England ripe for awakening and in Methodism's highly efficient system of organization, a system that proved itself admirably suited to the needs of scattered frontier settlements in America too. The conservative social gospel of Methodism exerted powerful and successful pressure (directly through Methodism and indirectly through such Anglican evangelicals as William Wilberforce) to end slavery, to reform a vicious legal code, to reduce poverty, drunkenness, profanity and gambling, while promoting the Christian virtues of charity, self-help, industry, thrift, sobriety and loyalty to the God-ordained political order. When Wesley died in 1791 he had travelled twenty-five thousand miles around Britain on horseback, preaching and visiting, and the Methodists numbered 135,000 on two continents. To John's inspired sermons and simplified Anglican liturgy, his brother Charles Wesley had added more than six thousand hymns for popular use in the Methodist societies.

The Church of Scotland, restored as the national church in 1690, underwent in the eighteenth century a marked relaxation of its previously harsh Calvinism.[6] The hierarchic system of church courts, rising from the congregational session through presbytery and synod to the highest court, the General Assembly, remained intact; but Calvin's keystone dogmas of man's total depravity and salvation for God's elect alone were gradually eroded by the more optimistic and humanistic view of redemption for all mankind. Within the Kirk two distinct groups struggled for control of the assembly, the larger group being known as the Moderates, purveyors of an uninspiring orthodoxy, who dominated the church and sought only "the tranquility of order." Opposing the comfortable apathy of the Moderates was the small but growing body of Scottish evangelicals, who, true to Calvinist doctrines, were theologically at odds with the incipient Arminianism of the Moderates.

Although the Moderates were ready to accept more state control over the Church, Parliament's restoration in 1712 of the medieval practice of patronage—the appointment of clergymen to particular congregations by lay patrons instead of by church courts—caused the secession of Ebenezer Erskine and a handful of fellow clergy to form the Associate Presbytery in 1732. This seceding body was in turn split in 1747 into Burghers and Anti-burghers, depending on whether they accepted or rejected an oath required of burgesses in Edinburgh, Glasgow and Perth, which implied recognition of the Church of Scotland. The patronage question caused a further split in the established Church in 1752 when the Reverend Thomas Gillespie denied the right of the General Assembly to force or intrude a minister on an unwilling congregation. Other ministers who supported "non-intrusion" joined Gillespie to form the Relief Presbytery in 1761. Despite the laissez-faire attitude of the Moderates the issue of church-state relations continued to simmer in Scotland for another four generations.

The lack of religious vitality within the Presbyterian body curtailed all missionary impulses throughout the eighteenth century. More serious, it led to the growth of Unitarianism among English Presbyterians. But until the nineteenth century formalism, traditional differences of opinion on church-state relations, the gradual sapping of Calvinism by deist influences, and the lack of spiritual vitality and sense of mission left the Church of Scotland in particular and Presbyterianism in general as a ineffective religious force in old Scotland and British North America.

THE RELIGIOUS BACKGROUND OF THE OLDER BRITISH COLONIES

In England's oldest American colony, Virginia, the colonial assembly established the Church of England as the official religion in 1619. Subsequently parishes were erected on the English pattern and all citizens were required to pay tithes. Nevertheless the established clergy suffered from meagre salaries and difficult travel conditions which discouraged capable priests from leaving their comfortable situations in England to serve the colonists. Neighbouring Maryland, first settled in 1634, had been a haven for persecuted Roman Catholics until the Glorious Revolution of 1688 when it was converted into a royal and Anglican colony. Lacking a bishop and a sufficient supply of priests, many of the twenty-five thousand Roman Catholics in America who depended on the religious services of a handful of dedicated Jesuits found a new refuge in William Penn's "Holy Experiment," Pennsylvania, where all religions were treated as equals. North of Maryland, however, the Church of England was never really established, although it was prominent in New York, New Jersey and Pennsylvania, and present in New England.[7]

The need of the colonial church for support from home had been partially met by the founding of the Society for the Promotion of Christian Knowledge in 1698 (to foster Christian education) and by the founding in 1701 of the Society for the Propagation of the Gospel in Foreign Parts (to obtain and support missionaries). With the help of the two societies and an extensive recruiting program for clergymen the condition of the colonial church improved considerably by the first half of the eighteenth century. Yet the church's difficulties were compounded throughout the whole colonial period by the adamant refusal of English church and state alike to sanction a colonial episcopate, the Bishop of London having been vested with control of the church in all overseas possessions in 1667. Without a bishop in the colonies ordination and confirmation could only be had in England, though communion was not strictly reserved to the handful of confirmed church members.

In those colonies where Anglicanism was established, the Church of England paid a high price in religious indifference because of its connection with the English government, while in New England it faced open hostility from the dissenting majority who harboured memories of persecution in England. Weak as the Church of England was in the colonies, non-Anglican Americans in the eighteenth century reacted violently against every suggestion that bishops be sent to the New World, in the belief that such plans were a reactionary plot by the mother country to curb the independence of Englishmen in America. By the time of the American Revolution many colonists were ready to turn the dictum of James I, "No bishop, no king," to their own political purposes.

The settlement of New England, that beautiful but rugged area of the North Atlantic coast, began in the Cape Cod area in 1620 when the Pilgrim Fathers, a separatist group from the Church of England, sought refuge from persecution by fleeing to the New World. In old England the harsh repression of the Puritans, the reforming group within the Church of England, led to the founding of a second asylum-colony in Massachusetts Bay in 1628, and it in turn gave birth to New Hampshire, Rhode Island and Connecticut primarily as a result of further religious divisions among the Puritans themselves. The Puritan preference for congregational autonomy within the Anglican Church soon developed in America into Congregationalism, a distinct denomination and avowed enemy of Anglicanism after the collapse of Cromwell's Puritan Commonwealth in 1660.

Puritan theology in New England was the Calvinism of the English dissenters—Bible-centred and regulated by the Westminster Confession (though modified in the various confessions adopted in the colonies). Original sin had left man totally depraved, and salvation through a personal religious experience was available only to God's elect. Since salvation was required for church membership, and that membership was a prerequisite for political rights, the New England colonies were supposedly ruled by saints who imposed a rigid code of personal behaviour. The Puritans prohibited by law such recreations as dancing or card-playing, the celebration of Christmas and other "popish" festivals, and all forms of physical labour on the Sabbath. Puritan enthusiasm for "holy living" could and did carry it into excesses of zeal, against immoral persons, against other denominations, and even against suspected deviates as in the case of twenty "witches" executed at Salem. In the judgment of a leading American church historian, "Toleration came slowly, painfully and bloodily."[8]

By the end of the seventeenth century, the iron grip of the "saints" on the government of the New England colonies was gradually relaxing as new laws extended political rights to all Englishmen except Roman Catholics. Although Congregationalism predominated in those colonies, just as Anglicanism did in the southern colonies, both regions were moving towards the religious pluralism already in evidence in the middle colonies —New York, New Jersey, Pennsylvania and Delaware. Popular opposition to the Baptists and their ideal of freedom of conscience had lessened and in 1707 the first continuing Baptist Association in the New World was formed at Philadelphia. Like the Baptists, the Quakers suffered violent persecution in New England until they found a refuge after the 1670's in New Jersey and Pennsylvania, two colonies owned by Quakers and dedicated to political and religious freedom.

Religious persecution in Germany had been responsible for the migration to America of three other religious groups—the Mennonites, Moravians and Lutherans—the first descended from sixteenth-century Anabaptists, the second a product of the mystical German pietist movement that had influenced John Wesley. By 1710 two waves of Mennonites, the first German, the second Swiss, had reached Pennsylvania where their simplicity of dress and deportment made easy their absorption into the "Plain Folk" atmosphere founded by the Quakers. The Moravian Brethren, or Unitas Fratrum, came to America first as missionaries to the Indians in 1735, but a regular Moravian settlement was soon formed in Pennsylvania. Most of the early Lutheran settlers had also been deeply influenced by pietism, but a shortage of ministers delayed until 1742 the organization of a separate synod. The Dutch Reformed Church dated its origins in America from the Dutch settlement at Manhattan in the early 1600s.

Most Presbyterians in America had arrived from Ulster after 1700 and by 1716 a synod of four presbyteries, containing forty churches, was established. This American Synod was soon torn by the issue of subscription to the Westminster Confession as a requirement for ordination, a conflict postponed rather than solved by a compromise declaration adopted in 1729.

In the New World these denominations had usually identified with the growing sense of a separate colonial existence, expressed most frequently in the formation of indigenous religious organizations whose cultural heritage from the old world was balanced by institutional autonomy. Only a few churches, like the Dutch Reformed, remained under the direct jurisdiction of their European parental bodies. Characteristics of colonial life in the eighteenth century were general acceptance of the principle of toleration, a growing belief in the separation of church and state, a tendency to puritanical morality, a sense of independence arising from neglect by the mother churches, and a spiritual vitality engendered through the American revivalistic movement known as the Great Awakening.

The Great Awakening swept the American colonies in the mid-eighteenth century, and was perhaps the most momentous development in American religious history.[9] As early as the 1720s a revival movement had begun in New Jersey within the Dutch Reformed Church, and William Tennent opened his "Log College" in Pennsylvania in 1727 to train Presbyterian ministers for revivalistic work. A less sensational revival began about 1733 among Congregationalists in various Massachusetts towns through the preaching of Jonathan Edwards. But the greatest impetus and unifying force for these separate groups came from the Calvinistic Anglican George Whitefield, a former associate of John Wesley. During his second visit to the colonies in 1739 Whitefield preached his sensational message of personal conversion to nearly six thousand people at one time in Philadelphia and in the autumn of 1740 he spent six weeks touring New England. Whitefield inspired many of the leaders of the Great Awakening and set the pattern for future revivals with his emotional preaching and itinerant ministry. The fire of revivalism lit by Whitefield spread quickly throughout the New England colonies, sweeping up members of most Protestant churches and many merely nominal Christians.

Although the effects of the Great Awakening were felt in all the colonies, its greatest impact was in New England where it spawned a separatist movement within the established Congregational churches. The separatists, or "New Lights," wanted to reestablish personal conversion as a test of church membership and restore the practice of ordination by congregations rather than by ministerial associations. Despite the implied Arminianism of the Awakening the separatists emphasized the doctrine of election, urged maximum use of the means of grace as a necessity for salvation and sought for visible proofs of salvation in their ministers and themselves. Copying Whitefield's example they adopted the use of itinerant clergy and exhorters which the Congregational establishment had so firmly opposed. In a vain attempt to stop the spread of revivalism, New Lightism and separatism, the conservative group, or "Old Lights," imposed increasingly stringent rules, but by 1800 some two hundred and fifty separatist Congregational churches had been formed in New England.[10]

Among American Presbyterians the seeds of division had already been planted by the subscription controversy before Whitefield's revival promoted the separation of the "Old Side" conservative Presbyterians from the evangelical New Side in 1741. The reunion of the two sides seventeen years later was an unqualified victory for revivalism since the New Side had more than tripled its strength while the Old Side had lost members. Although the Baptist fellowship in the colonies was relatively unaffected by the Great Awakening, the fact that many separatists also rejected infant baptism led a majority of the separated churches to merge with the Baptists in New England, New York, New Jersey and Pennsylvania. This has helped to make the Baptists the largest Protestant denomination in the United States.

NOVA SCOTIA AND NEWFOUNDLAND—NEGLECTED COLONIES IN THE NORTH

In the year 1760 Britain held all the explored regions of North America north of Florida. In addition to the thirteen older colonies on the seaboard, the Hudson's Bay Company territories in the north and Britain's oldest overseas possession, Newfoundland, she had, as a result of the war with France, consolidated her hold on Nova Scotia by capturing the fortress of Louisbourg on Cape Breton in 1758 and had united and safeguarded all these vast lands in 1759 by conquering New France. It was a glorious prospect for an undivided transatlantic empire that greeted the youthful new king, George III, in 1760; yet within a generation its richest parts had been lost in the holocaust of the American Revolution. All that then remained of the transatlantic empire were the lands on the northern periphery—Nova Scotia, Newfoundland, Prince Edward Island, Quebec and the vast, empty territories of the Hudson's Bay Company—the remnants of a dream that had failed, but the nucleus of the future kingdom of Canada.

Nova Scotia had been acquired from France in 1713 by the Treaty of Utrecht, although the colony's western boundaries remained so ill-defined that France effectively controlled the area of present-day New Brunswick for the next half-century. The Acadians—French Roman Catholic settlers in Nova Scotia—had been encouraged by Britain to remain on their farms and, since the treaty guaranteed their freedom of religion, the Bishop of Quebec sent priests to serve them by permission of the governors of Nova Scotia.[11] No effort was made by Britain to send English settlers into the colony, so that thirty-five years after the area became British the French-speaking Roman Catholic Acadians still composed virtually the whole of its population. The only difficulty between Britain and the Acadians had arisen over a proposed oath of loyalty to the new sovereign which the Acadians rejected out of fear that they might be compelled to fight against France. Unwilling to lose such valuable settlers British officials did not press the issue of the oath for several years until it became apparent about midcentury that Britain and France must inevitably and soon fight a war for total domination in North America.

By the peace terms of 1713 France had retained Ile St-Jean (now Prince Edward Island) and Cape Breton, and on the latter island France had begun in 1719 to construct the great naval fortress of Louisbourg, the Gibraltar of the Atlantic. Louisbourg was intended to protect France's remaining colony, New France, the settlement along the St. Lawrence River, but the fortress also threatened British interests in the fishing banks and the ocean approaches to the American colonies. Thus it was to offset Louisbourg's strategic influence and the uncertain loyalty of the Acadians that Halifax was founded in 1749 and some twenty-seven hundred "foreign Protestants"—Germans and Swiss members of several Reformed churches who were fleeing religious persecution in Europe—were settled at Halifax and Lunenburg in 1750 and 1751.[12] Finally, after fighting had begun in North America, the efforts of French agents such as the priest Jean-Louis Le Loutre to stir up the Acadians against British authority provided Governor Lawrence with the excuse to move this potential Acadian fifth column from the colony and from proximity to French power at Louisbourg and Quebec. Victims of a struggle between the two most powerful nations of the day, six thousand Acadians were rounded up in 1755 and deported to the British colonies further south. Another two thousand escaped, most to Prince Edward Island and some to French-held New Brunswick. After the British captured Louisbourg in 1758, and particularly after the Seven Years' War ended in 1763, many of these Acadians and those exiled in 1755 made their way back to the colony of Nova Scotia to settle on Cape Breton, Prince Edward Island and around the Bay of Chaleur.

The religious needs of the Protestant settlers at Halifax were first met by resident missionaries sent by the Society for the Propagation of the Gospel in 1749. Although the British government provided for a salary of a Lutheran minister for the German settlers, no clergyman was obtained and from 1750 Jean Baptiste Moreau, S.P.G. missionary to the French-speaking Protestant Swiss, conducted Anglican services in English for the other Lunenburg settlers. After the expulsion of the Acadians, however, the decision to invite New Englanders to fill up the vacant lands, and so consolidate Britain's hold on Nova Scotia, led to an important change in religious policy. A law passed by the first Nova Scotian Assembly in 1758 had established the Church of England as the state religion, but promised "free Liberty of Conscience" to Protestant dissenters. The following year Governor Lawrence issued a proclamation reiterating the promises of religious toleration and exemption from any taxes to support the Church of England.[13] Apparently reassured by Lawrence's "Charter of Freedom," about seven thousand New England "planters" or colonists arrived in the next few years to take up lands along the southwest coast of Nova Scotia, the Bay of Fundy shore and the banks of the Saint John River, and to provide the province of Nova Scotia with further elements of its growing tradition of religious pluralism and toleration.

Newfoundland, Britain's oldest overseas territory, was still not recognized as a colony and was practically without religious institutions as late as the middle of the eighteenth century. Each summer the arrival of the fishing fleet from England temporarily doubled the population of seven thousand permanent residents scattered in tiny villages along the south coast. Since English and Irish comprised virtually the whole population of Newfoundland, only the churches of England and Rome were represented on the island. Early in the eighteenth century the newly-formed S.P.G. established a permanent mission at Bonavista, and added two more at St. John's and Trinity in 1730, while outlawed Irish Roman Catholic priests, disguised as fishermen, probably visited their coreligionists intermittently. Until the 1760s, however, the story of Newfoundland was a story of neglect by church and state alike.

THE CATHOLIC HERITAGE OF NEW FRANCE

In contrast to the retarded religious condition of these northern seaboard territories in 1760, the newly conquered province of New France possessed a transatlantic heritage as old, as rich and as well-established as that of any English colony in North America. From the beginnings of French fur trade and settlement at the opening of the seventeenth century, the Roman Catholic Church, as the establish religion of France, had an official and vital role in the growth of the colony, both in ministering to the settlers and in the mission work for the conversion of the Indians. Laval, the first bishop to the colony, had been appointed in 1657 and from that date forward Canada, or New France on the St. Lawrence, had been an integral part, in jurisdiction, in organization, in liturgy and in ideals, of the Church of Rome. By the time of the British conquest a century later the substantial churches, schools, colleges, hospitals and orphanages, and the solidly Roman Catholic population of New France, made the diocese of Quebec the proud possessor of a French and Catholic transatlantic heritage—and an important part of the far-flung realms that owed allegiance to the papacy.

The eighteenth century was not one of the golden ages of the papacy but neither was it an age of decay. The office of pope passed through the hands of several men who if not remarkable for their vigour or leadership were nevertheless faithful custodians of the See of St. Peter and men above reproach in their personal lives. The papal administration moved slowly but efficiently through the complex structure of its world-wide organization. The worst forms of corruption within the church's civil service had been eliminated during the Counter-Reformation a century before, when a purified papacy had combined with its militant arm, the Society of Jesus, to stop and even to reverse the Protestant tide in Europe.

Officially the religion of France was Roman Catholicism but even before the Reformation the French kings had claimed control over the church in their domains. In spite of this Gallicanism—the movement to make Roman Catholicism effectively a national religion of the French people under the immediate control of the French king—the Roman Catholic Church enjoyed a position of prestige and influence in France unequalled by the church in any other Catholic country. It still provided all educational and social services; it controlled an estimated 20 per cent of the land; it enjoyed extensive immunities from taxation. But this very power and affluence caused the church to be viewed with jealousy. It was too obviously a mouthpiece for government policies; it did not carry a fair share of responsibility in national affairs; it was too close to secular life for its own good. Pluralism, nonresidence, immorality and luxury were proofs that the vitality of the church in France had been sapped and that reforms were badly needed; yet no reformer stood forth within the church. Religion continued to be attacked and ridiculed by the *philosophes* until the disaster of the French Revolution purged the church and almost destroyed it in the process.

In New France, the only developed French colony in continental North America, the church's position seemed similar to its position in Old France, but in fact its condition was immeasurably better. The climate of irreligion fostered in France by the *philosophes* had not taken root in the colony which as yet had neither printing presses nor a leisured middle class. The church held over a quarter of the land granted in the colony but, in view of the social services it provided and of the almost unlimited amounts of land available, this was not a cause for jealousy. In fact the only reason for dissatisfaction with church was its custom of filling senior offices with French-born clergy and thereby largely confining native Canadians to parochial duties, a type of class discrimination that was also reflected in the religious orders, both male and female.[14]

The sixty thousand or more inhabitants of New France were exclusively French and legally Roman Catholic. For more than a century Protestant worship had been forbidden although the presence of a few Huguenot merchants had been tolerated. From his cathedral in the city of Quebec the sixth Roman Catholic bishop, Henri de Pontbriand, ruled a vast diocese comprising all French possessions in North America, from the mouth of the St. Lawrence to the mouth of the Mississippi. The exact boundaries of his diocese were unknown and unimportant, for with the exception of one small region the French possessions constituted for the church one immense mission field. That exception was the valley of the lower St. Lawrence—roughly from Montreal to Rimouski—where parochial institutions on the European pattern were firmly rooted within the civil and economic framework of the seigneurial system.

This St. Lawrence heartland of the diocese was divided into three ecclesiastical "governments"—Quebec, Trois-Rivières and Montreal—each under a vicar general and containing respectively fifty, twenty and forty-one parishes. Two Indian missions, at Jeune Lorette and Caughnawaga, were operated by the Jesuits, while far to the west were the two missionary "governments"—the Great Lakes and the Illinois country—each under the superintendence of a vicar general.

Quebec City, capital of the colony, boasted several large and handsome religious buildings—the bishop's palace, the Jesuits' college, the seminary for training priests, the nursing convent of the Hôtel-Dieu, the Ursuline convent and its school for girls, the house of the Recollets and the parish church which also served as the cathedral—all sheltered within the walled city atop Cape Diamond. Below and outside the citadel lay the mercantile lower town where the General Hospital stood. The only other urban centre was Montreal, less than a mile long and three hundred and fifty yards wide. Reflecting the town's missionary origin in 1642, one-fifth of Montreal was occupied by religious foundations—the Hôtel-Dieu, the General Hospital operated by the Grey nuns, the houses of the Jesuits and Recollets, and the Gentlemen of St. Sulpice, the community of secular clergy that had acquired the whole Island as a seigneury in 1663. Thanks to the unsettling influence of the fur trade the rest of Montreal was little more than a rough frontier village, scene of unrestrained debauchery when the flotilla of fur-laden canoes arrived each summer. The other settled parts of New France were entirely rural. Most of the seigneuries fronted on the St. Lawrence River, and the close and regular succession of farm houses, seigneurs' manors and tin-roofed churches gave the visitor then as now the impression of a continuous village stretching along both shores for some two hundred miles.

Such, briefly, was the physical and religious condition of New France when that French and Catholic colony surrendered to the English-speaking and Protestant empire of His Most Britannic Majesty, King George III, in 1760.

NOTES TO CHAPTER ONE

1. A general introduction to the philosophical background of this period can be obtained from Crane Brinton, *The Shaping of Modern Thought* (Englewood Cliffs: Prentice-Hall, 1950), particularly chapters 3 and 4, and more extensively in Sir Leslie Stephen, *History of English Thought in the Eighteenth Century* (2 vols.; New York: Harcourt, Brace and World, 1962).
2. For a brief but authoritative analysis of Enlightenment philosophy see G. R. Cragg,

The Church and the Age of Reason (1648-1789), The Pelican History of the Church, Vol. IV (Harmondsworth: Penguin Books, 1960), particularly Chapter 15.

3. Of many excellent studies of the Church of England during the eighteenth and nineteenth centuries, the most useful are *Eighteenth Century Church and People* (London: Murray, 1959), and *Church and People 1789-1889* (London: S.C.M., 1934), both by S. C. Carpenter.

4. The relation of religion to politics in pre-Revolutionary America is the subject of *Mitre and Sceptre* (London: Oxford University Press, 1962), by Carl Bridenbaugh.

5. The literature on Wesley and Methodism is immense. John Wesley's *Journal* makes fascinating reading and J. W. Bready, *England: Before and After Wesley*, is a sympathetic and scholarly account of the changes that flowed from Wesley and his movement.

6. The most useful book on Scottish Presbyterianism is J. H. S. Burleigh, *A Church History of Scotland* (London: Oxford University Press, 1960).

7. Of the many histories of religion in the United States one of the most attractive, readable and recent is E. S. Gaustad, *A Religious History of America* (New York: Harper & Row, 1966).

8. Gaustad, *op. cit.*, p. 55.

9. W. W. Sweet, *Revivalism in America* (New York: Abingdon, 1944), is a popular study of this movement; but more recent and definitive is E. S. Gaustad, *The Great Awakening in New England* (New York: Harper and Row, 1957; paperback reprint, 1968). David S. Lovejoy, *Religious Enthusiasm and the Great Awakening* (Englewood Cliffs: Prentice-Hall, 1969), is a stimulating selection of controversial first hand accounts of the Great Awakening to which the editor has added notes and a useful introduction.

10. See C. C. Goen, *Revivalism and Separatism in New England, 1740-1800* (New Haven: Yale University Press, 1962).

11. See J. S. Moir, *Church and State in Canada 1627-1867: Basic Documents*, Carleton Library No. 33 (Toronto: McClelland and Stewart, 1967), pp. 23-30.

12. W. P. Bell, *The "Foreign Protestants" and the Settlement of Nova Scotia* (Toronto: University of Toronto Press, 1961), represents a lifetime of research on this topic.

13. See Moir, *op. cit.*, p. 34.

14. For a detailed analysis of the condition of the Roman Catholic Church in New France at the time of the conquest, see Marcel Trudel, *L'Eglise canadienne sous le Régime militaire, 1759-1764* (2 vols.; Montreal, 1956; Quebec: Les Presses Universitaires Laval, 1957).

TWO

"Unlimited Toleration"

The founding of the naval base of Halifax and the settling of the "foreign Protestants" had been the first step in the British policy of transforming Nova Scotia into an English colony. The second step was the expulsion of the Acadians and the final stage was the promotion of Nova Scotia in 1758 to the status of a royal colony, complete with a popularly elected legislative assembly, English common law, and the Church of England as the established religion. These English institutions and the availability of the Acadian farm lands would, it was hoped, attract a large northward migration of planters from New England, and Governor Lawrence repeated the invitation to settlement in 1759 with his proclamation of complete religious toleration for Protestants in the new royal colony. Thus from its inception as a royal English colony Nova Scotia acquired a pattern of religious diversity and harmony.

By contrast Britain's two other northern seaboard possessions, Prince Edward Island and Newfoundland, were ignored in official policy. The only inhabitants of Prince Edward Island were a few hundred Acadians who, having fled there to escape the expulsion of 1755, seemed to be forgotten by both church and state. Similarly, residents of Newfoundland were left to their own devices without the benefits of civil government, law or order, and with the most minimal of religious services provided by two or three Anglican missionaries of the Society for the Propagation of the Gospel, and by occasional and clandestine visits of Irish priests in the case of the Roman Catholics. It was little wonder that life in Newfoundland had become synonomous with immorality and social disintegration.

THE PLANTERS AND THEIR CHURCHES

The majority of the pre-Loyalist planters from Massachusetts, Connecticut and Rhode Island brought with them the Puritan moral code and the religious institutions of New England. Nearly a dozen Congregationalist churches sprang up at Halifax, Chebogue, Barrington, Liverpool, around Minas Basin, at Fort Cumberland on the Chignecto Isthmus, and Maugerville near present-day Fredericton on the Saint John River.[1] Several Harvard graduates came as preachers, but the Congregational ministry lacked continuity in Nova Scotia since many stayed but a short time. Ironically, Nova Scotia also offered a haven from the repressive theocracy of New England Congregationalism and for Baptists, who believed in the principle of complete religious freedom—"soul liberty"—and in the absolute separation of church and state. In 1760 the first Baptist preacher, Ebenezer Moulton, arrived at Chebogue and visited Yarmouth and Barrington before returning to Massachusetts. About 1763 a Baptist group settlement at Sackville set up its own church, but the church died when most of the settlers returned to Massachusetts in 1771. The scattering of Baptists throughout the widely dispersed Nova Scotian settlements, the independence of Baptist congregations and the Baptists' insistence that preachers have some private source of income—to avoid a "hireling ministry"—all combined to retard any substantial Baptist growth in the early years of the colony.

The decade of the sixties also witnessed the arrival of some New England Presbyterians who settled at Truro, Londonderry and Halifax where they were joined by others from Ulster and Scotland. In 1767 the *Hope* carried a group of Presbyterians to Pictou from Philadelphia, and six years later the *Hector* brought another migration to the same place directly from Scotland. Despite the considerable numbers of these settlers, few ministers came to the colony. James Lyon arrived from the Presbytery of New Brunswick (New Jersey) in 1764, and for several years worked at Truro, Onslow and Halifax. Samuel Kinloch of the Associate or Burgher Synod in Scotland arrived in 1766 for a three-year pastorate. In 1770 Daniel Cock replaced Kinloch at Truro where he remained until his retirement in 1798. David Smith, another Associate Synod missionary, was appointed in 1770 and laboured in Londonderry until his death in 1795. Cock and Smith ministered occasionally in neighbouring communities such as Cumberland, Pictou and Cornwallis, but they laboured alone until after the American Revolution. The rival Scotch General Associate or Antiburgher Synod in 1766 sent out James Murdoch who settled at Horton and served that town and the Windsor-Cornwallis area for thirty-three years.[2]

The wide dispersal of the few clergy inevitably delayed the organizational growth of all the churches and forced a reliance on local initiative to overcome obstacles by irregular means. A historic example of such inventiveness was the ordination of the Dutchman Bruin Romkes Comingo. In the presence of the Governor and some of his Council, the Presbyterians Murdoch and Lyons in 1770 joined two Congregational ministers, John Seccomb and Benaiah Phelps, to form an ad hoc presbytery at Halifax and ordain the self-educated Comingo, whom sixty Lunenburg families had chosen as their minister.[3] To the audience Murdoch explained the reasons for this action—Comingo's was a case of necessity and every procedural precaution had been taken to prevent injury to the cause of religion. Comingo was then pronounced to be a minister of the Reformed Presbyterian churches and, however unusual his ordination may have been, he served his Lunenburg congregation for half a century.

The German Lutherans at last obtained the pastor for whom they had so often petitioned when the S.P.C.K. ordained a German-speaking Swede, Paulus Bryzelius, in 1767, and sent him to Lunenberg in hopes of winning the Lutherans to the Church of England.[4] But Bryzelius was rejected by the Lutherans, who began to build their own church and received the Reverend Friedrich Schultz from Baltimore in 1772.

The only Roman Catholic priest in the colony was Pierre Maillard, the Apostle to the Micmacs, who had escaped to Pictou County from Louisbourg in 1758 and two years later moved to Halifax with some one hundred Acadians.[5] Despite the penalty of "perpetual imprisonment" provided for "Popish priests" by Nova Scotia law, Maillard was permitted to say mass in a Halifax barn and was given a government salary of £100 as missionary to the Acadians and to the Micmac Indians, whom he reconciled to English rule. When he died at Halifax in 1762, an Anglican doctor-turned-missionary performed the burial service as Maillard had requested. The Catholics were without a priest until Charles-François Bailly was despatched to Halifax in 1768 by Bishop Briand of Quebec and made Vicar General of Nova Scotia and the adjacent islands. But Bailly soon encountered official opposition because English-speaking Catholics attended his services and he left the colony in 1772. In the area of New Brunswick before the Revolution the only priest was Joseph-Mathurin Bourg, an Acadian, sent to the Saint John River in 1778 with a government salary of £100, to ensure the loyalty of the local Indians to Britain.[6]

By 1769 the colony of Nova Scotia (which still included New Brunswick) contained seven Congregational ministers, two Presbyterians and six Church of England missionaries supported by the S.P.G. But the lack of roads in the colony left all clergymen in virtual isolation so that they frequently served Protestants of several denominations in their own area but seldom met the clergy of their own or any other church. Since denominational organization was almost nonexistent, one positive result was the development of a generous spirit towards fellow Protestants. No serious state-church issue arose because both the provincial assembly and the council contained non-Anglicans and because the so-called "church-state party" in provincial politics consistently tried to treat all denominations reasonably if not equally.[7] The results of these policies can be seen in the absence of any anti-Anglican political group, in the social deference paid to the established church (status-seeking dissenters actually rented pews in St. Paul's, Halifax) and in the general climate of interdenominational cooperation and harmony which became a hallmark of Maritime religious life.

A census taken in 1767 indicates both the patchwork pattern and the local homogeneity arising from the group migrations of the settlements.[8] In a population of some 11,800 in Nova Scotia (not including the later area of New Brunswick), 6,000 were Americans, with King's County a solidly American and Protestant plantation. Of almost 1,900 Germans reported, 1,450 lived in Lunenburg County which, together with the other central counties, King's and Halifax, boasted half the population of the province. Over nine hundred Acadians were recorded, half of them in Halifax and another 30 per cent on Cape Breton. Interestingly the census showed only one hundred and fifty Scots in the whole province. Roman Catholics numbered only seventeen hundred but Halifax and Cape Breton together contained almost fourteen hundred of them. The census of New Brunswick for the same year provides even more startling figures. Of a total population just under twelve hundred, almost nine hundred were Americans and over a thousand were Protestants. New Brunswick contained only one hundred and fifty-two Roman Catholics and all but five of them were Acadians.

Prince Edward Island had been sold in 1767 to persons who acted as absentee landlords, a move that lay at the heart of that colony's troubles for generations after. The population of five hundred was divided evenly between Protestants and Roman Catholics: 40 per cent were Acadians who had escaped deportation in 1758; the remainder consisted of about equal numbers of Irish and English. The Island was separated from Nova Scotia and given its own government in 1769, but it continued without religious care until 1772 when Father James MacDonald arrived with a "swarm" of Highland Catholics.[9] By 1775 the population had grown to only thirteen hundred, of whom nine hundred had arrived in the preceding five years. Similarly on Cape Breton the population was small, amounting to perhaps a few hundred Acadians around Arichat on neighbouring Madame Island, all without spiritual guides.

NOVA SCOTIA AND THE AMERICAN REVOLUTION

Considering its exposed geographical position and the preponderance of New England immigrants in the population, Nova Scotia's involvement in the American Revolution was surprisingly limited. Britain's control of the Atlantic waters restricted the hostile operations of the revolutionaries to a few filibustering raids against Nova Scotia and Prince Edward Island, while the presence of the garrison at Halifax and Britain's naval superiority discouraged any sympathetic rebellion within Nova Scotia itself. In 1776 an abortive attempt by some Maine rebels to seize Fort Cumberland was repulsed by its small garrison with the aid of Yorkshire Methodists who had settled in the area. For a short time the American inhabitants of Maugerville openly adhered to the American cause, but the arrival of British troops ended this brief and fruitless flirtation with treason. It was in the political and economic self-interest of the isolated Yankees of Nova Scotia to remain loyal or at least neutral in this imperial war. For Nova Scotia, the most important result of the American Revolution was the Loyalist migration.

The most significant religious development during these war years was undoubtedly the arrival of the Great Awakening, or New Lightism. In Nova Scotia the seeds of religious division were planted by Henry Alline, a man in deep torment over the salvation of his soul.[10] Born in 1748 at Newport, Rhode Island, Alline had come to Falmouth in 1760 with his Congregationalist family. From early childhood he seemed emotionally disturbed, and was so seriously depressed by the Calvinistic doctrine of total depravity that he existed in perpetual expectation of imminent damnation. At the age of twenty-seven, after a conversion experience, Alline began preaching the gospel of the New Light in Falmouth, only to meet opposition on all sides from entrenched and respectable Congregationalism. Undeterred by threats to his life, Alline delivered his fiery message of repentance throughout the area west of Pictou, in New Brunswick and in Prince Edward Island.

Alline's emotional preaching of a modified Calvinism, that balanced God's love for mankind with God's terrible condemnation of sinners, was particularly effective in the rural Congregational churches. In the towns of Chebogue, Barrington, Liverpool, Chester, Kingsport, Granville, Fort Cumberland and Maugerville Alline caused the separation from Congregationalism of "New Lights" who subsequently formed Baptist churches. Always a supporter of congregational independence, he assisted in founding many Baptist churches and was present at the first Baptist ordination, held in 1778. Yet in part this Baptist expansion was also due to the close identification of Congregationalism with the Revolutionary cause in the Thirteen Colonies. In Loyal Nova Scotia Congregationalism smacked of treason, and this, added to Alline's disruptive influence, led to the absorption of Congregationalism into the strong Baptist fellowship that became such an important religious ingredient in Nova Scotian life.

Henry Alline's efforts were not confined to preaching. Despite his lack of formal education he showed considerable writing talent. In two published volumes he expounded his individualistic faith, and his posthumous *Life and Journals* give a rare insight into a tortured and mystical soul. By 1783, however, Alline's work was virtually over—consumption ended his life in 1784. He had laboured alone for six years, ignoring denominational lines and leaving no organization to perpetuate his cause.

As the Revolutionary War drew to a close the city of New York became a haven for Loyalists and when peace came in 1783 Guy Carleton, Commander-in-Chief in America, supervised their mass exodus. Even before the peace treaty was signed he had arranged with Governor Parr for their settlement in Nova Scotia and had despatched the first groups in British transports. In a matter of months thirty thousand Loyalists were moved to Nova Scotia, more than doubling the colony's population and altering drastically, permanently and almost overnight, the social composition of Nova Scotia. Despite generous government assistance the Loyalist settlers encountered such hardships that they soon gave their new home the nickname, "Nova Scarcity," and many migrated to England in search of a future. Some ten thousand refugees had crowded into the fishing village of Shelburne, but that boom town withered in a couple of years to a village of a few hundred when the economic resources of the area proved incapable of supporting such a multitude. Another fourteen thousand from Loyalist regiments were settled more permanently in blocks along the banks of the Saint John River, where the great timber resources of the area provided the basis of a prosperous trade in masts and spars for the Royal Navy.

One immediate result of the Loyalist migration into the valley of the Saint John was the imperial decision to divide the unwieldy colony of Nova Scotia in three. Many Loyalists questioned the loyalty of Governor Parr and his pre-Loyalist government officials and blamed them unjustly for every detail of mismanagement in the Loyalist settling. Because of this political opposition, but basically for geographic reasons, New Brunswick and Cape Breton Island were given separate colonial governments in 1784, and the colony of Nova Scotia was limited to the mainland peninsula.

Carleton, and William Knox, Under-Secretary of State for the Colonies, were both anxious that the conditions which had encouraged revolution in the Thirteen Colonies should not be repeated in the remaining British North American colonies. Knox, a High Church Tory, was given the congenial task of planning a constitution for New Brunswick and an Anglican establishment for the Maritime colonies. Loyalty to Britain must be promoted, and the Church of England, whose work had been frustrated so regularly in the revolted colonies, was one vehicle for preserving loyalty. Carleton was sure that virtually all Loyalists were Anglicans, so that the full establishment of the Church of England, with a bishop and a college, appeared to be a simple step in that direction.[11] Both he and Knox were convinced that Presbyterian principles lay behind the Revolution and to discourage republicanism Knox was even prepared to extend religious toleration to Roman Catholics. At least, when the first elections were held in 1784, Roman Catholics were eligible to vote provided they would deny the Pope's right to interfere in secular matters.

In New Brunswick Governor Thomas Carleton, younger brother of Guy, and his secretary, Jonathan Odell, a Loyalist and former S.P.G. missionary, proceeded to lay out parishes in every township. Only the pre-Loyalist settlement of Maugerville had a dissenting majority, and there New Lightism had destroyed Congregational unity. New Brunswick seemed then the ideal location for the Church of England experiment, and the colony's first legislature re-enacted the Nova Scotia law establishing the Church of England. Experience was soon to show, however, that a mere law could not make British North American colonies Anglican in fact. The S.P.G. provision for six clergymen and four church buildings was hopelessly inadequate for the size of the province. Ambitious plans to create an Anglican bishopric and university in New Brunswick died for lack of funds. Above all, New Brunswick, like her sister colonies, had a religiously pluralistic population which resisted Anglicanization by the church-state. In the end New Brunswick Anglicanism had to be content to be a minority, to share a bishop and college with Nova Scotia and to remain dependent on English missionaries for religious services.

CHARLES INGLIS, A MISSIONARY BISHOP

By 1785 the British cabinet had accepted the plans of Carleton and Knox for consolidating the remains of the empire in North America. These plans included the establishment of the Church of England with a colonial bishop, the first in the empire's history. The choice of a bishop was settled in the spring of 1786 as Carleton prepared to return to Quebec—the person agreed upon being the scholarly, Irish-born Charles Inglis, sometime teacher in Pennsylvania and later rector of Trinity Church, New York City. An outspoken Tory, Inglis had seen his church burned in 1777 by the revolutionaries whom he had so often denounced and defied, had returned to London just before the mass exodus of Loyalists to Nova Scotia and had acted as spokesman there for his church's interests in North America.[12] As a man who shared Carleton's opinions and acquaintance, Inglis was an excellent choice as bishop.

There was no room for doubt in Inglis's mind about the role which the established church should play in any British colony. "Government and Religion are therefore the pillars . . . on which society rests, and by which it is upheld; remove these, and the fabric sinks into ruin. . . . Whoever is sincerely religious towards God . . . will also . . . be loyal to his earthly Sovereign, obedient to the laws, and faithful to the government which God hath placed over him."[13] He was sure religious dissent encouraged "wild notions . . . which militate against Order in both Church and State." "Fanatics are impatient under civil restraint, and run into the democratic system. They are for Leveling [*sic*] every thing both sacred and civil . . . ." Yet Inglis's experiences in the revolutionary colonies had taught him "to avoid in my conduct what would give [dissenters] disgust and shock their prejudices. The whole secret lay in this, and in observing a candid and brotherly behaviour, and convincing them that the zealous discharge of my duty which did not in [ter] fere with them, was the only object I aim at."

Such were the views of Charles Inglis who was consecrated first bishop of the diocese of Nova Scotia (including Bermuda as well as the northern British colonies) on August 12, 1787. Nine weeks later Inglis was in Halifax ready to play an active role in the development of the colonial church and the promotion of loyalty to the empire. Beginning in Nova Scotia and New Brunswick during the summer of 1788, he held regular triennial visitations of his clergy throughout his "primitive Bishoprick."[14] In Nova Scotia he found only one finished church, at Halifax; in New Brunswick there were two, in Fredericton and Saint John. The next year he visited the province of Quebec, stopping on the way at Prince Edward Island where Theophilus DesBrisay was the only clergyman of any denomination. With the support of the S.P.G. he recruited more priests for his vast diocese, so that by 1790 he could report to the Colonial Office that New Brunswick contained six missionaries and one dissenting clergyman, while Nova Scotia had thirteen Anglican and seven Presbyterian clergy, as well as "a multitude of Methodists and sectaries."[15]

Anglican churches were built rapidly with government aid, and that same year—1790—Inglis performed at Shelburne the first Protestant consecration of a church in British North America. Within ten years of Inglis's arrival seventeen new churches had been built, although the number of communicants was still under one thousand. The bishop was critical of the laity's "backwardness"[16] in supporting the church financially, a condition that he blamed on poverty, indifference and sectarianism. One of Inglis's steps to encourage loyalty and to prevent the importation of American clergy and American politics was the founding of his Anglican academy at Windsor in 1788 with seventeen pupils and £400 from the Nova Scotia legislature.[17] Some of the college governors had grandiose ideas of creating a university overnight and Inglis had to insist on the removal of several regulations from the college statutes to ensure a sufficient supply of students. Although the imperial government promised a charter and a £1,000 grant to King's College in 1790, the charter did not arrive until 1802, and its terms changed what had started as a nonsectarian institution into a college so exclusively Anglican that even Inglis protested.

Few governors were such strong supporters of Anglican establishment as Inglis would have wished but his relations with all of them were generally satisfactory. John Parr, his first governor in Nova Scotia, described the bishop in 1789 as "a high Churchman, one who never drank the Glorious memory of King William 'till I made him; we agree very well in general, but differ in some points." Those points included Inglis's emphasis on "dead Languages" and "antient [sic] Learning" in his academy's curriculum.[18] Another issue between Inglis and Parr concerned the right of presentation, particularly to St. Paul's Church, Halifax. After ten years of wrangling Inglis concluded it was best to acknowledge the custom of viceregal appointments in Halifax—"especially in these times of Democratic rage and delusion."[19] Parr had set the tone of church-state relations but Inglis was never reassured about the dangerous encroachments of the Methodists, or the New Lights ("almost to a man, violent Republicans and Democrats"). Similarly Inglis watched the growth of Roman Catholicism in the Maritimes with a "jealous eye." He personally liked John Brown, the Presbyterian minister in Halifax, and obtained a £75 government salary for him—but not as a right of the Kirk.

Inglis's care to protect and foster the established church did, however, lead to difficulties over endowments and marriage laws. In Nova Scotia modest land reservations had been made for glebes and schools, but in New Brunswick some of the lots so reserved had been taken over by dissenters, and the civil authorities seemed reluctant to prosecute the interlopers. In the matter of marriages Inglis also struggled against official indifference towards the rights of the national religion. The Church of England viewed marriage as a sacrament reserved to itself, whereas dissenters considered it primarily a civil contract. Given the shortage of Anglican clergy in the diocese, Inglis had difficulty in countering the practical proposal of the governors in both New Brunswick and Nova Scotia that justices of the peace be permitted to perform marriages by licence. The intervention of the Colonial Office was required in 1800 to block such a measure by the latter province where it would have destroyed religious harmony, according to the bishop. "It had been suggested to the Governor," Inglis reported to the Archbishop of Canterbury, " 'that he as *supreme ordinary* had a right to give out marriage licences in any manner he chose' . . . I very bluntly replied that it was *supreme nonsense* to talk so. . . ."[20] Inglis had won his point—the marriage laws remained unchanged for another three decades—and no doubt he would have agreed with the governor's private opinion of his episcopate to date: "There is a good foundation laid for the Church of England, and this is the happiest time to cultivate it."[21]

POST-REVOLUTIONARY GROWTH OF OTHER DENOMINATIONS

The Roman Catholics in Nova Scotia received few additions from the Loyalist migration, but in the post-Revolutionary period the arrival of large numbers of British Roman Catholics, particularly Highland Scotch, made the Roman Church a major factor in the religious mosaic of the Lower Provinces. One significant development of the Revolutionary years had been the extension of religious liberty to Roman Catholics in Nova Scotia by an act of 1783 which removed all restrictions on public worship and land-holding by Roman Catholics. The Halifax community marked its new freedom by beginning to build a church.

Bishop Desgly of Quebec now took an interest in the long neglected Nova Scotian Catholics, sending Vicar General Bourg to Halifax in the summer of 1785. Four weeks later Father James Jones also arrived there, as Bishop Butler of Cork responded independently to a request from the English-speaking Catholics at Halifax for a priest. Desgly thanked Butler and asked for more Irish priests to fill the vacant missions in "Acadia,"[22] apparently happy to place the missions in other hands if that would solve the problem of an alien minority within the French diocese. Bourg was therefore removed to the Gaspé in 1786, leaving Halifax to Jones as superior of the Nova Scotian missions.

Jones's work in Halifax seemed very successful—the church and a parsonage were finished in 1787 and he was shortly joined by three other Irish priests, although one returned home quickly after some "scandalous behaviour." Each of these Irish missionaries served a large territory with members of different national origins, but the Acadians at Arichat continued to agitate for a French-speaking priest. Such a priest appeared briefly—a wandering and troublesome French Dominican who helped himself to the personal belongings of the late Father James MacDonald when passing through Prince Edward Island. A permanent French-speaking priest arrived at last in 1792 in the person of Father François Lejamtel, a refugee from St. Pierre and Miquelon fleeing the long arm of France's revolutionary government.

The first of two mass migrations of Highlanders took place in 1790. The group, two hundred and fifty strong, arrived on Prince Edward Island with their own priest, Angus Bernard MacEachern. Jones was glad to have the assistance of the Gaelic-speaking missionary who visited other Highland settlements in Merigomish, Miramichi, and in Pictou where the second major settlement, six hundred and fifty Highlanders, arrived in 1791 so utterly destitute that the provincial government had to provide them with the necessities of life. Despite a charitable welcome from the Pictou Presbyterians most of these newcomers followed MacEachern's advice to move to Cape Breton "where [Protestants] would not trouble them."[23]

With the Pictou immigrants had come another Father James MacDonald, who spoke English, Gaelic and French. In 1798, when MacDonald's health failed, MacEachern had to assume his duties on Cape Breton and the mainland as well as his own in Prince Edward Island. By that time there were seven missionaries in the Lower Provinces, but the shortage of priests and the preoccupations of the bishops at Quebec had combined to retard the church's growth in the region while orientating it away from the French-Canadian church and towards the Roman Catholic church in Britain.

The great influx of Loyalists also brought little increase in numbers to the Baptists, so that their growth after the Revolution was due not to British immigration but almost entirely to the collapse of Congregationalism in the wake of Loyalist political reaction and Henry Alline's preaching. From these two causes the Baptist membership increased during the next quarter of a century until it formed the third largest Protestant body in the Maritimes. In Nova Scotia, where most of this growth occurred, New Lightism influenced the careers of such Baptist "fathers" as James and Edward Manning, T. H. Chipman and Seth Harding, pastor at Horton from 1795 to 1855.[24] In Loyalist and Anglican New Brunswick, where Baptists had been without a resident pastor since 1771, Alline had left the nucleus of a new congregation at Sackville, which joined the Baptist fold in 1799; and the next year Joseph Crandall, Sackville's pastor, formed another church among the New Lights at Waterborough on the Saint John River. Except for these two churches, however, the Baptists in New Brunswick remained scattered and unorganized, ministered to by occasional visitors from Nova Scotia until the turn of the century. Baptist strength lay among the prosperous middle class of the small provincial towns that dotted Nova Scotia rather than in class-conscious, socially ambitious Halifax which remained a self-sufficient, self-satisfied and somewhat artificial administrative centre, remote in all but geography from the thriving countryside around it.

The growth of Presbyterianism, like that of Roman Catholicism after the Revolution, was almost entirely the result of emigration from Scotland. In 1786 Cock, Smith, and Hugh Graham (who reached Cornwallis in 1785) organized themselves by the authority of the Associate (Burgher) Synod of Scotland, as the Burgher Presbytery of Truro with George Gilmore, Loyalist and Church of Scotland minister, as a corresponding member. Its next addition, James Munro from the United States, was appointed to Onslow and three other congregations in 1792. Two more Associate Synod clergy from Scotland joined the presbytery in 1797, and three more were added before 1817.[25] Instituted on the principles of the creed and constitution "practised by the Church of Scotland in her purest times," this presbytery reflected in Nova Scotia the divisions of eighteenth-century Scotch Presbyterianism.

A second presbytery, calling itself the Associate Presbytery of Pictou and connected to the General Associate (Antiburgher) Synod of Scotland, had been formed in 1795 by James MacGregor, and by Duncan Ross and John Brown who arrived that year. MacGregor possessed "the two tongues"—he could preach in Gaelic and English—but each group complained that the other received the larger share of his bilingualism.[26] As no church building existed at Pictou when he arrived in 1786, MacGregor established an itinerant plan of preaching in private houses. He also travelled widely in the Lower Provinces to serve Antiburgher settlers. In 1790 he spent six weeks in Prince Edward Island, receiving aid and encouragement from the Anglican rector, DesBrisay, but despite numerous petitions from the Islanders to the General Associate Synod for a permanent minister, none was sent until 1795, a year after MacGregor had paid his second visit. Ross, also bilingual, settled at Pictou and Brown at Londonderry, which since the death of Smith of the Truro Burgher Presbytery had been without a minister. Brown's diplomacy soon united Burghers and Antiburghers in a single Londonderry congregation which he continued to serve for over half a century.

Unlike the more mission-minded Burgher and Antiburgher churches, the established Church of Scotland, largest of the Scottish branches of Presbyterianism, made virtually no effort to serve its adherents in the New World until moved by the new missionary spirit which produced the Glasgow Colonial Society in 1825. Three ministers of the Kirk, however, had come to the Lower Provinces long before that date but none of them under official church auspices. In 1783 Thomas Russell began a three-year pastorate at the Halifax Dissenting Meeting House (renamed St. Matthew's in 1815) which had previously been served by Congregationalists. After his departure the congregation applied for a minister to the University of Edinburgh which sent Andrew Brown in 1787, but he returned to Scotland eight years later. Until a new minister was obtained the ecumenically-minded congregation welcomed the Anglican George Wright to their pulpit. The next Presbyterian minister from the Kirk was Archibald Gray, who remained with the Halifax Dissenting Congregation for thirty years until his death in 1826.

WILLIAM BLACK AND THE METHODIST MISSION

Methodism was still essentially within the fold of the Church of England when followers of John Wesley first arrived in Nova Scotia from Yorkshire in the 1770s. This group settled in the Chignecto area where a local religious revival in 1780 produced the first and perhaps the greatest Methodist preacher in the Maritimes. William Black, son of one of these settlers, was converted at the age of nineteen and was authorized by Wesley to itinerate in Nova Scotia.[27] He commenced his active mission in 1783 with the first sermon heard at Shelburne. His audience was a Methodist class organized by Robert Barry, a New York Methodist who had arrived there with the first Loyalist convoy. The same year Black visited Prince Edward Island at the invitation of a Methodist convert but with few results. On the mainland at Shelburne and the Negro settlement of Birchtown, Methodist societies did appear briefly—for a short time Birchtown had no less than fourteen Methodist classes—but without any regular preachers the Methodist cause in Nova Scotia seemed doomed to extinction.

John Wesley had promised assistants to William Black in 1781 but after the independent American Methodist Episcopal church was organized in 1784 he preferred to leave Nova Scotia in its care. Black attended the first American General Conference at Baltimore, where Freeborn Garretson, the man who had ridden more than 1,200 miles in six weeks to call the Wesleyan preachers together,[28] volunteered for service in Nova Scotia. Garretson arrived at Halifax in 1785 to a warm welcome from Governor Parr and John Breynton, the Anglican rector, and from the handful of Methodists. Travelling through the colony Garretson found Anglican, Congregational and Presbyterian pulpits open to him, but among New Lights he encountered opposition to his mission. The fact that he was an American caused no political reaction since the presence of so many "old country" Methodists ensured conservatism and respectability in Nova Scotia.

When the first Nova Scotian Conference was held in 1786 the circuit work was regularized. The Methodists now had some six hundred adherents served by five preachers. When Garretson returned to the United States in 1789 Black emerged as the leader of Methodism in the colony, acting in effect as the superintendent of one district of the American Methodist Episcopal Church. Since Black and the two Mann brothers, James and John, were ordained by Coke and Asbury in 1789 the Methodist ministry in Nova Scotia was now on a formal basis. James Wray, the first British volunteer, had arrived in 1787 but soon left because his colleagues refused to enforce certain Methodist rules which they considered unsuited to a pioneer community. Wray believed American influences were making Nova Scotian Methodists hostile to England, an opinion apparently shared by Wesley himself when he commented "O, American gratitude! Lord, I appeal to thee".[29] In subsequent years preachers arrived from both the United States and Britain, but the American influence never brought charges of disloyalty as in Upper Canada. In the Maritime regions the Loyalist "fact" was so deeply rooted in the religious and political fabric that it never faced or feared Americanizing influences. Unlike the Canadas, the Maritimes received no "post-Loyalist" immigrants from the United States. Year-round communications with the mother country were possible, so that the Maritimes naturally looked eastward in religious as in all other matters. Above all, Methodism in the Maritimes continued that same deferential relationship to the "national" Church of England which Wesley himself maintained and urged.

William Black still made Halifax his headquarters and the other Methodist clergy similarly settled in a pastorate and itinerated only during a part of the year in a hybrid of the parish and the circuit systems that produced more of the disadvantages of each than advantages. Methodism in Nova Scotia received a temporary impetus when six preachers volunteered at the New York Conference in 1791 to return with Black. Another arrival of that year was Abraham John Bishop, a native of Jersey Island who responded to the request for a French-speaking clergyman to work among the Acadians at Memramcook. Armed with a letter of introduction to Governor Parr from the colonial under-secretary, Bishop was warmly received at Halifax and even offered ordination by Bishop Inglis.[30] Bishop altered his itinerary to visit some Methodists at Saint John who had been asking the New York Conference for a preacher. His stay there resulted in the immediate formation of several classes with a sizable number of Negro members, but New Brunswick was so solidly Anglican that nonconformity of any variety was rare. By 1800 membership was only eight hundred and fifty with three thousand adherents, of whom less than two hundred were in New Brunswick, while Prince Edward Island no longer reported. The lack of preachers was a serious handicap in Nova Scotia but desperate in New Brunswick—in 1795 the Methodists had eight preachers in the Maritimes but four years later this number had shrunk to six because of the withdrawal of all American preachers.

In the early 1790s Methodism in all the Atlantic colonies began to attract hostile attention from the Anglican church and state establishment, a development which reversed the previously tolerant and even friendly attitude towards Wesley's followers. This change in the religious climate became apparent first in New Brunswick where one preacher was temporarily silenced by court injunction obtained by the Anglican rector of Fredericton, and another barely escaped from a lynch mob in Sussex Vale. In 1792 Black was threatened with imprisonment at Saint John for preaching without a licence.[31] The attitude of the Maritime Methodists towards the "national church" had always been divided—a majority had no scruples about organic separation from the Church of England but a minority were, for a generation at least, unwilling to hold their services at the same hour as the "church" worshipped. It was probably Black's holding of concurrent services at the new Methodist chapel in Halifax that sparked Charles Inglis's letter to the S.P.G. in which he equated the Methodists with the New Lights and accused the former of "the greatest extravagances" since their "formal schism from the Church of England."[32] The bishop was not alone in these denunciations of "enthusiasts" and "fanatics" as the bitterness of denominational disputes began in the 1790s to erode the previous religious harmony and tolerant spirit of the Lower Provinces.

RELIGIOUS AWAKENING IN NEWFOUNDLAND

In the wake of the American Revolution the surviving British colonies had received considerable attention from the imperial government, but rather less attention from the Christian churches. Newfoundland, however, remained Britain's forgotten possession even in matters of religion for at least another generation. Two or three S.P.G. missionaries were present on the island at any given time; the first resident Catholic priest arrived in 1770; and Moravians established Eskimo missions in northern Labrador in 1771,[33] but that was the extent of religious facilities.

The most notable religious development in the latter half of the eighteenth century was the appearance of Methodist influences. In 1765 Lawrence Coughlan, one of John Wesley's followers, arrived in Newfoundland to find no church building and no school in existence, the only clergy being the S.P.G. missionaries at St. John's and Trinity.[34] After preaching at Harbour Grace and Carbonear for two years, Coughlan was accepted by the S.P.G. as their missionary, and was subsequently ordained by the Bishop of London. Coughlan's evangelistic message produced a religious revival and a remarkable reform of morals in the area of Conception Bay and Blackhead near St. John's. He continued to report the progress of Methodism in frequent letters to John Wesley until ill health forced him back to England in 1773.

Coughlan's successor at Harbour Grace was soon complaining that the "Dissenters and Methodists" in his new mission wanted a preacher of their own.[35] For ten years he met only distrust and coolness from his congregation while two of Coughlan's converts acted as lay preachers to the small and scattered bands of Methodists between Trinity Bay and Conception Bay. When the inhabitants of Old Perlican in 1779 requested that their local preacher be ordained, the Bishop of London replied that three missionaries were sufficient for Newfoundland. Wesley was highly critical of this rebuff, and of the S.P.G. missionaries in Newfoundland whom he characterized as men with "no claim to piety, nor even decency."[36] When another request for help reached Wesley, he turned to Coke and the newly created American Methodist church. But no missionary could be spared from that source, so that the English Methodist Conference of 1785 sent John McGeary, the first ordained Methodist preacher in Newfoundland, to Carbonear.

When McGeary left just three years later after quarrelling with the Methodist lay preachers, William Black came from Nova Scotia in 1791 to investigate the disorganized state of Methodism. He discovered that the fruits of Coughlan's revival had virtually vanished. The Methodist classes at Carbonear and Harbour Grace had each dwindled to a mere dozen women, but Black's preaching began a revival as spontaneous as Coughlan's a generation earlier. Newfoundland was obviously a field ripe for spiritual harvesting, but that task could not be met by occasional visitors. A continuous ministry was needed to give direction and permanency to the scattered Methodist classes that had been gathered by local workers. The English Methodist Conference had in fact appointed several preachers, but some failed to reach their missions and the few who arrived usually left within a couple of years.

At the end of the eighteenth century the religious state of Newfoundland was still distressing. Although the British government had provided salaries for five S.P.G. missionaries, as late as 1810 only two Anglican clergymen resided on the Island. Residents at several outports had built churches at their own expense in a vain attempt to attract clergy from England. Methodism remained largely dependent on the labours of local preachers. John Jones, an ex-soldier turned Congregational minister whom Black met at St. John's in 1791, found few parishioners in a population so generally lacking the middle class to which Congregationalism traditionally appealed.[37]

In contrast to Protestant neglect of Newfoundland, the Roman Catholic Church was successful in winning masses of converts. The papacy appointed James Louis O'Donel, an Irish Franciscan, Superior of the Mission of the Island of Newfoundland in 1784, the same year that "liberty of conscience" was proclaimed on the Island and the first Roman Catholic chapel built.[38] Under O'Donel's direction a small band of priests, mostly Irish, travelled by ship from one outport to the next, defying the hardships of sea and shore to bring religion to the spiritually destitute. Their converts were numbered in thousands—more than five hundred residents of one Conception Bay settlement were reported to have embraced Romanism in the space of six years.[39] O'Donel's efforts were credited with producing a large measure of peace and order on the Island, especially among the Irish settlers, and his diocesan statutes issued in 1801 effectively controlled some priests who hitherto had been both independent and restive. From its beginning the Roman Catholic Church in Newfoundland was intimately associated with Ireland—O'Donel and his successor in 1806, Patrick Lambert, as well as most of the priests, came directly from the Emerald Isle, and contacts with the diocese of Quebec were relatively few.[40]

It was the Methodists and Congregationalists of England rather than the Church of England, or any of the church bodies based in continental North America, that made the first concerted efforts to stem this tide of proselytism to Rome by filling the vacuum with Protestant clergy. Through the efforts of Jones, a Congregationalist minister was sent to Twillingate in 1799 by the interdenominational London Missionary Society, but the Society's interest in Newfoundland waned when a second missionary was captured by a French privateer. The year 1799 was also a turning point for Methodism as James Bulpit arrived from the English conference to establish a continuous ministry. After 1808 the number of Methodist preachers and class members increased steadily, and when the Wesleyan Methodist Missionary Society was formed in 1813 Newfoundland became a mission district with a fully established circuit system.

The determining influences in Newfoundland's religious growth continued to be the isolation of settlements in small pockets along the coast and the ethnic nature of those settlements. Irish Roman Catholics predominated in the southern part of the Avalon peninsula, English Protestants in the northern—and for both groups the ties were to Great Britain rather than either the United States or the other British North American colonies. This combination of settlement patterns and religious allegiances set Newfoundland apart from the mainstream of North American religious development and permanently influenced the church affiliation and educational system of her people.

NOTES TO CHAPTER TWO

1. I. F. Mackinnon, *Settlements and Churches in Nova Scotia 1749-1776* (Halifax: 1930), pp. 24-27, 70-76.
2. William Gregg, *History of the Presbyterian Church in the Dominion of Canada* (Toronto: 1885), pp. 60-64.
3. Juw fon Wearinga, "The First Protestant Ordination in Canada: The Story of Bruin Romkes Comingo, 1723-1820," *The Bulletin*, UCA, 1958, pp. 19-32.
4. C. R. Cronmiller, *A History of the Lutheran Church in Canada* (n.p., Evangelical Lutheran Synod of Canada, 1961), pp. 47-50.
5. N. McL. Rogers, "Apostle to the Micmacs," *Dalhousie Review*, VI ((July, 1926), pp. 166-76.
6. W. J. Osborne, "Joseph Mathurin Bourg, First Acadian Priest," *CCHAR*, 1950, pp. 31-36.
7. Norah Story, "The Church and State 'Party' in Nove Scotia, 1749-1851," *Collections of the Nova Scotia Historical Society*, XXVII (1947), 33-57.
8. *Census of Canada*, 1871, Vol. 4.
9. *RAPQ*, 1929-30, p. 96, H.-T. Cramahé to J.-O. Briand, 29 October, 1772.
10. For a modern and highly readable biography of Alline, see J. M. Bumsted, *Henry Alline* (Toronto: University of Toronto Press, 1971).
11. PAC, C.O. 5, v. 108, Guy Carleton to Lord Townshend, 26 October 1783, and Carleton to Lord North, 26 August 1783.
12. R. V. Harris, *Charles Inglis, Missionary, Loyalist, Bishop (1734-1816)* (Toronto: General Board of Religious Education, 1937), pp. 40-57.
13. Judith Fingard, "Charles Inglis and his Primitive Bishoprick in Nova Scotia", *CHR*, XLIX (3) (September, 1968), pp. 250, 251, 257.
14. PAC, *Report*, 1913, pp. 231, 232, 235, Journal of Charles Inglis; *ibid.*, 1912, p. 254, Charles Inglis to Dr. W. Morice, 15 November 1797.
15. *Ibid.*, 1912, p. 237, Charles Inglis to Grenville, 20 May 1790.
16. *Ibid.*, p. 244, Charles Inglis to Dr. W. Morice, 20 March 1792.
17. C. E. Thomas, "The Early Days of King's College, Windsor, Nova Scotia 1750-1810," *JCCHS*, VI (3) (September 1964), pp. 30-45.
18. PAC, Shelburne Papers, Vol. 88, p. 124, J. Parr to Lord Shelburne, 9 October 1789.
19. PAC *Report*, 1912, p. 252, Charles Inglis to Dr. W. Morice, 14 March, 1797.
20. J. S. Moir, *Church and State in Canada 1627-1867: Basic Documents*, Carleton Library No. 33 (Toronto: McClelland and Stewart, 1967), pp. 62-63, C. Inglis to Archbishop of Canterbury, 26 July 1800.
21. PAC, Nova Scotia "A", Vol. 132, pp. 158-61, Sir John Wentworth to John King, 8 November 1800.
22. *RAPQ*, 1930-1, p. 189, L.-P. Desgly to Butler, 23 October 1785. See also A. A. Johnston, *A History of the Catholic Church in Eastern Nova Scotia* (Antigonish: St. Francis Xavier U.P., 1960), chap. 22.
23. George Patterson, *Memoir of the Rev. James MacGregor, D.D.* (Edinburgh: Oliphant, 1859), p. 257.
24. G. E. Levy, *The Baptists of the Maritime Provinces 1753-1946* (Saint John: Barnes-Hopkins, 1946), Chaps. 2 and 3.
25. Gregg, *op. cit.*, chap. 3.
26. Patterson, *op. cit.*, p. 136. MacGregor described the wedding of a man who spoke only English and a woman who spoke only Gaelic—"How they managed to court or to converse afterwards I know not," *ibid.*
27. Matthew Richey, *A Memoir of the Late Rev. William Black . . .* (Halifax, 1839), pp. 47 ff.

28. Goldwin French, *Parsons & Politics* (Toronto: Ryerson, 1962), p. 33.
29. Quoted in T. W. Smith, *History of the Methodist Church . . . of Eastern British America* (2 vols.; Halifax, 1877, 1890), Vol. I, p. 208.
30. *Ibid.*, Vol. I, p. 220.
31. Richey, *op. cit.*, pp. 278-81.
32. Smith, *op. cit.*, Vol. I, pp. 350-51.
33. W. H. Whiteley, "The Establishment of the Moravian Mission in Labrador and British Policy, 1763-83," *CHR*, XLV (1), (March 1964), pp. 29-50.
34. Lawrence Coughlan, *An Account of the Work of God in Newfoundland . . .* (London, 1776).
35. Smith, *op. cit.*, Vol. I, p. 65.
36. Quoted in Smith, *op. cit.*, Vol. I, p. 72.
37. D. W. Prowse, *A History of Newfoundland* (London: Macmillan, 1895), p. 363; *Supplement*, pp. 49-51.
38. *Ibid.*, p. 363; *Supplement*, p. 27.
39. Smith, *op. cit.*, Vol. I, p. 354.
40. Lambert spent eleven months of 1811/12 in Ireland recruiting missionaries for Newfoundland. *RAPQ*, 1932-3, p. 85, Patrick Lambert to J.-O. Plessis, 12 June 1812.

THREE

Catholic Colony—Protestant Empire

Throughout the summer of 1759 General Wolfe's fleet blockaded New France's lifeline, the St. Lawrence, and his army pounded the citadel of Quebec with shot and shell. When the siege ended in September with the British victory on the Plains of Abraham, every building in Quebec had been damaged and one-third had been destroyed. The cathedral and the episcopal palace were empty shells; the Ursuline convent and school, the houses and chapels of the Jesuits and of the seminary were heavily damaged.[1] Seven parish churches and fourteen parsonages in the neighbourhood of Quebec lay in ruins while half of the city's population of thirty-five hundred had fled to the countryside. The Articles of Quebec's capitulation granted the free exercise of the Roman Catholic religion and permitted the bishop to use his religious authority "until the possession of Canada shall have been decided,"[2] but the ailing Bishop Pontbriand had already found asylum in French-held Montreal, leaving Jean Olivier Briand, his friend and fellow Breton, at Quebec as senior vicar general.

Throughout the winter of 1759/60 the citizens and the occupying army shared the shattered city. General James Murray, the military governor, took every possible measure to ensure equal treatment to conquered and conqueror alike. Military guards were posted to protect the lives and property of the religious community. When the Hôtel-Dieu was requisitioned as a hospital for the two thousand sick and wounded of the British army, Murray ensured that these services were fully paid for and that the nursing nuns received regular rations from the already strained resources of the army. The Ursulines, who also served as nurses, were given rations as well, and when harvest-time arrived the next summer soldier volunteers helped nearby farmers with their field work. The warm relationship established between the Canadians and the army in occupied Quebec was a bright omen for the future relations of British and French in Canada.

Quebec's hopes of liberation rose briefly in the spring of 1760 when a force from Montreal defeated the decimated British army outside Quebec, but hope was soon dashed by the arrival of British convoys. When no help came from France, Montreal surrendered without a fight one year after the capture of Quebec. Thus the French era closed, and although a peace treaty had yet to be signed the prospects for the Roman Church in Canada were uncertain. As France publicly celebrated its good fortune at losing the colony, one French priest commented from Canada, "It will cost the English little to make [the Canadians] appreciate the advantage of changing masters, since [the English] have only to do the opposite of what we [French] have done."[3]

THE CONDITION OF THE CHURCH

Not only were the conquerors Protestants but the church had lost its leader when Bishop Pontbriand died at Montreal in the summer of 1760. Without a bishop to ordain a priesthood, the sacramental life of the church was doomed to extinction. Without a bishop to administer the diocese, chaos and irregularities threatened.

The lack of a bishop was only one of many problems besetting the church under the occupation. The Articles of Capitulation for Montreal had been more specific on the matter of religion than the Articles for Quebec of the previous year. The free exercise of religion was reaffirmed, the property of the church protected, and communities of nuns were granted their existing rights, but the future of the Jesuits, Recollets and Sulpicians was to be decided by the British king. Meanwhile members of the male communities, mostly French-born, were given permission and encouragement to return to France. A request that the King of France might name future bishops was firmly refused, the care of the diocese being left in the hands of the vicars general appointed by the Cathedral Chapter in Quebec. This twelve-member chapter, established in 1684, had become more decorative than functional. At the Conquest one canonry was vacant, three officers (including the Canadian-born dean, Lacorne) had lived in France for several years, and three more canons resided outside Quebec city. Only six canons, five of them Canadian, remained at the cathedral and two of these soon went to France, leaving only four to meet in July 1760 and reappoint the vicars general to govern the diocese as the dead bishop had requested.[4]

One of the most serious problems confronting the church was the sudden decline in the number of clergy. At the beginning of 1759 the one hundred and ninety-six clergy included the bishop, nine canons, thirty Recollets, thirty-one Jesuits, thirty-four Sulpicians and ninety-one secular priests. Two years later they numbered only one hundred and sixty-three—six canons, twenty-four Recollets, twenty-five Jesuits, thirty Sulpicians, five Gentlemen of the Quebec Seminary and seventy-three seculars. Twenty-one, including Bishop Pontbriand, had died and twelve had left for France. Although 81 per cent of the canons and seculars were Canadian by birth, only one Canadian occupied an important post, while of the sixty Jesuits, Sulpicians and Gentlemen of the Seminary not one had been born in Canada.[5] Not only could no new priests be ordained after Pontbriand's death but the Jesuits and Recollets were forbidden by the British to receive any new members.

Unlike the male religious communities, the orders of nuns received preferred treatment from the conquerors. The Ursulines, the Hospitalières of the Hôtel-Dieu and of the General Hospital in Quebec, all received payment for services to the British as well as gifts, although the General Hospital, religious centre for the diocese during the occupation, lost General Murray's good will by spreading anti-British rumours.[6] Yet the expenses of these three communities and of the Montreal Hôtel-Dieu regularly surpassed their income. Only the small, independent Ursuline convent at Trois-Rivières and the Montreal General Hospital came through the occupation period without encountering serious money problems. The largest female order, the uncloistered Congregation of Nôtre-Dame, which taught reading and writing to young girls, contained almost a third of all nuns in the province and recruited its members from the poorer classes. For the congregation the Conquest and occupation brought the loss of four of its ten establishments through war damage, expropriation or abandonment.[7]

While the French colony awaited news of the peace treaty that would determine its destiny, the three British military governors—Murray at Quebec, Burton at Trois-Rivières and Gage at Montreal—reported to the British government on the state of their respective areas. Where Burton and Gage submitted perfunctory reports noting the general satisfaction of the inhibitants with their religious freedom, Murray's report was voluminous and detailed, and offered many suggestions for future policy. Commenting on the church he observed that because the Canadians were "extremely tenacious of their religion, nothing can contribute so much to make them staunch subjects to his Majesty as the new Government giving them every reason to imagine no alteration is to be attempted in that point."[8] Since many clergy, especially the "dignified part," had formerly come from France, Canadians must now be encouraged to enter the profession. This would require the continuation of the seminary and the early appointment of a bishop. In Murray's opinion the Jesuits were "neither loved nor esteemed" and if banished from the colony their vast properties—over twelve hundred square miles—would make a good endowment for a bishop. The mendicant Recollets might yet withdraw voluntarily for "a better living somewhere else," but the various orders of nuns were so popular that they should be preserved and encouraged by the British government.

As Murray's report suggests, there was never any real doubt that New France (or Canada, to use its popular name) would become a British colony. It remained to be seen how the government would fit a French-speaking Roman Catholic colony of some sixty thousand souls into the framework of an English and Protestant empire where dissent from the state church meant the loss of political rights. The Peace Treaty, signed at Paris in February, 1763, contained no surprises. Being a settlement to a global war, only one of its twenty-seven clauses mentioned Canada. That colony became part of George III's Protestant empire and its Roman Catholic population were granted freedom of religion—"as far as the laws of Great Britain permit,"[9] a proviso that left His Majesty's "new subjects" simply in a state of toleration. Details of policy regarding Canada were left to be worked out in the future.

THE IMPACT OF THE PEACE

The detailed plans for the future of Quebec, as the new colony was officially called, were laid down by the Board of Trade and Plantations which advised the British government on all aspects of colonial administration. One cause of the recent war had been the overflowing of British settlers beyond the Appalachian Mountains into the French-held Mississippi Basin. Now, thanks to the Conquest, Britain seemed on the point of solving the two related problems of providing new lands for colonists and of forestalling Indian troubles over white settlement in the interior. The Indian lands in the West could be closed to settlement and the tide of migration diverted to Quebec.

The board's report on Quebec, in June 1763, was an expression of pure mercantilism—the colony was examined only for what it could contribute to the strength of the British Empire. Three later documents clarified the board's intentions. The first, the famous Proclamation of October 1763, closed the Mississippi Basin to settlement, defined Quebec's boundaries and provided it with the constitution common to royal colonies—a governor and appointed council, an elected assembly, and a legal system "as near as may be agreeable to the laws of England."[10] Murray became the first governor of Quebec and his commission and instructions completed this outline for government. He was charged to respect and protect the Church of Rome in Quebec but not "to admit of any Ecclesiastical Jurisdiction of the See of Rome." The Church of England would be established "both in Principle and Practice" with government support under the direction of the Bishop of London, and the governor was authorized to fill all Anglican vacancies. Finally, all "new subjects" must take an oath of loyalty to King George or quit the colony."[11] As a result of this British policy the Roman Catholic Church found itself cut off from its physical and financial resources in France and its spiritual roots in Rome. The Roman Church had been the established church of New France; now it would be only a tolerated church of legally second-class citizens, controlled by an alien and Protestant king. Quebec was to become an English and Anglican colony—at least in theory.

Just two weeks after the signing of the Treaty of Paris, Lacorne, Dean of the Chapter of Quebec, arrived in London to seek a solution to the problem of the vacant bishopric, undoubtedly with an eye to his own advancement.[12] The British government, at Murray's urging, were prepared to grant this boon to the "new subjects," even though it would nullify the official policy of weaning the Canadians from Romanism to Protestantism. But the real issue was, who should name a new bishop—the Pope, the King of England, or the Chapter? English law prohibited either a royal nomination or a papal one, so it was privately agreed by the government that a bishop, to be recognized by Britain simply as "Superior of the Clergy," might, subject to the royal veto, be elected by the chapter and then discreetly consecrated by papal authority.

With French-born Vicar General J. O. Briand presiding, the four canons unanimously chose Etienne Montgolfier, Superior of the Sulpicians, to be the new bishop. Montgolfier left at once for England as did a prominent merchant, sent at a cost to the parishes of six thousand livres, to carry supporting petitions from the laity and to act as negotiator with the British government.[13] But their journey was in vain—Montgolfier was fated never to be a bishop. Murray's adverse report on him as a possible bishop was taken by the government as a virtual veto and, to clinch Montgolfier's rejection, Rome accused the chapter of usurping papal power by choosing its own bishop. In view of these unexpected developments Montgolfier withdrew his candidacy and returned to Montreal.

In September 1764 the chapter met again, and unanimously accepted Governor Murray's nominee, J. O. Briand, who was then simply recommended to the papacy to avoid another clash of authority.[14] Briand seems to have refused the nomination twice but was finally persuaded to accept. He arrived in England in November, only to encounter a rude setback in his plans for the diocese. J. B. Roubaud, an apostate Jesuit who had been welcomed into Governor Murray's own household in 1763 as a self-appointed adviser on all matters concerning the colony, had gone to London earlier in 1764. There his connection with Murray and his malicious statements regarding the religious wishes of the "new subjects" gained him the ear of certain British government officials who wished to believe that the Canadians might yet be converted to Protestantism.[15] The government's attitude towards Briand and the Roman Church hardened perceptibly.

For the next eleven months Briand waited in England to receive an honour he did not want and which, if conferred, he hoped soon to pass on to someone more capable of the heavy responsibilities. At last the British government gave its approval and the necessary papal bulls were obtained early in 1766. On March 16 Briand was consecrated seventh Bishop of Quebec in a private ceremony near Paris, thus assuring the continuation of the life of the church in Canada, at least during his lifetime. Soon a double assurance arrived in the form of bulls permitting Briand to choose and consecrate a coadjutor who would automatically succeed him. Never again would it be necessary to fight on two fronts—Rome and London—to secure the succession of bishops at Quebec. As a final mark of recognition the Assembly of the Clergy of France granted the unendowed bishop an annual pension of three thousand livres for life.[16] With a bishop consecrated and his successor provided for, the chapter had now outlived its usefulness. No more canons were appointed and after its last member died in 1795 the lack of a cathedral chapter was never felt.

Two other bodies that also disappeared under the British regime were the Jesuits and the Recollets—the Sulpicians, who hastened to entrench themselves by purchasing their Canadian property from the parent French body, were eventually left undisturbed because they were secular clergy. The Recollets, forbidden to receive new members, dwindled from twenty-four in 1764 to five in 1791, and vanished when the last one died in 1813. Two Recollets, Michel Houdin and Emmanuel Veyssière, were accepted as Anglican priests after the Conquest, and the Recollet chapel in Quebec was shared as a place of worship for several years with the Church of England. As for the Society of Jesus, which had played a dominant role in the religious history of New France since 1625 and had given the Church seven martyr saints, its golden age was ending in Europe almost at the moment Britain acquired Quebec. Feared for their political power as tutors and confessors of Catholic princes, the Jesuits' days were numbered in the plans of their many enemies and rivals.

To Protestants the Jesuit Order epitomized the most subtle and dangerous aspects of the Counter-Reformation, but its fate was sealed first by its exclusion from Catholic France in 1763 and completed by a papal order for its total dissolution in 1766. In Canada its extinction came more slowly. Since the Empire was officially Protestant the Pope's decree of 1766 could not be legally enforced in the colony, but British policy forbade recruiting by the Jesuits. They remained in Canada, protected by their Protestant king from the authority of their spiritual father until death removed the last Jesuit in 1800. Yet even in death the Society of Jesus left a troublesome legacy to its destroyers, for the disposition of the society's estates in Quebec provided a bone of contention between church and state as late as 1888.[17]

"THESE HAPPY BEGINNINGS"

The return of Bishop Briand to his diocese was like a Roman triumph. After a month-long visit to his family in France and another month spent in London he reached Quebec at the end of June, 1766, amidst a tumultuous welcome from the whole populace. A Jesuit who accompanied him reported, "The English vied with Roman Catholics in showing their joy. . . . The principal Anglican minister here himself showed and made his children show their respect and veneration."[18] "These happy beginnings," wrote Cardinal Castelli from Rome in a letter intended for Briand, "give us great hope that things will go well in the future."[19]

The "happy beginnings" were solidly grounded on the mutual esteem in which Briand and Murray held each other from the period of the occupation onwards. Without currying favour Briand and Montgolfier had responded to Murray's generous treatment of the church in a spirit of cooperation. Briand justified this policy of obedience and support for civil authority by citing St. Paul's famous dictum of Romans 13:1. In 1762 prayers for the Protestant King George III were introduced into the Mass and special prayers were said for his marriage. "They are our masters," remarked Briand, "and we owe them what we used to owe to the French."[20] In administering the diocese Briand regularly sought and received Murray's approval of changes that might involve government policy. Impressed with Briand's uprightness and good will Murray exempted his correspondence from the censorship imposed on all communications to and from the colony.

Murray, however, had left Quebec on the very day that Bishop Briand returned. He went home to answer the charges of English-speaking merchants that his actions were frustrating the imperial intention to make Quebec into an English colony. If this meant that he had not persecuted the Roman Catholics, Murray retorted, "I plead 'Guilty.' "[21] His Huguenot Attorney General, Francis Maseres, had decided on second thought that even the British government had been duped by the specious and sophistical arguments of Murray's secretary, H.-T. Cramahé, in favour of the "imprudent measure" to reestablish the Roman Catholic episcopate at Quebec. "I incline," wrote Maseres, "to think that, if during the seven years we have possessed this country, vigorous measures had been taken to patronise and introduce the protestant religion, though without the least persecution of the Popish, half the country would already have turned Protestants."[22] The Catholics, he was convinced, had given up hopes for a bishop, but now Briand, who was supposed to be only a "superintendent," publicly wore purple robes and a gold cross and was universally referred to as "the bishop."

If Briand was disturbed by this growing hostility towards the Roman Church in some government circles he was soon reassured about future church-state relations after the new governor, Guy Carleton, arrived in the autumn of 1766. A career soldier who had been wounded on the Plains of Abraham, Carleton's rather stiff dignity masked a reverence for honesty and justice which made him a more ardent admirer and protector of the "new subjects" in Quebec than even Murray had been. Briand soon formed a high opinion of Carleton. "Here we enjoy profound peace under the government of one of the most lovable men and religion is freely exercised, and more fervently by many than ever before. We have no further affliction to fear than losing him." "We hardly know we are under a Protestant government. In civil life Catholics and Protestants get along well together. The [holy] ministry goes on as it did in the time of the French."[23] Yet, however satisfying Carleton's support might be to the church, Briand still found it necessary to tread warily through the minefield of church-state relations. Commenting on a disciplinary matter involving the Montreal Congregation of Nôtre-Dame he warned Vicar General Marchand, "It won't do to be so tough on certain occasions; it was all right previously. Today things have changed, you know."[24]

The internal problems of the diocese facing Briand on his return in 1766 were almost overwhelming. The recruiting of priests had now been suspended for seven years and their numbers had been reduced by one-third. Many neighbouring parishes had been amalgamated because of the shortage of clergy. Although most of the war damage had been suffered in the region of Quebec City, the need to repair private homes and public buildings had to take precedence over rebuilding churches in the reconstruction era. The grants previously received from the King of France by all religious bodies except the seminary had now ceased. Credits in France were hard to collect and the French paper money was discounted as much as 75 per cent after the Peace. Parish curés repeatedly complained that this almost worthless currency found its way regularly into church collection boxes.

THE PROTESTANT PRESENCE IN QUEBEC

The Conquest was not without some beneficial results for the Roman church. The ties of the Canadian church with the government of France and with Gallicanism had been severed—hereafter its contacts were with bodies directly dependent on the papacy. Since church and state were no longer legally connected as they had been under the French, there was less political interference in matters of religion. The British government's policy called for the church to be Canadian in its personnel and British in its loyalty, and this process of Canadianization was promoted by the limitations put on the Recollets and Jesuits. Thus the importance of the secular clergy increased because they were largely Canadian and because the church was the only organized body which could speak to and for the Canadian people. Within two generations of the Conquest the church had become wholly Canadian, identified with and sometimes even identical to French-Canadian culture. Only the church could provide a dike against cultural assimilation of the Canadians to the English and Protestant way of life.

No threat of assimilation ever really developed. English settlers did not flock to Quebec and no attempt was made to provide an elected assembly in a colony where the vast majority of citizens were legally incapable of voting because of England's Test Act of 1673. The handful of Americans and

Scots who took over the fur trade and the economic life of the colony as their fruits of victory made little direct impression on its cultural life. But they were the real key to the provinces politics. A small but vocal and powerful minority, their charges that Murray kept old and new subjects divided "by most flagrant Partialities, by fomenting Parties,"[25] had forced his recall. Carleton's larger arts of diplomacy brought a brief armistice between the commercial and governmental groups. Yet the basic contradiction remained between the avowed imperial policy to make Canada British and the conciliatory practices of a fair-minded governor towards the French population.[26] Officially the religion of Quebec might be Anglican but the lack of settlers and of Anglican institutions ensured that the Roman Catholic Church remained the dominant, almost the exclusive, religious influence for years.

Protestant chaplains had been with the British army and fleet at Quebec, and on September 23, 1759, the soldiers attended a Thanksgiving service on the field of their recent victory.[27] On the twenty-seventh of that month the first public Protestant service was held in the Ursuline convent chapel by the Reverend Eli Dawson, chaplain of the flagship H.M.S. *Stirling Castle*. One week later several Huguenot merchants attended divine service in the same chapel and after November worship was conducted there regularly on Wednesdays and Sundays.

As the military subjugation of New France proceeded, Protestant church services were held by chaplains in other places. The Reverend John Ogilvie, S.P.G. missionary of Albany, accompanied the Royal American Regiment to Niagara in the summer of 1759 and performed a Church of England service in the chapel of the French fort. The following year he accompanied General Amherst to Montreal and remained there as garrison chaplain.[28] Hopeful of winning some French Canadians for his church, Ogilvie asked the S.P.G. to send French bibles, prayer books, and religious tracts "written in the spirit of moderation and Christian charity."[29] Michel Houdin, a former Recollet who had served in Canada before his conversion into an S.P.G. missionary, had come to Quebec with the 48th Regiment and had been retained there by General Murray for liaison with the inhabitants. The few Huguenots who had been allowed to settle in Quebec City before the Conquest now had in Houdin their own minister and were for the first time able to worship publicly. But Houdin left in 1761 and other chaplains did so soon after, so that by 1764 the Reverend John Brooke at Quebec and the Reverend Samuel Bennet at Montreal were the only Protestant clergymen left in the colony. Brooke successively shared the Ursuline and Recollet chapels with the Roman Catholics, and Bennet shared the Hôtel-Dieu chapel in Montreal. Bennet sought an appointment as an S.P.G. missionary but apparently departed with his regiment. In 1766 the Reverend D. C. Delisle, minister of a French church in London, was appointed garrison chaplain of Montreal and the Reverend

George Henry, former Church of Scotland chaplain to a Scottish regiment, organized the first Presbyterian congregation in a room of the Jesuit Barracks at Quebec.[30]

In 1762 General Murray had recommended the granting of a church for use of French Protestants and the appointment of a clergyman "of sound sense and good character." Two years later he reported the presence of one hundred and forty-four Protestant householders in Quebec and fifty-six in Montreal, but only ten were qualified for jury duty. On the eve of his departure he commented on the variety of religions represented at Quebec—Quakers, Puritans, Anabaptists, Jews, Presbyterians and Anglicans, as well as the great Catholic majority.[31] At the same time Brooke asked the governor to keep the former bishop's palace for the use of a future Anglican bishop, pointing out that seven years after the Conquest Anglicans were still without their own place of worship. Protestants in the colony were also concerned at the lack of educational facilities. A short-lived school for Protestant boys at Quebec had closed in 1764, and as there was no school for Protestant girls they were put under the care of the Ursulines. The only result of petitions to the government was a hundred-pound grant towards an English Protestant school opened in Montreal by public subscription.

This retarded growth of the established church was not entirely due to indifference on the part of the Church of England. In April 1764 the Archbishop of York presented the government with a lengthy document entitled "Thoughts upon the Ecclesiastical estabilshment in Canada," which proposed to devote the properties of the Jesuits and Recollets to the use of the Church of England.[32] In a further memo the archbishop pointed out the limited authority which the Bishop of London could exercise over the North American part of his diocese. The appointment of a resident colonial bishop, so long demanded by the Church of England in the older colonies, was again discussed, but it required the American Revolution to bring about such an appointment.

In 1767 the Archbishop of York suggested the expansion of Anglican church facilities to include two ministers at Quebec and two at Montreal, along with Anglican schools in those places staffed by bilingual teachers. The purpose of such an establishment was to win converts from Rome by means of language. The instructions issued to the new governor, Guy Carleton, in 1768 were a literal transcript of those given to Murray five years before, but privately he was recommended "particularly to countenance the Established church."[33] Still the plan for an Anglican establishment was doomed to disappointment. Canadians did not desert the Church of Rome despite the appointment of the Swiss David François de Montmollin to replace the English-speaking John Brooke as Anglican parish priest of Quebec. By 1770 de Montmollin was reporting that the number of his communicants had fallen from fifteen to three, and only two conversions had been recorded. Most Protestants, he explained, were dissenters who supported the Presbyterian George Henry. At Montreal, Chaplain Delisle's complaint was different. His congregation contained five hundred soldiers and four hundred civilians but no church was provided for their exclusive use. Delisle was anxious to become an S.P.G. missionary and be paid for his semi-annual visits to the garrison at Fort Chambly. At Trois-Rivières Veyssière was inducted as parish priest at the same time and on the same terms as de Montmollin, only because the home government had been unaware of Carleton's "mean opinion" of him.[34] The only remaining English-speaking clergy were Henry and a regimental chaplain at Quebec.

THE PERPETUATION OF THE ROMAN CHURCH

After the Conquest all priests who refused the oath of loyalty to the English king had been sent to France, and Carleton deliberately fostered the Canadianization of the church and the friendship of Canadians by restricting the immigration of foreign priests and by showing government preference to native-born clergy. The French clergy, remarked Cramahé, "have always had a thorough contempt" for Canadians, and Carleton, aware of this conflict, had suggested that "at present it would be judicious to throw what advantages there are rather into the hands of the Natives of Canada."[35]

The appointment of a coadjutor to Bishop Briand was discussed in 1767 when the bishop again expressed a wish to lay down his mitre. Before his consecration Briand had been afraid to preach but now he preached with such ease and effectiveness and was so well liked that his clergy would not hear of his resigning. When it was clear that no one but a Canadian would be acceptable to the British government—the precedent of Briand, a Frenchman, was not to be repeated—the bishop accepted Carleton's Canadian-born nominee, Louis-Philippe Desgly, the aging and deaf curé of St. Pierre on the Isle of Orleans. Briand did not think it his duty to oppose the vice-regal will in the matter of choosing his successor, but when Carleton asked that Desgly be consecrated without waiting for papal approval, Briand firmly refused to countenance such an irregularity.[36]

As the years passed it became apparent that the official British policy for Anglicizing Quebec was not being fulfilled. Quebec remained predominantly French and Roman Catholic. With a bishop empowered to choose his successor, the perpetuation of the Roman Church seemed assured. In the civil administration, difficulties of law and language confronted the government since the Canadians were unacquainted with the English legal system and unable to use the official language of the courts. The handful of English settlers enjoyed a power out of all proportion to their numbers, and contrary to Carleton's sense of fair play. So, as early as 1767 when the government began to reconsider its Quebec policy, Carleton had urged a new policy for the colony in the name of "the natural Rights of Men" and of British interests in North America. His ideal was the recreation of the old French order—church, seigneurs and habitants—for, "Barring a catastrophe shocking to think of," he concluded, "this Country must, to the end of Time, be peopled by the Canadian Race. . . ."[37] In 1770 Carleton went back to London to promote his new policy for the colony of Quebec—his dream of re-creating New France under British sovereignty.

While Carleton was away Briand's work went on with equal cooperation from Cramahé who was now promoted to lieutenant-governor. Besides routine matters the bishop was occasionally faced with novel situations. Desgly had been consecrated coadjutor of Quebec in the summer of 1772 without royal approval, and this irregularity was brought to the king's attention. Disturbed by possible political repercussions in Canada of a royal veto over Desgly, Cramahé warned the colonial secretary, Lord Dartmouth, that the maximum of religious freedom would be needed to ensure Canadian loyalty to Britain—the Catholic clergy would soon be entirely Canadian and consecration at Quebec of a coadjutor would forestall any trip abroad for that purpose.[38] Dartmouth agreed entirely. Since a new policy for Quebec would soon be announced, the Canadians would be assured of "all possible Satisfaction . . . on the Head of Religion," so that "all Foreign Jurisdiction [will] be excluded, and that those professing the Religion of the Church of Rome, may find within the Colony a resource for everything essential to the free Exercise of it, in the true Spirit of the Treaty."[39]

One foreign influence that was not excluded but actually promoted by the English presence was the cult of the Enlightenment. Even before the Conquest *philosophe* ideas had seeped into the middle class of New France despite the watchful eye of the church, but now, under the British regime, Voltaire's books circulated more freely.[40] The rapid and related rise of Freemasonry among the French of Montreal in the 1770s was stopped only by disciplinary action from the church.[41] But the solid strength of the church under Briand was seen most patently in its institutional progress. By 1774 twenty-five new parishes had been formed, and twenty-five priests ordained, although in those same eight years thirty-two priests had died and two others were not serving, so that repeated requests for priests from Canadian settlers on the Ohio could not be filled before 1774. Parish difficulties—over the location of churches, the control of pews, the clash of cliques and personalities—all absorbed the bishop's time. Briand had expected problems with the British and he had met them with a mixture of firmness and conciliation that won him respect from government officials as an honest man. He could not, however, have anticipated all the troubles that were caused by his own flock. For several years he was maligned by enemies and former friends as a haughty, ambitious, arrogant and bad-tempered man, and his opinion of his detractors was not more flattering. "They know everything about religion, more than the priests and the bishop. . . . You could go through the whole of Christendom and not find people more intractable or less religious."[42] His stubborn and protracted struggle with the church wardens of Quebec to make the rebuilt church his cathedral was happily settled by Cramahé's good offices and by instructions from Rome to the "iron-headed" bishop urging him to compromise.[43] Amid jubilant throngs Briand entered his cathedral church for the first time on the eighth anniversary of his consecration and in so doing reestablished yet another traditional tie with the religious life of New France before the Conquest.

When Governor Carleton finally returned to the colony in the autumn of 1774 his mission to England had been accomplished. The Quebec Act of which he had been the main promoter had been passed in June. Almost the whole of the policy of 1763 had been reversed. Quebec would not get a representative assembly—it would be ruled by a governor and appointed council as in the days of the French. French civil law would henceforth replace English common law. "All possible Satisfaction" to the Church included confirmation of the free exercise of the Roman Catholic religion and of the clergy's "accustomed Dues and Rights" from their flocks.[44] A new form of loyalty oath that avoided all reference to religion opened the government services for the employment of Roman Catholics, over half a century before the repeal of the Test and Corporation Acts in Britain itself. The Roman church had every reason to rejoice at the favourable terms of this act, a milestone in the history of the Canadians and their church. In Quebec the act was praised by Carleton, its godfather, and by the bishops and seigneurs whose gains in power were obvious. A contemporary cartoon entitled "The Mitred Minuet" portrayed four bishops performing a stately dance around a copy of the Quebec Act—a prophetic jibe at the religious results of Carleton's—and Britain's—new policy.

The inarticulate masses of Canada left no record of their immediate reaction to the Quebec Act, but this semi-establishment of the Roman Catholic religion in a North American colony did meet a hostile reception in other quarters. Rumblings of discontent were heard from the tiny English and Protestant minority and from a few Roman Catholic habitants who since the conquest had come to enjoy the reduced state of clerical authority. More important, the restive British colonies to the south claimed to see in the Quebec Act an instrument for the future oppression of colonial self-government and Protestantism. The Quebec Act, designed to keep Quebec British by leaving it French, was destined to inflame anti-British feeling in the other colonies without winning any expressions of general gratitude in Quebec itself.

NOTES TO CHAPTER THREE

1. Marcel Trudel, *L'Eglise Canadienne sous Le Régime militaire 1759-1764* (2 vols.; Quebec: P.U. Laval, 1957), Vol. I, pp. 9, 13, 35-36.

2. J. S. Moir, *Church and State in Canada 1627-1867: Basic Documents*, Carleton Library No. 33 (Toronto: McClelland and Stewart, 1967), pp. 772-73.

3. *Bulletin des Recherches Historiques*, XV, p. 296.

4. Auguste Gosselin, *L'Eglise du Canada après la Conquête. Première Partie 1760-1775* (Quebec: Laflamme, 1916), pp. 2-7.

5. Trudel, *op. cit.*, Vol. I, pp. 108-9, 111.

6. *Ibid.*, Vol. II, p. 312.

7. *Ibid.*, Vol. II, pp. 306-361, 335 ff., and Marcel Trudel, "Les Communautés des femmes sous le régime militaire" (*RSCHEC*, 1955-6), pp. 33-52.

8. Moir, *op. cit.*, p. 75.

9. *Ibid.*, p. 77.

10. Adam Shortt and A. G. Doughty, *Documents relating to the Constitutional History of Canada 1759-1791* (2nd and rev. ed.; Ottawa: King's Printer, 1918), p. 165.

11. Moir, *op. cit.*, pp. 78-79.

12. PAC, Q Series, Vol. I, p. 129, Lord Egremont to Sir James Murray, 13 August 1763.

13. *RAPQ*, 1929-30, p. 58, Petition of citizens of the city of Quebec, no date.

14. *Ibid.*, p. 61, Members of the Chapter to Abbé de la Corne, no date.

15. *Ibid.*, p. 62, J.-O. Briand to Etienne Marchand, 11 January 1765.

16. *Ibid.*, pp. 64-65, J.-O. Briand to the bishop of Orleans, 1 May 1766.

17. For a full and scholarly study of the history of these lands see R. C. Dalton, *The Jesuits' Estates Question 1760-1888* (Toronto: University of Toronto Press, 1968).

18. *RAPQ*, 1929-30, p. 67, A.-J.-M. Jacrau to Cardinal Colonna, 20 August 1766.

19. *Ibid.*, p. 68, Cardinal J. M. Castelli to the abbot of Ile-Dieu, Paris, 17 December 1766.

20. *Ibid.*, p. 50, J.-O. Briand to Etienne Montgolfier, 1762?

21. PAC, Murray Papers, Letter Book III, 241-43, *Memorandum*.

22. W. S. Wallace, ed., *The Maseres Letters 1766-1768* (University of Toronto Library, 1919), p. 54.

23. *RAPQ*, 1929-30, p. 79, J.-O. Briand to Sebastien Meurin, 26 April 1769.

24. *Ibid.*, 1947-8, p. 101, J.-O. Briand to Etienne Marchand, 14 July 1766.

25. Shortt and Doughty, *op. cit.*, p. 233, Petition of the Quebec Traders, 1764.

26. A. L. Burt, *The Old Province of Quebec*, Carleton Library Nos. 37, 38 (2 vols.; Toronto: McClelland and Stewart, 1968), particularly chapters VI and VII; Chester Martin, *Empire and Commonwealth*, Oxford, O.U.P., 1929, p. 94 ff.; Moir, *op. cit.*, Part Three.

27. *An Historical Journal of the Campaigns in North America . . . by Captain John Knox* (3 vols.; ed. A. G. Doughty; Toronto: Champlain Society, 1914), Vol. II, p. 143.

28. A. H. Young, "The Rev. John Ogilvie, D.D., An Army Chaplain at Fort Niagara and Montreal, 1759-1760," *OH*, XXII (1925), pp. 296-337.

29. *RAPQ*, 1948-9, p. 300.

30. *RAPQ*, 1948-9, p. 308, "Church and State Papers for the Years 1759 to 1786," extract from the Papers of the Board of the S.P.G., 14 April 1766; William Gregg, *History of the Presbyterian Church in the Dominion of Canada* (Toronto: Presbyterian, 1885), p. 146.

31. PAC, Murray Papers, Letter Book III, pp. 241-43, *Memorandum*.

32. PAC, Shelburne Manuscripts, Vol. 59, pp. 30-36. Thoughts upon the Ecclesiastical establishment in Canada, by the Archbishop of York, 11 April 1764.

33. Shortt and Doughty, *op. cit.*, p. 325, Lord Hillsborough to G. Carleton, 12 October 1768.

34. PAC, Q Series, Vol. 5-II, p. 726, G. Carleton to Lord Hillsborough, 21 July 1768; p. 757, Lord Hillsborough to G. Carleton, 12 October 1768.

35. *Ibid.*, Vol. 8, p. 160, Cramahé to Lord Hillsborough, 25 July 1772; Vol. 4, p. 321, G. Carleton to Lord Shelburne, 30 October 1767.

36. *RAPQ*, 1929-30, p. 85, J.-O. Briand to the papal nuncio in Paris, 17 July 1770; H. Têtu, ed., *Mandements, Lettres Pastorales et Circulaires des Evêques de Québec* (Quebec, 1888), Vol. II, pp. 241-43.

37. Shortt and Doughty, *op. cit.*, p. 284, G. Carleton to Lord Shelburne, 25 November 1767.

38. Moir, *op. cit.*, p. 89.

39. Shortt and Doughty, *op. cit.*, p. 485, Lord Dartmouth to H. T. Cramahé, 1 December 1773.

40. Seraphin Marion, "Le Problème voltarien," *RSCHEC*, 1939-40, pp. 27-41.

41. *RAPQ*, 1947-8, pp. 89-90, Etienne Montgolfier to J.-O. Briand, 20 January 1771; Gosselin, *op. cit.*, Première Partie, pp. 380 *ff.*

42. Quoted in Hilda Neatby, "Servitude de l'Eglise Catholique: a Reconsideration," *CCHAR*, 1969, p. 22.

43. *RAPQ*, 1929-30, p. 104, J.-O. Briand to M. Mérineau, 10 March 1774.

44. Moir, *op. cit.*, p. 97.

FOUR

Quebec and the American Revolution

During the decade between the Conquest of Canada and the passing of the Quebec Act, the thirteen older colonies along the Atlantic coast had moved from crisis to crisis towards their War of Independence. Their unrest had in fact contributed to those peculiarly un-British clauses of the Quebec Act. That act may have been greeted rapturously by the clergy and seigneurs because it restored their pre-Conquest position in society, but the English colonists of Quebec found in it no cause for rejoicing. Despite the promises of 1763, an elected assembly was now denied to them and the threat of losing their rights to habeas corpus and trial by jury hung over them. In anger and desperation some of these "old subjects" turned for sympathy and aid to the American revolutionary movement. As for the great mass of Canadians, events were soon to show how wrong had been Carleton's prediction that what pleased the Roman Catholic Church would necessarily please its flock.

The results of Carleton's political miscalculation became evident in events outside Quebec as well. The disaffected colonists to the south viewed the Quebec Act as just one more of the "Intolerable Acts" by which a tyrannical British government was attempting to destroy the British birthright of Englishmen in America. Even before fighting began at Lexington and Concord, the Americans had taken steps to win the support of Quebec to their cause. In September 1774 the Continental Congress meeting at Philadelphia invited the Canadians to join in the coming struggle for liberty—or else be treated as enemies. The Boston Committee of Correspondence sent an agent to the northern colony to promote the cause of independence and Carleton was soon made painfully aware of the success of American propaganda. Unrest, spreading from the English merchants at Montreal to the Canadians during the early months of 1775, came to a head in that city on May 1, the day that the Quebec Act came into force, with the desecration of the king's bust in the Place d'Armes.

THE REACTION IN QUEBEC

Bishop Briand had good reason to be thankful for the return of Carleton to the colony. The governor had proved himself a true friend and a protector of the church while he was in the colony from 1766 to 1770, and had won its further gratitude by obtaining extensive powers for it under the Quebec Act. The friendship and confidence of former years was now resumed between the two leaders. When the bishop had objected to the form of oath in the draft of the Quebec Act the British government had altered the oath to make it acceptable to Roman Catholics. When Briand protested the use of the word "supremacy" in the act—referring to King George's constitutional relationship to the religion of his subjects—Carleton explained to him that the term "supremacy" has been essential for the passing of the act, but since the obnoxious word was omitted in the oath he advised the bishop to "swear, and think what you please."[1]

Briand had also good reason in 1774 to be pleased with the spiritual state of his diocese. His church had made remarkable progress since those dark days of the Conquest and not a little of that progress was owing to the support of the liberal-minded English governor, Sir Guy Carleton. All classes of society, he believed, were now more pious than they had been under the French regime. But the loyalty, gratitude and even piety of Briand and his flock were soon put to the test. An abortive American invasion of the province in May 1775 forced both clergy and laity to choose between supporting the rebellious colonists or their British sovereign. For the clergy there was not a moment's hesitation in showing their gratitude for past favours received from Carleton and the British government. As Carleton prepared to rush to the defence of Montreal, Briand in the space of three hours not only composed a *mandement* directing all Canadians to repel the threatened invasion but got copies prepared for distribution. Without exception the clergy gave unstinting support to the British cause throughout the empire's civil war in America.

Among the civilian population the reaction to the Revolution was quite different. A handful of the English merchants at Montreal who had opposed the Quebec Act now joined the rebel forces in response to the call of the second Continental Congress for a united front of all "fellow-sufferers." Among the Canadians the reaction was even more diverse and unexpected than among the English. A few hundred disaffected habitants supported the second American invasion in the autumn of 1775, while a small minority who shared the fervour of the priests took up arms to defend their native land. But the vast bulk of the Canadians remained neutral, viewing Britain's struggle with her colonists as no concern of theirs. The army of Canadians that Carleton had expected to raise never took form as the habitants of Quebec remained indifferent to the struggle and to the confiicting pleas of their curés and the revolutionaries. When the invaders took Saint Jean in November after a two-month siege and then moved north to occupy a defenceless Montreal, some disaffected persons, both English and French, boldly welcomed their American "liberators."

The church's hold on its subjects was now obviously weak. Its call for support of Carleton and the British cause remained unheeded. "Some say the priests preach war," commented Bishop Briand. "No, I do not preach it, but [I preach] obedience and subordination, loyalty to the oath and to their king as they have sworn."[2] Curés were ordered to withhold the sacraments from any who refused to obey the law of the land, and when a parishioner at St. Michel publicly denounced the government during the mass, Briand demanded the name of the culprit. In the bishop's eyes any Canadian who aided the hated *bostonnais* was a heretic, and he was prepared to interdict the whole diocese if necessary to enforce obedience and loyalty. But the "evil will" and "insolences" of parishioners still increased, as Briand sadly informed Montgolfier. "I write and I punish. But what do people say? They say that I and the priests are afraid." Despite these religious pressures few of the recalcitrants were convinced of the error of their ways. To Briand the crying need was simply more troops. "They would be better persuaders than the word of God that we preach to them."[3]

Throughout the winter of 1775/6 Montreal remained in the hands of the Americans, and Quebec City remained encircled by the enemy. The second "siege" of Quebec was, however, nothing like that of 1759. The American forces were too weak to threaten Carleton's position and the arrival of the first convoy of British reinforcements in May sent the Americans scurrying towards Montreal. For political reasons Carleton allowed the invaders to escape from a trap at Trois-Rivières and to retreat southward from Montreal into American territory. His failure to destroy the enemy had disastrous consequences the following year when General Burgoyne's army was forced to surrender to a superior rebel force at Saratoga in northern New York. Henceforth the Americans controlled the Richelieu-Lake Champlain-Hudson River route which in British hands could have linked the two British strongholds of Quebec and New York city, and divided the rebel colonies of the north from those in the south. But at least by July 1776 the colony of Quebec was free of invaders and thereafter the scene of battle shifted southward for the remainder of the Revolutionary War.

The year 1776 marked the end of Quebec's direct involvement in the American Revolution. Seditious utterances were no longer heard in Canadian parishes and the trickle of volunteers to the enemy dried up completely. Bishop Briand had the final victory over the rebellious minority in his flock—until they had been pardoned by their king the dissident Canadians were not allowed to make peace with their mother church. The danger that Quebec might become the fourteenth state of the young

Union ended in the spring of 1776 when convoy after convoy sailed up the St. Lawrence to ensure that the colony remain British.

FRENCH INFLUENCE AND THE CANADIAN CHURCH

After the exciting events of 1775 and 1776 the province of Quebec returned to a state of comparative quiet. The civil government was completely occupied by the great military struggle in the colonies to the south, and the correspondence of the governors from 1776 to 1783 contains little relating to religious matters. In 1777 Carleton was replaced by the French-speaking, Swiss-born soldier of fortune, Lieutenant-General Frederick Haldimand, who had been military governor of Trois-Rivières for a time during the occupation. Honest to a fault and scrupulously courteous in even the smallest matters, Haldimand was in every way the superior of Carleton whose liberality towards the French Canadians barely masked a vindictive and egotistical nature. As governor of Quebec until 1784 Haldimand had to deal during the rest of the Revolutionary War with the problems of Loyalist refugees entering the province and with the continuing delicate relations between the Protestant state and the Catholic church.

Haldimand's attitude towards the Canadians and their religion was as sympathetic as Carleton's but not quite so naïve. His basic criticism of the church was that its clergy, drawn for the most part from the lower social classes, tended to be either inferior in quality or dangerous in character. The restoration of the episcopacy in 1766 could not alone restore the damage done to the church by the loss of French-born and educated gentlemen and by the long interruption from 1759 to 1766 in the education and ordination of priests. Briand had tried to fill vacant parishes by ordaining semiqualified students and the seminary in turn had been forced by the government ban on foreign clergy to fill vacant professorships with Canadians academically unprepared.

Haldimand was concerned that the remaining French-born priests wielded an undue influence over their Canadian colleagues, directed more to the interests of France than of Britain. This influence seemed all the more dangerous after France entered the Revolutionary War on the American side in 1778. Despite British suspicions, the French government never tried to establish contacts with its former subjects in America, even during the American Revolution, but that did not discourage a few Canadians from trying to interest Louis XVI in the affairs of his former colony.[4] In 1779 Haldimand had Bishop Briand arrange the deportation to England of a pro-French priest, one of several disturbers and security risks within the bishop's fold. The governor was convinced that the low standards, French influence and doubtful loyalty among the clergy could be remedied by importing priests from the kingdom of Savoy. Such men would be sympathetic to Britain, acceptable to the French-speaking Canadians, and would make good professors and reliable curés to preach loyalty among the Canadians.[5]

The home government agreed to Haldimand's plan, but when the first four Savoyard priests were captured in 1783 by the French while en route to Quebec no further recruits were sent. Haldimand subsequently learned from Montgolfier that two Sulpicians dressed as laymen had arrived from France and had been admitted to the Montreal Seminary. Disturbed by this increased threat of French political influence and doubly disturbed by a public announcement from the two French priests that more of their kind could and would come to Canada, Haldimand ordered the two Frenchmen deported in spite of pleas from Briand, Montgolfier, and the citizens of Montreal.[6]

Despite numerous ordinations by Briand vacant parishes still existed, and in 1783 some of the clergy circulated a petition asking full self-government for the Roman Catholic Church in Canada and the admission of foreign priests. Significantly Briand did not sign the petition and when the rumour spread that this omission was due to his fear of Carleton, he hastened to advise the former governor that he had never feared any man in his life, but had not signed because Quebec diocese needed professors, not parish priests.[7] Briand did not give his opinions on the request for church self-government.

For Briand the failure to obtain reinforcements for his hard-pressed clergy was a matter for regret, but for the average Canadian the episode had a deeper significance. The exclusion of the French priests, at a time when Britain's prestige was everywhere suffering from her defeat at the hands of the colonies, seemed unjust and impolitic. Canadians were once more fearful of some danger to their religion and their way of life, particularly when they saw the tide of Loyalist refugees—all presumably English and Protestant—flooding in their direction. Haldimand was aware of this growing uneasiness on the part of the Canadians and did all in his power to reassure them and keep them loyal to the British Crown. This task was successfully accomplished by Carleton who returned to Quebec in 1786 with the title of Lord Dorchester and the task of finding a constitutional solution to the problems posed by the presence of the English-speaking Protestant Loyalists within the French-speaking and Catholic colony.

THE CATHOLIC CHURCH AND FRENCH-CANADIAN NATIONALISM

Late in 1784 Briand, supposedly ailing from an incurable sickness, resigned the bishopric in favour of Desgly. Briand had now served eighteen years in an office he had never wanted. Under his care the church had made great strides in reconstruction and reorganization; the episcopal succession was now assured and Briand had during his episcopate ordained no less than ninety priests to perpetuate the parochial work of the church.[8] By 1784 the three governments of Quebec diocese—Quebec, Trois Rivières and Montreal—contained ninety-nine curés serving nearly one hundred thousand Catholics in one hundred and eighteen parishes. The church had been the sole surviving cultural institution from the days of New France, and the British policy of religious "Canadianization" had made it the preserver of French Canada's sense of identity. Briand could look back on his achievements with satisfaction, and look forward with reasonable hope of the future growth of the Roman Catholic faith in Canada.

The choice of Desgly as coadjutor in 1772 had been virtually dictated by Carleton. That aging cleric (born in 1712, three years before Briand) had never expected or hoped to become Bishop of Quebec and he now refused to leave his parish on the Island of Orleans to reside in Quebec City. His episcopal functions would have to be performed by a coadjutor if they were to be performed at all. One of his first acts, therefore, was to seek the appointment of Jean François Hubert, missionary at Detroit since 1781, as his coadjutor. He asked the papal nuncio at Paris to impress on Rome the urgency of issuing Hubert's bulls. "The shortest route seems to be also the surest," he remarked, perhaps anticipating some difficulties in London similar to his own in 1772.[9] More than six months elapsed from the time Desgly approached Rome until he personally asked Colonial Secretary Lord Sydney for royal approval of Hubert. The British government had at first wanted the consecration of the seventy-two year old Montgolfier who had been rejected in 1763,[10] but accepted Hubert's name when Montgolfier declined the honour. Hubert's consecration was further postponed when the papal nuncio delayed the despatch of the bulls, and when Lieutenant-Governor Hope insisted on waiting for Carleton's arrival with the British authorization. In the end Carleton gave permission in October 1786, five months after receipt of the bulls, and Hubert was consecrated coadjutor the following month. The choice of the forty-nine year old Hubert was the best thing that Desgly did for his diocese.

Part of Desgly's difficulties were financial—the bishop had no endowment in Canada and until 1787 the French pension of three thousand livres still went to Briand. Desgly had to make do with an inadequate income of some sixteen hundred livres paid to him by the Paris Hôtel-de-Ville. In his vast diocese—which included five modern provinces of Canada—the bishop faced a continuing shortage of priests. He was willing (but the government was not) to ignore the nationality of any foreign priests who could be recruited to serve in his diocese. The first source of acceptable recruits was Bishop Butler of Cork, who sent several Irish priests to work among the Roman Catholics of Nova Scotia. A vicar general was appointed to supervise the Gaspé and Nova Scotia, and a superior of missions was added when the number of Irish priests increased. But financial shortages bedevilled this missionary expansion of the diocese because the Quebec and Montreal seminaries were unable to assist missionaries arriving from abroad. Desgly warned his vicar general in London that Irish priests sent to Nova Scotia would require an independent income.[11] Finances also prevented Desgly from sending any missionaries into the Illinois country in the west.

Desgly's poor health, probably the result of paralytic strokes, and his advanced age made it necessary for Hubert to undertake the bishop's visitations. On the first pastoral visit made in fourteen years Hubert confirmed ten thousand souls—nine thousand in the district of Montreal alone.[12] Hubert, who had been critical of Desgly's refusal to perform the episcopal duties and of his poor relations with other members of the clergy, had scarcely departed on his second pastoral tour in 1788 when he received word of Desgly's death.

After Hubert's assumption of the title as well as the duties of bishop he reconfirmed the episcopal powers of Briand who, although retired at Quebec, still exerted influence as the elder statesman of the Church. Desgly had had some correspondence with his former superior, but Hubert frequently called on Briand for advice with diocesan problems. On his earlier pastoral visit Hubert had noted the piety of the laity but had commented adversely on the laxity of some priests.[13] He now intended to use his episcopal broom to sweep clean some of the less satisfactory corners of diocesan administration, but instead he encountered unexpected difficulties. His first reverse came when Dorchester vetoed his plan to create a diocesan synod of deans to assist the bishop.[14] The next disappointment was Charles-François Bailly de Messein, his choice for coadjutor. Bailly had held several church posts—vicar general of Nova Scotia from 1768 to 1772, professor at the Quebec Seminary until 1777, and then curé of Pointe-aux-Trembles. That he had been seriously wounded defending Quebec against the American invaders and that he had entertained Inglis overnight during the latter's tour of 1789 were indications of his pro-British feelings. Perhaps more significant in explaining his subsequent collaboration with the English governing class was the fact that he had been tutor to Lord Dorchester's children, and that he had tried to become Briand's successor in 1784. He was consecrated in the summer or 1789 and before a year had passed he was involved in a bitter controversy with his bishop.

Bailly approved of a plan of Chief Justice William Smith, Dorchester's friend and associate, to establish an integrated educational system of free parish schools and a publicly endowed, nondenominational university where no theology would be taught and where Protestant and Catholic, French and English would be mixed together. Hubert replied, to Smith's enquiry, that this scheme would endanger the Roman Catholic religion and the French-Canadian way of life by its inclusion of Protestants.[15] This opinion Bailly criticized in a letter to Smith's legislative committee investigating the state of education, adding that he was convinced the document was "a forgery made in the name of our dear bishop."[16] Supported in his opinion by the

Quebec parish clergy, Hubert issued a *mandement* to inform the laity of the Church's official attitude. As Hubert told one of his vicars general, he wanted to ensure that no one threw stones at "our nation" without Canadians knowing of it.[17] In the bishop's estimate Bailly was an ambitious traitor to French-Canadian interests and the controversy caused an estrangement between the two men that continued until Bailly's death in 1794.

The aging Briand warned Lord Dorchester that Bailly as a titular bishop had no business interfering in diocesan matters—his real motives were to get himself promoted as a bishop in his own right.[18] Hubert had suggested establishing a second bishopric at Montreal before the row began over Smith's educational plan. He had sounded out the Congregation of the Sacred Propaganda in Rome, adding that if Rome approved he would himself approach the British government to avoid any British suspicions that Rome was interfering in the colony. Apparently Dorchester had already given verbal approval to division of the diocese, but when the Prefect of the Congregation authorized Hubert to seek the necessary arrangements with Lord Dorchester he ignored Hubert's broad hint against Bailly's candidacy and suggested that Bailly as Bishop of Montreal and Hubert as Bishop of Quebec should each have a coadjutor.[19] Hubert abandoned his project of dividing the diocese rather than permit the advancement of the unreliable Bailly.

The opening years of Hubert's episcopate posed other problems for the French-Canadian church and French-Canadian people besides that of Bailly. Echoes of the French Revolution were heard in Montreal where European events had influenced many citizens. There was much talk of liberty and independence, and pressure from church-wardens to run the spiritual as well as the temporal affairs of the parishes; but the only priest who supported the Revolution was Bailly.[20] When a number of young French refugees arrived in Quebec in 1790 the bishop was forced by the government's fear of revolutionary influences to refuse them admission to the seminaries and the ranks of the clergy, but he did offer them employment as school teachers.[21] The religious vocation was still attracting too few candidates, and those who did enter were drawn largely from the upper classes. Although the diocese now contained one hundred and forty-six priests and two hundred and thirty-six nuns, this was a distressingly small number to serve adequately the rapidly increasing French-Canadian population. The magnitude of the problem was evident on Hubert's first pastoral visit as Bishop of Quebec when he confirmed twenty-eight thousand.

To a degree which the bishops could not or would not recognize, the Roman Catholic Church in Quebec had since the Conquest become a national church of the French Canadians, so closely identified with the survival of the "Canadian nation" that the presence of non-French Catholics within the diocese was only grudgingly admitted. Both Desgly and Hubert were reluctant to face the fact that considerable numbers of English-speaking

Catholic Loyalists had settled in Nova Scotia and the section of Quebec west of Montreal. Neither bishop was prepared to reduce still further the number of priests in Quebec by sending clergy to these new settlers, or even to spend much time on supervising the few priests who were working in those regions.

LOYALISTS AND THE "NATIONAL" CHURCH OF ENGLAND

The Protestant churches in central Canada date their real beginnings from the American Revolution, rather than from the Conquest. It was the arrival of Loyalist refugees that altered the course of the country's religious history. From being an insignificant minority in the midst of an overwhelmingly French and Roman Catholic population, Protestants grew rapidly in the years after the Revolution to a sizable English-speaking group claiming membership in one or other of the larger Protestant churches. These changed conditions were most immediately reflected in the new status of the Church of England which until the Revolution had been only the shadow of an establishment. Now the mass of Loyalists required spiritual care, and the imperial government was convinced from its experiences with the rebellious colonies that only the Church of England would ensure loyalty to Britain within the remnant of empire in North America. While never denying toleration to dissenters, the government's fixed policy was to promote Anglicanism as the surest antidote to those democratic tendencies which seemed to be in the very air of North America.

Hostilities had barely commenced in the Thirteen Colonies when the first Loyalists began to arrive in the colony of Quebec. After the British defeat at Saratoga in 1777 the northward flow of refugees from the interior settlements of New York and Pennsylvania increased further and by 1780 the noncombatant Loyalists were being clothed, fed and housed in camps near Trois-Rivières and Sorel, while some Loyalist soldiers of Butler's Rangers had begun farming at Niagara to supply the local garrison with food. The peace treaty in 1783 turned this Loyalist migration into a small flood. Travelling overland, members of Loyalist regiments and their families, as well as some civilians, reached the upper St. Lawrence River and settled in blocks from Cornwall to Prescott. Two groups evacuated from New York City in 1783 were later located at Kingston and around the Bay of Quinte. The loyal Six Nations Indians had also retreated to the haven of British soil and were given reservations along the Grand River and on the Bay of Quinte. In all some six thousand Loyalists arrived in the western part of the colony but unlike the Loyalists in the Maritimes who were largely drawn from the professional and middle classes of the sophisticated culture of the old seaboard colonies, the new settlers in Quebec were almost exclusively from the frontier regions of New York and Pennsylvania, men already skilled in pioneering but lacking in formal education and political experience.

Since the diocesan powers of Bishop Inglis extended to the colony of Quebec as well as all the present-day maritime provinces, he proceeded to Quebec in June 1789 to investigate the religious state of its newest settlers. Here he found the condition of the church "deplorable." No church building existed at Quebec City for the exclusive use of Anglicans, and the governor general, Lord Dorchester, was unwilling to purchase the shared Recollet chapel from the three surviving friars. In Bishop Inglis's estimate Lord Dorchester was religiously overliberal for he made "too little distinction between the National church and other denominations."[22] Chief Justice William Smith, the most important political figure after the governor, was not an Anglican but a Presbyterian. Inglis saw that the Canadians were "as firmly attached to the Church of Rome as ever," and the establishment of Anglican schools seemed the best hope of "enlightening" them religiously.

Inglis approved of the work at Quebec of the English clergyman Philip Toosey (who had arrived on his own from England in 1785), but Montmollin, the French-speaking pastor there, had almost no command of the English language and no idea of church discipline. Under pressure from the bishop, Montmollin retired on full salary and left the Anglican congregation in Quebec city entirely to Toosey. At Trois-Rivières, where most of the twelve Protestant families were Presbyterian, Inglis was unable to understand a word of Veyssière's sermons and prayers. Instead of attracting converts, clergy like Veyssière and Montmollin could only degrade Protestantism in the bishop's opinion. In Montreal, half of the 1800 Protestants were nominally Anglican but Inglis encountered the same difficulties regarding the local church and its priest Delisle who, in deportment and command of English, was only a slight improvement over Montmollin and Veyssière. The congregation were anxious to get an English assistant for the minister and Inglis was equally anxious to secure outright possession of the Jesuits' church which Delisle was using. At Sorel the bishop did find church affairs in good order under the energetic direction of a Loyalist, the Reverend John Doty, who had built the second Protestant church in the colony.

From this rapid inspection of the colony one fact emerged clearly in the bishop's mind—the old plan to Anglicanize and Anglicize the Canadians by employing French-speaking ministers had failed utterly—they remained French "as much as when they were conquered."[23] Worse than that, the position of the Church had been weakened by the estrangement of many Protestants. The Church of England in the colony of Quebec needed capable English ministers and its own places of worship if it hoped to serve the Protestant minority effectively. Inglis returned to Quebec city to consult with Lord Dorchester and hold a visitation. Eight of his nine clergy appeared at the visitation, including John Stuart and John Langhorn who had travelled almost four hundred miles from Kingston and Bath on Lake Ontario.

Besides holding confirmation services Inglis took several steps before leaving Quebec to put the Church on a firmer basis in the colony. Stuart, Toosey, Doty and Langhorn were officially licensed. J. M. Tunstall, S.P.G. missionary at Quebec city for the past year, was appointed Delisle's assistant. Toosey was appointed Bishop's commissary for the eastern portions of Quebec and Stuart for the western, where more than thirteen thousand Loyalists, soldiers, and "late Loyalists" were now settled. In the matter of church buildings Inglis had less success because Lord Dorchester preferred to have Anglicans build their own rather than acquire Roman Catholic ones. As for education, the uncooperative attitude of some Canadians led Inglis to remark that they "would prove to be spoiled children: that they seemed to consider themselves as a distinct people from the English and wished to continue so."[24]

By 1791 the Church of England, the state religion of the colony of Quebec for nearly three decades, had only three parishes and three missions in the whole province. At Quebec, Trois-Rivières and Montreal the incumbents of the Anglican parishes were paid by the British government, while the missionaries at the three Loyalist centres of Sorel, Cataraqui (Kingston) and Ernest Town (Bath) were paid jointly by the government and the S.P.G. Progress had been disappointingly slow, and the bulk of the Protestants, who were in the western settlements, had only the three missionaries while the established parishes with far fewer Anglicans had three resident priests. Still, Inglis deserved to feel considerable satisfaction with his personal efforts to organize the Church of England in the colony.

THE CONSTITUTIONAL ACT

The physical problems facing the Loyalists in the "Western District" of Quebec were problems that they had encountered before and which they were well skilled to meet—clearing land and building homes in a forest wilderness. Gifts of tools and supplies from the government helped them through the difficult early years, yet there were other problems besides that of mere survival. The Loyalists now living under The Quebec Act disliked its terms almost as much as the Revolutionaries had in 1775. Governor Haldimand believed that Loyalists who had suffered so much at the hands of democratic assemblies would be happy to live under Quebec's system of nonrepresentative government, French civil law and seigneurial tenure; but his error of judgment was made obvious by a petition received in April 1785 from several leading Loyalists. Bluntly they demanded a separate government for the western settlements, along with the benefits of the British constitution for which they had fought and suffered loss and exile.[25] Loyalists in Nova Scotia and New Brunswick enjoyed self-government, English law, trial by jury and freehold tenure—Loyalists in Quebec deserved equal treatment. This and similar petitions gladdened the hearts of English merchants in Quebec who had lost their earlier battle against the Quebec Act.

But defenders of the Quebec Act could and did point to the undeniable fact that French Canadians still comprised 95 per cent of the population and in any case the Loyalists had been aware of Quebec's system of government and land tenure before they chose to settle there.

Lord Dorchester was convinced that some constitutional change was needed to satisfy the Loyalists' complaints, but he admitted his inability to suggest a solution to this conflict of two ways of life within a single colony.[26] In the summer of 1789 William Grenville became colonial secretary and by that autumn had single-handedly formulated a new constitution which, while maintaining the conservative and anti-democratic spirit engendered in government circles by the recent Revolution, recognized "the Loyalist fact." The Constitutional Act, an amendment to the Quebec Act, acknowledged the bicultural pattern of Quebec by authorizing its division into two colonies—Lower Canada containing the French population, and Upper Canada comprising the Loyalist settlements along the upper St. Lawrence River and the lower Great Lakes. Upper Canada would receive English common law and freehold tenure, and each colony was to have an elected assembly as in the plan of 1763.[27] The Constitutional Act was a victory for the Loyalists but a defeat for the mercantile group at Montreal and Quebec City who continued to oppose this division of the natural economic unit of the Great minority in an overwhelmingly French-speaking province where French votes would undoubtedly control the popular assembly.

For the next half-century the Constitutional Act provided the governmental framework for the two Canadas and for the relations of church and state therein. To bolster the new provinces against the destructive spirit of democracy the two governors (a lieutenant-governor in Upper Canada) and their appointed councils were given extensive powers, and provision was made for an Erastian religious establishment. Clause 36 of the act authorized "a permanent Appropriation of Lands in the said Provinces, for the support and maintenance of a protestant Clergy." These Clergy Reserves were to be "equal in Value to the Seventh Part" of all lands granted in every township. Clause 38 further authorized the governors "to constitute and erect, within every Township . . . one or more Parsonage or Rectory . . . according to the Establishment of the Church of *England*" and "to endow every such Parsonage or Rectory" with as much land as might seem expedient. The two assumptions of church establishment were that religion was a useful support for civil government and that the state religion was the faith of a majority of the population. For the Canadas the first assumption was the unquestioned reaction to the recent revolution in the older English colonies, but the second assumption certainly could not apply in Lower Canada and would only become fact in Upper Canada if the Church of England were provided with the clergy and church buildings necessary to attract the settlers.

To the layman the purpose of these clauses might be crystal clear—the Church of England became, by imperial statute rather than by colonial law as in Nova Scotia and New Brunswick, the state church of the two Canadas. But closer examination of the clauses could raise serious legal doubts about their precise meaning. Only the Church of England would receive endowed rectories, but could rents from the Clergy Reserves be given to the other British establishment, the Church of Scotland? Did the phrase "a Protestant Clergy" mean only the Church of England ministers, or should it include those of the Church of Scotland, or even those of other Protestant denominations who were not established, such as the Congregationalists, Baptists, or perhaps even Methodists? The projected rectories were to be endowed "according to the Establishment of the Church of *England*" but this did not specify that the Church of England was necessarily established in the two Canadas. These uncertainties, whether deliberately or accidentally embodied in the Constitutional Act, made the relations of church and state a major source of political controversy for a later generation of legislators, and the Clergy Reserves especially became a veritable Pandora's box of religious dissension in the colony of Upper Canada.

Since the Constitutional Act was only an amendment of the Quebec Act, designed to cope with the problems created by the arrival of the Loyalists, most of the Quebec Act still formed the constitution of Lower Canada. Although the powers of the governor and council were somewhat reduced by the granting of an assembly, the Constitutional Act altered the religious situation in Lower Canada only slightly. Any doubts about the status of Anglicanism as the state religion were now dispelled, yet Roman Catholicism retained its peculiar position as a semi-established church within an officially Protestant Empire. The Quebec Act had allowed Roman Catholics to enter the governor's council by permitting a loyalty oath that made no mention of religion. After 1791 Roman Catholics could vote for and even become members of the assembly, almost forty years before such political rights were given to their co-religionists in Great Britain. On Christmas Day, 1791, the Constitutional Act came into force and the old province of Quebec ceased to exist. For the moment the Constitutional Act marked a political watershed in the country's development rather than a religious one.

NOTES TO CHAPTER FOUR

1. *RAPQ*, 1929-30, p. 109, J.-O. Briand to ? , 10 March 1775.
2. *Ibid.*, p. 111, J.-O. Briand to A.-H. Lagroix, 1 October 1775.
3. *Ibid.*, p. 112, J.-O. Briand to Etienne Montgolfier, 5 November 1775.
4. Claude Galarneau, "Le Canada et la France (1760-1815)," *CHAR* 1970, pp. 81-88.
5. PAC, Q Series, Vol. 21, pp. 264, 298 *ff.*, Sir Frederick Haldimand to Lord North, 19 June, 15 July 1783.
6. *Ibid.*, Vol. 23, p. 55, Lord Sydney to Sir F. Haldimand, 8 April 1784.

7. *RAPQ*, 1929-30, p. 129, J.-O. Briand to Sir Guy Carleton, 30 June 1784.
8. H. Têtu, ed. *Mandements, Lettres Pastorales et Circulaires des Evêques de Québec* (Quebec: 1888), Vol. II, p. 186.
9. *RAPQ*, 1930-1, p. 188, L.-P. Desgly to the apostolic nuncio at the court of France, 2 January 1785.
10. PAC, Q Series, Vol. 24-I, p. 214, Lord Sydney to Lt.-Gov. Henry Hamilton, 30 April 1785.
11. *RAPQ*, 1930-1, p. 191, L.-P. Desgly to Hussey, 19 September 1786.
12. *Ibid.*, p. 202, J.-F. Hubert to F. de Villars, 1787.
13. *Ibid.*
14. PAC, Q Series, Vol. 42, pp. 32, 33-47, Lord Dorchester to Lord Sydney, 7 June 1789, and draft plan by Desgly.
15. Têtu, *op. cit.*, Vol. II, pp. 385-96.
16. *Ibid.*, pp. 398-409; Lucien Lemieux, *L'Etablissement de la première Province ecclésiastique au Canada 1783-1844* (Montreal: Fides, 1967), p. 27.
17. *RAPQ*, 1930-1, p. 228; Têtu, *op. cit.*, 399.
18. *RAPQ*, 1929-30, p. 134, J.-O. Briand to Lord Dorchester, 2 May 1790.
19. *Ibid.*, 1930-1, pp. 219-20, J.-F. Hubert to Cardinal Antonelli, 24 October 1789.
20. *Ibid.*, 1947-8, p. 114, G.-J. Brassier to J.-F. Hubert, November 1789.
21. Têtu, *op. cit.*, Vol. II, pp. 427-32.
22. *RAPQ*, 1953-4, 1954-5, p. 89. The full text of Inglis's Journal is printed here, pp. 85-110.
23. *Ibid.*, p. 89.
24. *Ibid.*, p. 108.
25. Adam Shortt and A. G. Doughty, *Documents relating to the Constitutional History of Canada 1759-1791* (2nd and rev. ed.; Ottawa: King's Printer, 1918), pp. 473-777, Petition of Sir John Johnson and Loyalists, 15 April 1785.
26. *Ibid.*, p. 947, Lord Dorchester to Lord Sydney, 13 June 1787.
27. The full text of this Act is printed in Shortt and Doughty, *op. cit.*, pp. 1031-51; the clauses relating to religion are printed in J. S. Moir, *Church and State in Canada 1627-1867: Basic Documents*, Carleton Library No. 33 (Toronto: McClelland and Stewart, 1967), pp. 108-10.

FIVE

Rivals for Establishment in Lower Canada

The three decades that followed the passing of the Constitutional Act brought marked changes in the religious condition of Lower Canada. The internal stability of the colony and the Roman Catholic diocese of Quebec plus British preoccupation with the French revolutionary and Napoleonic wars combined to prevent the effective implementation of that Church of England establishment projected by the terms of the Constitutional Act. Even after the American Revolution and the arrival of Protestant English-speaking Loyalists, the proposal to appoint an Anglican bishop in Quebec met with determined opposition in the British cabinet; and the appointment of Inglis as Bishop of Nova Scotia in 1787 seemed to preclude any early steps to divide his diocese. But the passing of the Constitutional Act reopened the question of a Canadian bishopric—or even of two bishoprics. Lieutenant-Governor Simcoe was urging a separate diocese for Upper Canada as a bulwark against republicanism and democracy, but an Upper Canadian diocese was shelved for nearly half a century by the decision in 1792 to make a single Anglican diocese of the two Canadas.

JACOB MOUNTAIN, BISHOP OF QUEBEC

The choice for bishop fell on Jacob Mountain, examining chaplain to George (Pretyman) Tomline, Bishop of Lincoln and former tutor of Prime Minister Pitt in whose hands the gift of the bishopric really lay. Jacob Mountain had risen steadily up the clerical ladder to his chaplaincy, making his reputation as an administrator and scholar (and incidentally as a poet). Just forty-three years of age, he was of pleasant but undistinguished appearance, father of four small children and *pater familias* to the little band of thirteen souls—including his two sisters, his clergyman brother and family, and a spinster sister-in-law—who comprised his entourage when he reached Quebec in November 1792.

Governor Lord Dorchester's welcome to Mountain may not have been too warm—his own two nominees for the bishopric had been rejected. But Attorney General James Monk was pleased, and hastened to explain the facts of Lower Canadian political life to the new bishop. Monk was critical of the British government's failure to implement its avowed religious policy for the colony. Former governors had not supported the Protestant church or controlled the Roman church. Tithes had not been collected or the proper use of the Clergy Reserves determined. With Mountain in the executive and legislative councils of the two Canadas (his title "Lord Bishop" secured him these honours which Inglis had not received) all could be put right by a bishop who would give direction to policy. But Dorchester expressed misgivings about Mountain's council appointments, fearing they would "awaken much jealousy on the part of the Canadians, that their Bishop does not receive the same honour."[1]

Mountain, viewing the executive council as the counterpart of the cabinet at home, was convinced that there, rather than in the legislative council, "I can politically serve the church."[2] Inglis, however, offered him some sage advice on church-state relations: "Being the first Bishop sent to the British Colonies in America, & aware of the prejudice that prevailed against that measure, I deemed it prudent on my arrival to go through my duty with as little noise, or offence as possible. . . ."[3]

Quebec Diocese, named for the old province rather than the city, contained in 1792 only nine clergy in its three parishes and four missions. No change in locations had occurred since Inglis's arrangements made during his 1789 visit. The ninth clergyman was Robert Addison who had occupied the new Niagara mission only since 1792, itinerating regularly through the region and visiting the Mohawks on the Grand River. One of Mountain's first acts was to appoint Toosey and Stuart, Inglis's Canadian commissaries, as his own—henceforth with a government salary of £150. Their duties continued to be purely administrative—the bishop's power to ordain, confirm and consecrate could not be delegated.

In his first episcopal year Mountain carried out his first visitation. Replies to his preliminary questionnaire must have forewarned him of some of the less satisfactory aspects of the church in the Canadas. At Quebec, Sorel and Trois-Rivières there were no wardens, and no catechizing because no children attended church. Leaving Quebec early in July 1794 Mountain visited Trois-Rivières, Sorel and Montreal, and by the end of the month was enduring a hot and unpleasant journey through the upper province as far as Niagara. Mountain reported the religious state of the settlers as "truly deplorable." The crying need was for more churches and more clergy. Mountain approved of the few Presbyterian and Lutheran clergy but he formed a very low opinion of the Methodist preachers—"a set of ignorant Enthusiasts whose preaching is calculated only to perplex the understanding & corrupt the morals, to relax the nerves of industry, and dissolve the bands of Society."[4]

Mountain held his second visitation at Kingston in 1803. The first decade of his episcopate had now passed, with disappointingly small progress for the church. Just one building—the cathedral at Quebec—had been erected in Lower Canada during that period, and it would be completed only in 1804 from an annual government grant of £400. Only two clergy had been added in the lower province and two in the upper. In the next decade—to the beginning of the war with the United States—the church's situation did not improve noticeably. By 1811 the Quebec cathedral was in serious disrepair, even before its interior was finished. Toosey, Deslisle and Veyssière were dead by 1800; Doty had resigned in 1802. The most notable addition to the clergy in Lower Canada was Charles James Stewart, third son of the Earl of Galloway and Mountain's successor as bishop, who had volunteered for the mission of St-Armand in 1807.

Four related problems—tithes, rectories, reserves and education—attracted Mountain's attention during those years. To him the right to collect tithes seemed essential to any church establishment, but as early as 1796 the British government agreed with Simcoe that their collection would be inexpedient. The issue of establishing rectories as legal corporations had been raised before Mountain's arrival, but by 1816 the provincial government had not erected a single parish and Mountain suspected this reluctance stemmed from a fear that "umbrage might be given to the Church of Rome."[5] Significantly, all Lower Canadian Anglican parishes were legally established soon after the postwar reorganization of the Roman Catholic diocese of Quebec.

The existence of the Clergy Reserves—almost 675,000 acres in Lower Canada—was probably responsible for the government's parsimonious support of the "Protestant religion" in that province. Potentially the reserves were a magnificent patrimony, but they would remain potential until the demand for land gave them real value. Their management by a committee of the executive council—a system first adopted in Upper Canada in 1798—was opposed as early as 1803 by Bishop Mountain who wanted control vested in a clergy corporation that would make a more active interest in their development for profit. Such a scheme was finally sanctioned in 1816. As late as 1823, however, the income from the lower Canadian reserves barely covered administrative expenses, and by that date the first rumblings of the storm over the right of the Church of Scotland to share in the "Protestant Clergy Reserves" were being heard in the Canadas.

After viewing the unsatisfactory state of education during his first visitation Bishop Mountain urged the establishment of Protestant parochial schools, with low fees to attract French pupils who might "embrace by degrees the Protestant Religion."[6] The Royal Institution for the Advancement of Learning, created in 1801 to supervise a system of free schools, remained a dead letter until 1818 when James McGill's bequest of £10,000 and a house for a university led to the appointment of trustees for the institute and of Mountain as its first principal. But only two grammar schools had been opened and, except for Catholic parish schools, the field of elementary education remained chaotic. In the education of ordinands in Canada the first steps were taken under Mountain on a plan proposed by John Strachan and supported by the S.P.G. Six promising students were to get £200 annually while they lived and studied with parish clergymen. The plan was instituted in 1815 but the two Lower Canadian students were ordained that year so that effectively the first four scholars were drawn from Upper Canada. Until the opening of Bishop's College at Lennoxville in 1845 this scheme was the only local means of recruiting and training priests for the diocese.

Mountain had early expressed his dissatisfaction with the contrast between official government policy towards his church and actual government practice, between his own circumscribed position and the freedom enjoyed by the "Romish Superintendent." Every governor's instructions since 1764 had offered "the most pleasing expectations" of "all possible encouragement . . . to the support of the Protestant Religion to the end that the Church of England might be established both in principle and practice." Mountain's appointment had raised Protestant and lowered Roman Catholic hopes, but "both parties have long since been undeceived." "No Bishop in the world . . . enjoys such privileges & exercises such powers, as the Roman Catholic Bishop of Quebec! Not only is the whole patronage of his diocese . . . at his sole disposal, but he removes his Clergy from one Cure to another, arbitrarily. . . ."[7] Yet Mountain's only patronage was the two commissaryships and the Governor's approval was required for every change in Anglican cures.

Colonial Secretary Lord Portland answered these complaints in 1801 with a despatch to Lieutenant-Governor Milnes ordering full implementation of his instructions regarding the royal supremacy over the Church of Rome in Canada, even if this should require an increased government allowance "almost to any extent" for the Roman bishop.[8] Attorney General Sewell then drew up a list of steps necessary to redress the imbalance and restore the royal authority. He proposed to remove all French émigré priests, to require the Roman bishop and his coadjutor to reside in Quebec and to recognize both by imperial statutes as crown appointees (so that the king could name all curés who would hold their livings through royal pleasure). Finally Sewell proposed to make both bishop and coadjutor into civil servants, liable to correction, by appointing them to the executive and legislative councils.[9]

Milnes, however, was reluctant to grasp the Roman nettle which his predecessors had avoided. He was saved from his unpleasant duty by the retirement from the Colonial Office of Mountain's supporter, the Duke of Portland, whose successors were inclined to join Milnes in procrastination. Nevertheless Mountain continued to press his case, invoking the aid of his friend and patron Bishop Tomline. Since Mountain would be bound to oppose the illogicality of two established churches in one diocese, he was not invited to joint in the discussions with the Roman Catholic authorities. Both Mountain and Milnes had gone to England in 1805 just before Bishop Pierre Denaut's death early in 1806 offered a heaven-sent opportunity to end the absurdity of a Roman Catholic bishop in a Protestant diocese. But the precipitate action of Thomas Dunn, administrator of the province in the absence of the governor, cut the ground from under both Mountain and Sewell by recognizing J.-O. Plessis as the new bishop and B.-C. Panet as his coadjutor without awaiting British approval. Reporting to Mountain this action by Dunn (whose wife was a French-Canadian Catholic), H. W. Ryland, the governor's secretary, exclaimed, "Where is the layman sufficiently free from vanity, who at seventy-three years of age would let slip an opportunity of making a Bishop?"[10] When Mountain, still in England, urged his claims against the continued existence of the rival Roman establishment, Lord Castlereagh, a political realist, commented curtly that interference with the Roman Catholic Church in Quebec would be "a very delicate matter."[11] Threatened by a war with the United States, imperial statesmen were still prepared to accept religious toleration as the price of French-Canadian loyalty to Protestant King George.

Returning to Canada in May 1808 after a futile attempt to resign his bishopric, Mountain believed he had Castlereagh's promise that the new governor, Sir James Craig, would be directed to consider the unsatisfactory state of the Anglican establishment—but Craig received no such instructions.[12] Mountain did manage to have the whole issue reopened in 1810, and when Ryland went to England that summer he pressed the issue of royal supremacy over the Roman Catholic Church in Canada before the Law Officers of the Crown. The law officers admitted the royal right but cautioned against any "appearance of hardship" in practice.[13] A despatch embodying Mountain's aims was actually drafted, only to be shelved because *"the Lord Chancellor had doubts."*[14]

The outbreak of the war with the United States in 1812 ended any possibility that the imperial government would risk estranging Roman Catholic opinion in the Canadas by interfering with its bishop. Mountain's urging of his case for an Anglican establishment merely irritated Governor Prevost whose hands and time were full with Canada's war for survival. By 1817 Mountain's ambitions were hopeless. Not only had Plessis been acknowledged as Bishop of Quebec but his government salary had been raised to £1000. The loyalty of French Canadians during the recent hostilities demanded rewards, not rebuffs—one reward was to admit Plessis to the legislative council. The "French fact" and the War of 1812-1814 had combined to perpetuate the limited co-establishment of Romanism and Anglicanism, just as similar circumstances four decades earlier had led Carleton to treat Bishop Briand and his church as close allies. Thereafter the Roman bishop was reassured of complete independence of action and Mountain was privately informed by a member of the British government that Plessis' church "must be considered as the Established Church of Canada."[15] Bitter in his defeat, Mountain again threatened to quit as bishop unless Anglicanism was publicly declared the religion of Canada, a demand adamantly rejected by the imperial government.

The war of 1812-14 had increased the work of Mountain's clergy without increasing their numbers. The handful of missionaries obtained for the diocese barely offset the losses by death or retirement. At least no church property in Lower Canada was damaged by hostilities. In the midst of the war Mountain made a confirmation tour as far as York, but with peace restored he set off in 1816 for a full three-month visitation which took him for the first time as far west as Sandwich. Immediately afterwards he left on his second trip to England where he stayed until 1819, vainly pleading his case for better treatment of his diocese. By the latter date both the diocese and the provinces had entered a new age of rapid development as thousands of immigrants left a depressed and restless Britain for brighter futures in the New World. Mountain, now seventy years of age and fast nearing the end of his physical resources, could look back on an episcopate of more than a quarter-century seemingly filled with disappointments. His achievements may have appeared to be few in number, but they were limited as much by the conditions of the times as by his own shortcomings which have been attacked more by later historians than by his contemporaries.[16]

J.-O. PLESSIS—STATESMAN IN TRAINING

When Hubert's troublesome coadjutor Bailly died in 1794, the bishop chose Denaut, one of Briand's first ordinands, as his successor. Perhaps his experience with the ambitious Bailly influenced this choice, for Denaut was quiet and withdrawn. When Hubert retired in 1797, just six weeks before his death, Bishop Denaut retained the large cure of Longueuil with its fourteen hundred communicants and remained there until his death, visiting Quebec City only when the most urgent business required.

The results of Denaut's physical separation from the church's centre at Quebec were important and long lasting. The thirty-four-year-old Joseph-Octave Plessis, residing in the city as coadjutor, took charge of many aspects of diocesan affairs, especially of relations with the government. Born in Montreal in 1763 of a working-class family that had descended on one side from a New England youth captured by the Iroquois, Joseph-Octave had displayed outstanding scholastic ability at the Sulpician college in Montreal and at the Petit Séminaire in Quebec. Immediately after receiving the tonsure from Bishop Briand in 1780 he was employed at the Montreal college to teach literature and rhetoric, but only three years later he was called to Quebec by Briand to be secretary of the diocese. His reputation for a prodigious memory, his aptitude for business and his proven discretion in church matters had placed Plessis on the first rung of the ladder to the episcopate when he was only twenty years old. As Denaut explained to the Prefect of the Propaganda in Rome, the choice of a coadjutor was "a very delicate business under a Protestant government which considers the position only from a political viewpoint . . . ,"[17] but the choice of Plessis proved a happy one for the Church. An energetic and competent administrator, a diplomat and politician of consummate ability, Joseph-Octave Plessis, coadjutor for one decade and bishop for two, was the most important and powerful figure in the history of the Roman Catholic Church in Canada during the century from the Conquest to Confederation.

Few problems arose for his church during Denaut's ten years as bishop. The church was not involved in the widespread disaffection towards the government that arose in the colony in the wake of the French Revolution. Denaut continued to submit all changes of cures for the governor's approval. "I never overlook anything that will recommend me to the government," he boasted to his coadjutor when congratulating Plessis on his friendly relations with Bishop Mountain and government officials at Quebec.[18] Nevertheless in 1798 Plessis was embarrassed by Denaut's reluctance to order a church celebration of Nelson's victory "over French Republicans" at the Nile. In the end Denaut agreed to the governor's request—"We owe it to the paternal interest the King takes in us and to the protection we receive always from his representative in this province."[19] Denaut also became exercised over the custom of having Roman Catholics take oaths on Protestant Bibles. He blamed Attorney General Jonathan Sewell for this "innovation" which he feared as "the beginning of a *persecution*" designed to push the royal supremacy "step by step towards a distant goal."[20] His conscience was not salved by the opinion of the Archbishop of Dublin that such oaths were permissible.

Much more serious for the church than these local issues was the repeated interruption of communications with the papacy as a result of the Revolutionary and Napoleonic wars. A year after Plessis' nomination as coadjutor, no bulls had been received for him, and Denaut explained to Pius VI the necessity for continuity in the Canadian episcopate and the need for local authority to consecrate successors when communications with Rome were broken. Pius was in fact a captive in France when this letter reached Rome, and his death in 1799 further delayed the bulls for Plessis. In the autumn of

1800 the documents arrived in Lower Canada—and although their validity was questionable because they named the Bishop of Quebec as "Jean-François,"[21] Pierre Denaut consecrated his successor in January 1801. The confusion regarding his own name was not corrected for two more years.

Early in 1805 Denaut became aware that Bishop Mountain was working actively for a new policy which would establish the primacy of the Church of England in the Canadas in fact as well as name by curtailing the authority of the Roman bishop. In this "dangerous crisis" for his church Denaut felt sure of Lieutenant-Governor Milnes' good will—"but I fear the bishop who puffs and the attorney general who is his echo."[22] Specifically, the Anglican party proposed royal control over all appointments of parish priests, but in return for this acknowledgment of the "supremacy" Denaut would be recognized and paid as Roman Catholic bishop instead of Superintendent of the Roman Church. Denaut saw clearly that effective political control of appointments would relieve him of all administrative powers, making his function purely sacerdotal. He much preferred "my present state, such as it is, to the *solid establishment* that is offered me."[23]

In view of King George's coronation oath to maintain "the Protestant reformed religion," how could the crown establish the Roman Catholic Church? Denaut warned Plessis not to be surprised at his answer—it would not pay to panic. Denaut wanted only the boon of toleration, enjoyed since the Conquest. By their support of the Constitution and their actions in the American Revolution—"the Canadian people, above all the clergy, have deserved it"—and he would go to the foot of the throne or even quit as bishop if it were denied them.[24] Plessis had already become directly involved in the controversy during an interview with Sewell on 26 April 1805. The coadjutor stoutly defended the status quo, rejecting the supposed advantages of establishment and arguing for separation of church and state, or at least independent coexistence. "I do not wish to see the Bishop in splendor, but I wish to see him above want.—I do not wish to see him in the Legislative or Executive Council, but as an Ecclesiastic only, entitled to the rank which is due him in Society."[25]

Plessis prepared a defence in the form of petitions to the governor and the king though Denaut felt the government's preoccupation with other business would weigh against the church's case. The return of Milnes to London in August 1805 probably brought a respite from the pressures applied by the Anglican party. As administrator Thomas Dunn did not press the question of church-state relations any further. Writing to Milnes in November Denaut again stressed that protection of his church in Lower Canada was the surest guarantee of French-Canadian loyalty, as Lord Dorchester would testify.[26] On January 17, 1806, Denaut died at Longueuil, and the astute, energetic, forty-two-year old Plessis became bishop. After taking the oath of loyalty before Dunn, he knelt in prayer at the city gate and then entered his cathedral amid the singing of hymns, mounted his throne and received the homage of his clergy. The accession to the bishopric of this man inaugurated a generation of forceful policy and solid advances for the Roman Catholic Church in Canada.

Apparently Plessis felt competent to carry his diocesan burdens alone, for his choice as coadjutor was Bernard Claude Panet, ten years his senior and more self-effacing than Denaut. Refused admittance to the Sulpicians' house, Panet spent the next twenty years at the isolated fishing hamlet, Rivière-Ouelle, near Kamouraska, virtually ignored by his bishop and playing a most insignificant role in diocesan affairs. The diocese of Quebec now contained two hundred thousand Roman Catholics, served by one hundred and eighty priests. To cope with the physical problem of such a vast jurisdiction Plessis proposed to the Congregation of the Propaganda a plan to establish three auxiliary bishops. A division of the unwieldy diocese had been suggested by Hubert in 1796 and vaguely considered by Denaut. But Plessis saw reorganization and devolution of authority as an urgent necessity, and he pressed perseveringly for division until it was finally achieved years later.

Such a division may have been connected in Plessis' mind with his defence against Bishop Mountain's manoeuvres. François Bourret, vicar general in London, had met Mountain at Milnes' home and heard the Anglican bishop speak highly of the Roman Church in Canada, but he agreed with Plessis that Mountain was "an adversary to be feared and watched" because of his ambitions for the Church of England.[27] The death of Prime Minister Pitt in 1806 reduced the influence Mountain had exerted on the government through Bishop Tomline, Pitt's old tutor, but by the summer of 1807 Bourret was reporting Mountain's latest move—to have Plessis named Patriarch of the Roman Church in North America, thereby leaving the title "Bishop of Quebec" entirely to the Anglicans.

While Bourret lobbied with the Colonial Office and with Sir James Craig, newly appointed governor of Quebec, emphasizing his church's past support for the government of Canada, Plessis opened a new front in his campaign for division of the diocese. Alexander Macdonell, vicar general in Upper Canada, was sent to Francis Gore, lieutenant-governor of that province, to request his approval for the appointment of a missionary bishop already authorized by the Holy See. The papacy in fact wanted to make Canada an ecclesiastical province but as this was politically impossible at the moment the Propaganda was prepared to appoint three or four more auxiliary bishops *in partibus infidelium*. Gore agreed to recommend this plan to the British government but no action followed.

LOYALTY REWARDED

Craig arrived in Quebec in October 1807, only to fall seriously ill for several months. Plessis found the ailing governor "gentle and very honest"[28] but soon complained that Craig was unsympathetic to the church because he refused to allow French refugee priests into the colony. Later Plessis decided that Craig was in fact well-intentioned but hindered from acting independently by the web-like oligarchy of local officials that surrounded him—the same complaint against colonial governors voiced thirty years later by the political reformers in the British North American colonies.

Early in 1810 political developments in Lower Canada presented an opportunity for Plessis to prove the loyalty, and the usefulness, of his church to Governor Craig and his superiors in Britain. Craig's support for the English party in the provincial legislature had brought him into headlong conflict with the French-Canadian popular or reform party (*parti canadien*) and with its outspoken journal *Le Canadien* which, in Plessis' opinion, was a "miserable paper" that "tends to nullify all principles of subordination and set fire to the province."[29] When the reform majority in the newly elected assembly attacked undue government influence, Craig dissolved the legislature without warning on February 26, seized the presses of *Le Canadien* and arrested the leaders of the popular party. "The coming elections will be very hot," Plessis wrote to one of his vicars on March 15, "Recommend all the curés you see not to get involved in any way."[30]

On Monday the 19th, however, Craig summoned the bishop to council to inform him that an uprising was feared because of the *Canadien*'s seditious influence. He asked the clergy to declare themselves for the government "in the most decided manner," and asked th bishop to support his proclamation against sedition. Craig went on to complain that many curés subscribed to the *Canadien* and praised its principles, a charge supported by evidence found in the paper's offices, that the clergy at large were infected with "*almost criminal apathy*."[31] Plessis warned his vicars general that the clergy were being watched—they must do nothing to justify Craig's criticism. Officially the church would support the government—"Our business is not to examine, but to second the measures of the Executive as I promised the Council. . . ."[32]

The governor's proclamation was read in the Anglican Cathedral by Bishop Mountain who also preached personally on the virtue of submission to authority. Plessis however was in a quandary—the custom of the Roman Church was merely to publish royal documents outside the churches after divine service. He had already issued a circular to his clergy—everything in it had been dictated by the governor. Exhortations on loyalty delivered from parish pulpits received mixed responses. Most curés reported their parishes undisturbed by the revolutionary spirit, but at Laprairie the curé stirred up such antagonism that he expected the popular party to impeach the clergy at the bar of the assembly if it won a majority.[33] Finally Plessis decided to order the reading of Craig's proclamation from the pulpits. Again the results were not good. The election went strongly against the governor.

Plessis feared that the clergy's loyalty might induce their enemies to renew attempts to curb the bishop's power. The issue of royal supremacy over Catholic bishops in the empire was in fact being discussed by the imperial Parliament in 1811, and many Catholics in England supported the crown's claim to a positive veto over the appointment of the Bishop of Quebec. In Lower Canada Craig revived the government's demand to control all nominations to parishes, to which Plessis replied indignantly that his acceptance of the principle would be treason to his church, that his support for Craig at the election had already alienated the affections of too many of his flock! In Britain Catholic hopes for emancipation had been disappointed, but in Lower Canada "they want to *demancipate* us."[34] This renewed offer of a respectable position and more money had been rejected by Plessis "with horror" as a parallel to the Devil's temptation of Christ. "This firmness has disconcerted, at least for the moment, calculations which would have soon made my church an Anglican church."[35]

The replacement of Craig by the friendly Sir George Prevost in the autumn of 1811 reduced political tension in the province but, as Plessis anticipated, Prevost repeated the offer of "a respectable footing" for the episcopate. Plessis prepared a memorandum on the Quebec bishopric to explain its essential differences from Anglican episcopacy. Unwilling to concede an inch of authority he suggested that future coadjutors be "*proposed* by the bishop, confirmed by the Holy See and approved by the government"—essentially the existing practice and a compromise with the royal veto theory.[36]

The effectiveness of this memorandum on the British government cannot be measured. A few days after its transmission the United States joined Napoleon in his war with Britain. During the war years Prevost was busy defending British North America, and Bishop Plessis' correspondence declines in historical importance. On Prevost's recommendation Plessis' salary was raised to £1000 in 1813, a tangible recognition of the bishop's loyalty and zeal for the war effort. Now a bishop of Quebec was, in Plessis' opinion, twice blessed—with a liberal salary, and "with as much freedom and independence as in any country in the world, although he has not yet obtained civil and legal recognition as bishop . . . because of the principles of the British constitution."[37]

In 1817 Plessis did obtain civil and legal recognition as bishop from the imperial government. Acting on the advice of the new governor, Sir John Sherbrooke, the crown ordered Plessis' appointment to the Legislative Council "by the style and title of the 'Bishop of the Roman Catholic Church in Quebec.' " This honour was further recognition of the bishop's "merits and public services." Regardless of the letter of the British constitution, British statesmen were prepared to give practical proof of their appreciation of Roman Catholic loyalty to the Protestant king. Their liberal spirit, combined with more harmonious relations between Britain and the papacy, provided the basis for the next great development for the Roman Catholic Church in British North America—the division and reorganization of the diocese made possible by Plessis' new and official status as bishop.

Four times during 1815 Plessis had written to the Propaganda regarding division—and no answers had been received. In April 1816 Cardinal Litta, Prefect of the Propaganda, informed the bishop that Edmund Burke was in Rome, and would be made vicar apostolic of Nova Scotia, if only Plessis would answer the Propaganda's earlier letter! This was the beginning of a confused series of letters in both directions, several of which never reached their destination. Before the cardinal's letter could reach Plessis, he had despatched Alexander Macdonell to Europe with orders to unearth the famous memorandum of May 1812 and try to get some action on it.

Plessis was satisfied with Burke's appointment as vicar apostolic of Nova Scotia (excluding Cape Breton) though he would have preferred a full bishop and was not convinced that the British Government would have objected. At least he would have "one province less on his conscience."[38] The next step should be two vicars apostolic, for the rest of the Maritime region and for Upper Canada. Ideally, Plessis told Cardinal Litta, the Church in British North America should have a metropolitan with suffragan bishops but he did not expect this in his lifetime unless Rome showed more initiative in dealing directly with the British government![39] There the matter rested for almost a year. In August 1817 Sherbrooke reported that the memorandum was being favourably considered by the imperial government but Plessis should not expect to get all he asked for. Again a veil of silence descended around Plessis. Then in the early months of 1818 Sherbrooke suffered a paralytic stroke and Plessis privately asked the Ursulines to pray for their governor—"The religion of this country is more interested in this than people think."[40]

Probably with the intention of expediting his division plan, Bishop Plessis sailed for Europe at the end of June 1819. Hours after his ship dropped down the river from Quebec an incoming vessel brought papal bulls naming Plessis Archbishop of Quebec, and Macdonell and McEachern as his suffragans and vicars apostolic for Upper Canada and for Prince Edward Island and New Brunswick. A courier raced forty-five miles to Cap-Saint-Ignace, in vain. The outbound ship bearing the unsuspecting archbishop was beyond reach.

The news of his elevation that greeted Plessis in London was decidedly embarrassing, for the Propaganda had not bothered to consult British authorities in the matter. From his asylum near Nottingham, Sherbrooke sent his congratulations and then added bluntly, "Common courtesy should have induced the [Court of Rome] to have communicated its intention, and its having omitted to do so may have a tendency to create a coolness which cannot but be disadvantageous to the Roman Catholic Religion in the Canadas. I am willing to hope however that your presence in England may prevent any serious effects."[41] Colonial Secretary Lord Bathurst was, however, the essence of English hospitality and gentility. Plessis was entertained at the Bathurst estate near Cirencester as a start—and better things followed in a flood. The government approved the appointments already made and also those of two more suffragans—Plessis' travelling companion to London, J.-J. Lartigue, for the district of Montreal, and J.-N. Provencher for the district of the Northwest. In all this no mention was made of the archbishopric—for all its liberal treatment of a "tolerated church" the British government was not yet ready to recognize any dignitary superior to the bishop of the national church at Quebec.

Having conquered London, the happy bishop progressed to Rome where he obtained the necessary bulls for his latest suffragans, reversal of his appointment as archbishop, and also a direct papal order for Lartigue to accept consecration regardless of the Montreal Sulpicians who viewed Lartigue's elevation with suspicion. Plessis' mission was finished and his arrival in Quebec on August 7, 1820, was greeted deservedly as a triumph equal to that of Bishop Briand fifty-four years earlier. Since 1806 Plessis had successfully defended his authority against the Erastian claims of the Protestant conquerors. The firm loyalty of the Roman Catholic Church during the war of 1812-14 had now been properly rewarded with legal recognition and unstinting cooperation in the reorganization of a diocese of five hundred thousand souls into five districts. True, the bishops were only vicars apostolic, not diocesans, but the measure of Plessis' achievement would have been unbelievable in the dark hours after the Conquest, just three generations ago.

PARISH LIFE OF THE CHURCH

Even while Bishop Plessis was working to ensure the independence of his church from state control, two related developments—the British policy of "Canadianizing" the church, and the granting of representative government under the Constitutional Act—combined to create a variety of challenges to religious authority at the parish level.[42] Despite the acquisition of forty-five émigré priests during the French Revolution the church still had fewer clergy than at the time of the Conquest, although the size of the Catholic population had tripled. Moreover, at least twenty-five of Plessis' priests were engaged in teaching because the government had banned the importation of scholars for the seminary faculties. As a result the clergy were too few in number to meet parochial needs and so overworked that nervous breakdowns became a frequent occurrence. The quality of the priesthood suffered in proportion since parish clergy were inadequately trained and were ordained perforce without discrimination as to physical and psychological capability for their work. Too few college students were offering themselves for the priestly vocation, complained Bishop Plessis, because the creation of the assembly and the burgeoning of the provincial economy offered new employment opportunities for the ambitious. Since 1790 the church had increasingly to share its leadership of the Canadians with the rising educated élite of doctors, lawyers, notaries, journalists, small merchants and well-to-do farmers who were building a native middle class such as New France had never possessed.

These new leaders of society were quick to take advantage of the peculiarly unsatisfactory legal position of their church. Since no parishes had been incorporated by law since 1721 most parishes could not enforce the payment of tithes, nor could other religious bodies be sure of collecting any dues from seigneuries they held. Bishop Plessis was forced to buy back the seminary of Nicolet from the avaricious niece of Bishop Denaut after the latter had tried to circumvent the lack of any legal corporation for the institution by willing it to the lady, on the mistaken assumption that she would piously transfer the property to his successor as Bishop of Quebec. Church authorities were unwilling to test their position in the courts because an unfavourable judgment would only serve to publicize the weakness inherent in the church's position relative to the new law of the land. Commenting on a case in 1805 involving the contested division of one parish, Chief Justice Sewell said, "There is no Catholic Bishop of Quebec by law. His office became extinct at the Conquest, and the patronage of the benefices . . . is devolved to His Majesty." Fully aware of the delicacy of his own position Plessis tried to settle parish and diocesan problems by quiet diplomacy out of court, and to stay neutral in the growing confrontation between the government and the governed, as in the issue of Craig versus the *parti canadien*. Unfortunately this left both the bishop and his clergy vulnerable to subtle forms of blackmail by the laity, of whom Plessis charged that the leaders showed a "certain indifference" to religion while the masses were ignorant and passive followers of the trouble makers. The traditional habitant trait of independence towards all authority was encouraged by the political situation. The Superior of the Sulpicians reported in 1812 that "the emboldened churchwardens exclude us from everything, they even try to bar the curé from the parish assemblies . . . and they openly blame the Grand Vicar for having placed a statue of Christ in the Church without the advice of the Church warden's trustees."[43]

Regular church attendance was the rule among the laity, if a priest was conveniently close, but religious observance among the populace was motivated more by custom than piety. The French-Canadian capacity to enjoy life resulted too frequently in debauchery. Excessive drinking, even on Sunday, and a distressing rate of criminal and immoral behaviour were the constant and bootless complaints of the church. The feasts of patron saints became so often the occasion and the excuse for unbridled revelry that the bishop suppressed most religious holidays. A disturbingly high percentage of illegitimate births—twice as high in the cities as in the countryside—was admitted to exist despite all the pleadings, remonstrations and threats of the clergy. Prostitution seemed to flourish in the urban centres, and Quebec city, with a population of some thirteen thousand in 1810, was reputed to have as many as six hundred professional women of easy virtue. Visitors to the province commented that women's behaviour and dress, especially in the leisured classes, seemed designed to encourage immorality and to create scandals.

One redeeming feature of parish life was, however, the welfare work of the devout female religious orders. Schools, hospitals, orphanages, refuges for the aged, asylums for the insane were maintained, and relief work among the poor was undertaken in a spirit of charity and with a degree of concern for the individual unfortunate that evoked praise from all sides. "Two out of three institutions," wrote the English Protestant traveller John Lambert in 1809, "bestow their time, attention and property, upon the sick and aged poor. The other devotes the services of its sisters to the education and instruction of young females."[44] But the contrast with the general tone of society was only made the more obvious by the piety and virtue of Quebec's nuns. Church officials, and especially the bishop, had only limited success in curbing those anti-social and irreligious tendencies in the life of the average parish which were so far removed from the picture of Victorian piety painted by a later generation of idealistic historians.

NOTES TO CHAPTER FIVE

1. PAC, Q Series, Vol. 71-I, p. 7, Lord Dorchester to Henry Dundas, 25 May 1794.
2. *Ibid.*, Vol. 69-II, p. 366, enclosure in Bishop of Lincoln to Henry Dundas, 30 December 1793.
3. Quoted in T. R. Millman, *Jacob Mountain, First Lord Bishop of Quebec: A Study in Church and State 1793-1825* (Toronto: University of Toronto Press, 1947), p. 33.
4. *Ibid.*, p. 57.
5. *Ibid.*, p. 133.
6. PAC, Q Series, Vol. 74-II, pp. 207-13, Bishop Mountain replying to the opinion of the Attorney General, 15 July 1795.
7. *Ibid.*, Vol. 83, p. 338, Bishop Mountain to Lord Portland, 15 April 1799.
8. *Ibid.*, Vol. 86, pp. 3-9, Lord Portland to Sir R. S. Milnes, 6 January 1801.
9. Millman, *op. cit.*, p. 63.
10. J. S. Moir, *Church and State in Canada 1627-1867: Basic Documents*, Carleton Library No. 33 (Toronto: McClelland and Stewart, 1967), p. 129, H. W. Ryland to J. Mountain, 3 February 1806.
11. PAC, Q Series, Vol. 108, pp. 155, 157-72; a paper on church establishment in the Canadas, and observations on same, 7 September 1806.
12. *Ibid.*, Vol. 113, pp. 112ff., J. Mountain to Sir James Craig, 8 March 1810.
13. *Ibid.*, Vol. 115, pp. 176-80, Report of the law officers of the Crown on patronage of Roman Catholic Church, 3 July 1811.
14. Robert Christie, *History of the Late Province of Lower Canada* (6 vols.; Quebec: 1848-55), Vol. VI, p. 304.
15. Quoted in Millman, *op. cit.*, p. 76.

16. For a discussion of interpretations of Mountain by historians, see Millman, *op. cit.*, pp. 277-83.
17. *RAPQ*, 1931-2, p. 137, P. Denaut to Cardinal Gerdil, 10 September 1799.
18. *Ibid.*, p. 142, P. Denaut to J.-O. Plessis, 22 November 1797.
19. *Ibid.*, pp. 155-56, P. Denaut to R. Prescott, 24 December 1798.
20. *Ibid.*, pp. 172-73, P. Denaut to J.-O. Plessis, 18 September 1800.
21. *Ibid.*, p. 176, P. Denaut to J.-O. Plessis, 23 October 1800.
22. *Ibid.*, p. 231, P. Denaut to J.-O. Plessis, 25 April 1805.
23. *Ibid.*, p. 232, P. Denaut to J.-O. Plessis, 4 June 1805.
24. *Ibid.*
25. Moir, *op. cit.*, p. 125. The full text of the interview is printed in A. G. Doughty and D. A. McArthur, *Documents relating to the Constitutional History of Canada 1791-1818* (Ottawa: King's Printer, 1914), pp. 304-09.
26. *RAPQ*, 1927-8, pp. 239-40, P. Denaut to Sir R. S. Milnes, 16 November 1805.
27. *Ibid.*, 1932-3, pp. 32-33, F. Bourret to J.-O. Plessis, 30 September 1806.
28. *Ibid.*, 1927-8, p. 259, J.-O. Plessis to J.-H. Roux, 19 November 1807.
29. *Ibid.*, p. 270, J.-O. Plessis to J.-H. Roux, 4 December 1809.
30. *Ibid.*, p. 272, J.-O. Plessis to F. Noiseux, 15 March 1810.
31. *Ibid.*, p. 272, J.-O. Plessis to J.-H. Roux, 22 March 1810.
32. *Ibid.*, p. 272-73, J.-O. Plessis to P. Conefroy, 22 March 1810.
33. *Ibid.*, 1932-3, p. 66, J. Boucher to J.-O. Plessis, 28 March 1810.
34. *Ibid.*, 1927-8, p. 282, J.-O. Plessis to E. Burke, 1 June 1811.
35. *Ibid.*
36. *Ibid.*, p. 290, J.-O. Plessis to J.-H. Roux, 19 May 1812.
37. *Ibid.*, 1932-3, pp. 102-3, J.-O. Plessis, Mémoire sur l'état du diocèse de Québec, 14 September 1814.
38. *Ibid.*, 1928-9, p. 93, J.-O. Plessis to Edmund Burke, 10 September 1816.
39. *Ibid.*, p. 95, J.-O. Plessis to Cardinal Litta, 15 October 1816.
40. *Ibid.*, p. 115, J.-O. Plessis to F.-X. Noiseux, 4 March 1818.
41. *Ibid.*, 1932-3, p. 148, Sir J. C. Sherbrooke to J.-O. Plessis, 3 September 1819.
42. J.-P. Wallot, "Religion and French-Canadian Mores in the early Nineteenth Century," *CHR*, LII (1) (March 1971), pp. 51-91.
43. Quoted in *ibid.*, p. 75.
44. John Lambert, *Travels Through Lower Canada* (3 vols.; London, 1810), Vol. I, p. 66.

SIX

Old Subjects in a New Land

Until the Loyalist migration into the old province of Quebec, the Protestant presence in that Catholic colony had been limited to a few government officers and businessmen. The coming of the Loyalists, who were almost exclusively Protestants, altered the religious composition of the colony only slightly, since the Loyalists numbered less than six thousand in a population of over one hundred and fifty thousand. Furthermore, the Loyalists settled primarily in that portion of Quebec west of the Ottawa River, where they were soon demanding their rights as Englishmen in recognition of their recent sacrifices for the empire. Free land, tools and rations were not enough—they must have an elected assembly, English common law, trial by jury and freehold tenure, all of which were denied to them by the Quebec Act. The pragmatic solution for this Loyalist problem was to divide the vast colony of Quebec roughly along the Ottawa into two parts, linguistically and religiously distinct—the French-speaking region to be called Lower Canada, and the Loyalist settlements, Upper Canada, the first land-locked colony in the history of the empire.

The Constitutional Act of 1791 acknowledged the Loyalist fact in Upper Canada by endowing the province with English institutions. Upper Canada would, as far as humanly possible, become another England beyond the Atlantic, with the image and transcript of the English constitution, civil and religious. Such was the plan for the St. Lawrence valley in the post-Revolutionary era, but time and circumstances decreed that the future province of Ontario should become instead a religiously pluralistic society and, for its first generation at least, a society that seemed very American in many of its attitudes and habits.

THE PROTESTANT MINORITY IN LOWER CANADA

In 1789 Bishop Inglis had described the condition of the Church of England in the colony of Quebec as "deplorable"—only three parishes and three missions (two of the latter in Upper Canada) existed. The church that he ruled was indeed an establishment in name only, yet the condition of other Protestant denominations in Lower Canada was little better. Alexander Henry, minister to the Church of Scotland congregation in Quebec city, had acquired an assistant, Alexander Spark, in 1784, and five years later Spark took over the full duties of the ailing Henry. Six years after the congregation petitioned the king, in 1802, for a building lot, Governor Craig did provide them with land in the Upper Town; and on St. Andrew's day, 1810, a church built by public subscription was opened and named for St. Andrew. The only other Church of Scotland congregation in the colony was one formed in Montreal in 1786 by John Bethune, Loyalist and chaplain to the 84th Regiment.[1] When Bethune left Montreal after only one year to settle among the Scottish Loyalists of Williamstown near Cornwall (where his ability to preach in Gaelic made him particularly welcome), the Montreal congregation was without minister until John Young, a Scot ordained by the Presbytery of Albany, New York, arrived in 1791. The congregation, which included most of the wealthy Scottish managers of the fur trade, worshipped in the Recollet chapel until land adjoining the Champs-de-Mars was purchased in 1792 and the first Presbyterian church in Lower Canada was completed six months later.[2] This church was known by various names but is remembered by its latest appellation, St. Gabriel Street.

In 1803, when Young departed, the Montreal congregation accepted James Somerville, a licensed preacher of Scotland's Relief Synod. Somerville's ordination presented a problem since there was no presbytery in the Canadas, but this was overcome by the ad hoc creation of the "Presbytery" of Montreal, consisting of Spark, Bethune and an elder of St. Gabriel Street congregation. The "presbytery," which had no authority from any body in Scotland, justified its action in ordaining Somerville as being "for the good of religion." An earlier "Presbytery of Montreal" had been formed by Spark, Bethune, Young and their respective elders in 1793 when Young and his Montreal congregation severed their connection with the presbytery in New York State, but there is no evidence that it ever met.[3] Somerville's ordination in 1803 was the first Presbyterian one in the two Canadas. Like Comingo's ordination at Halifax in 1770, this was the act of a self-constituted presbytery, but unlike the Comingo case in that the participating ministers were all from a single branch of Presbyterianism.

Somerville's call to St. Gabriel Street Church had not been unanimous and the dissenting minority withdrew into a separate congregation temporarily under Robert Forrest, a minister of the Scottish Associate Synod. In 1804 it got a permanent minister, Robert Easton—also from the Associate, or Burgher, Synod—who had come to the United States with Forrest and two others in response to an American request for clergy. With substantial aid from American Presbyterians Easton's congregation soon erected its own church but declared its adherence to the Burgher Synod, an action never acknowledged by that body. This uncertain relationship and the presence of American and Scottish elements within the congregation caused yet another split in later years.

From Somerville's ordination until the arrival of Henry Esson from the Church of Scotland in 1817 to be Somerville's associate at St. Gabriel Street, no other Presbyterian minister came to Lower Canada, although a rival to Spark had appeared in Quebec in 1800. Responding to a request from some Protestants in that city, the Congregationalist-dominated London Missionary Society sent out Clark Bentom who organized a congregation of two hundred souls on the principles of the Church of Scotland but independent of any British ecclesiastical body. Bishop Mountain, who described Bentom as "a very young man . . . possessing that noisy and random eloquence which captivates weak and enthusiastic people,"[4] denied the legality of marriages and baptisms performed by Bentom and refused him access to the Protestant burial ground. Although Bentom's request for a register was rejected by the courts in 1803 he continued his "Clerical Duty" until convicted of usurping "the office of a Priest or Minister." In the meantime he published in New York State a pamphlet defending himself and attacking the bishop with such biblical passages as "Fear not thou worm Jacob, thou shalt thresh the Mountains and beat them small," which brought his conviction for libel, imprisonment for six months, a £50 fine, and ended his Canadian career.

Other Protestant denominations besides Anglicans and Presbyterians were represented in Lower Canada but by similarly insignificant numbers. From 1780 to 1783 a British soldier named Tuffey preached in Quebec city to a small group, presumably fellow soldiers, who followed John Wesley's teachings, but no Methodist congregation was organized in Lower Canada until after the turn of the century when American Methodist preachers extended their work from Upper Canada.

In 1802 Joseph Sawyer was sent by the New York Conference to Montreal where he formed a society of seven Methodist Loyalists. Three years later that number had only grown to twenty, and an attempt to organize a circuit on the Richelieu River had been abandoned.[5] Serious Methodist efforts in Lower Canada began in 1806 with the organization of three cricuits, one of which included the Upper Canadian side of the Ottawa River. That year the redoubtable travelling American missionary, Nathan Bangs, gathered a dozen hearers in Quebec City where a previous attempt to form a society had failed. Subsequently, preachers on the Quebec station were responsible for serving immigrants from Europe and raftsmen in the timber trade. Two more preaching stations were established in 1806 in the Eastern Townships, but the work in Lower Canada grew so fitfully that the total membership of five circuits reporting in 1811 was only two hundred and forty-two.

Like other Protestant denominations Methodism in Lower Canada was an almost exclusively urban phenomenon—the rural population of the colony remained overwhelmingly French and Roman Catholic. Outside of the cities Protestantism was limited to one specific area, the Eastern Townships, and two denominations. Despite Dorchester's intention to keep the Eastern Townships as an uninhabited *cordon sanitaire* between the United States and the Canadas, these border lands were gradually filled after 1792 by Loyalists and "late Loyalists" (Americans who had not served against Britain but who had followed the original Loyalist exodus from the revolted colonies). Among them the Baptist communion flourished early when settlers at Caldwell's Manor formed a congregation and sought the services of a pastor in the wake of a missionary tour by two Vermont preachers in 1793. When no more missionaries were forthcoming the congregation licensed and later, in 1796, ordained William Marsh, a Loyalist and member of the congregation who established several other churches locally before leaving the province in 1825. In 1799 an American-ordained preacher founded a church at Abbott's Corners where he had settled, and after 1806 the Massachusetts Baptist Missionary Society began sending preachers on annual tours of the area. Although records of these visits are fragmentary, the numbers of Baptists must have been growing since the last of these itinerating missionaries reported that prospects for further development were "quite flattering."[6] After 1811, however, no more American visitors came to the townships and the next epoch of Baptist history in Lower Canada began with the arrival of French-speaking Swiss Baptists twenty years later.

LOYALISTS AND RELIGION IN UPPER CANADA

By 1791, when the new colony of Upper Canada came into existence, the original population of some six thousand Loyalists had probably been doubled by later arrivals. The thin and broken line of settlement was still confined to the banks of the St. Lawrence River, the Kingston-Bay of Quinte region, the Niagara area, and the neighbourhood of Detroit (which was not surrendered to the United States until 1795), with additional small isolated pockets close to the shores of lakes Ontario and Erie. Except for Indian trails no roads existed, so transportation and communication depended on the water route along the "front" or southern edge of the settlements on the St. Lawrence-lower Great Lakes. Coming as they had from interior settlements of the northern colonies, especially New York and Pennsylvania, the earliest settlers had the advantage of previous experience in coping with the problems of opening new land. At the same time they were "more illiterate" than the Loyalists in other British colonies and quick to oppose any "Caprice and partiality" in government policies.[7]

Because the Loyalists had been settled in groups largely according to their membership in Loyalist regiments (which in turn had often been raised from a particular area in one of the older colonies), these bloc settlements possessed from the outset a social cohesion that was normally lacking in frontier expansion. But no provision existed for their religious welfare, and the first clergyman to visit the "western settlements" had been the Reverend John Stuart, former S.P.G. missionary to the Six Nations Indians at Fort Hunter in the Mohawk Valley, who was a military chaplain at Montreal in 1782. In 1784 Stuart visited the Loyalists at Kingston, held services at Niagara for the garrison, and at the Grand River for his former congregation of Joseph Brant's Six Nations Indians, baptizing seventy-eight children and five adults, and giving communion from the church vessels sent by Queen Anne to the old Mohawk River chapel in 1712. The following year these Indians built the first Protestant place of worship erected in the colony, the present Chapel Royal of the Mohawks on the Grand River. On his return trip from the Grand River Stuart stopped briefly at the other Mohawk reservation on the Bay of Quinte and then visited every settlement en route to Montreal. This missionary journey was only the first of the herculean labours of Stuart, "Father of the Anglican Church in Upper Canada," who the following year settled among the five hundred inhabitants of Kingston, served as pastor to them and to the widely dispersed Loyalists and even opened a school.[8]

The second S.P.G. missionary, John Langhorn, soon joined Stuart in the vast field of Loyalist settlements. Coming directly from England, Langhorn arrived in Bath in 1787, but his unsociable character and eccentric manners—he bathed daily—soon led his flock and his fellow clergyman to wish that he had stayed in Britain.[9] John Bryan, like Stuart an American refugee, was "elected" pastor of Prescott at a town meeting in 1784 and later, in 1786/7, was appointed to the parish of Cornwall by Lord Dorchester. For the next three years Bryan preached, baptized, married and buried to the general satisfaction of all, until in 1790 Stuart discovered that Bryan's clerical certificates were forgeries and that he had never been ordained, whereupon the counterfeit cleric departed suddenly and permanently for the United States.[10]

Because Anglicanism had been so closely identified with Loyalism during the American Revolution it was assumed in government circles that a majority of the Loyalists either were, or wanted to be, connected with the established Church. There is little evidence to support any analysis of their religious affiliations but other Protestant denominations were certainly represented among them. John Stuart reported that his Kingston congregation included Presbyterians, Baptists and Quakers—only seven families were Anglican—and Langhorn reported only eleven Anglican communicants at Bath in a settlement of more than fifteen hundred souls.[11]

Other than Stuart and Langhorn, the only clergy in the six-hundred-mile-long colony were Bethune of the Church of Scotland in Williamstown, and F.-X. Dufaux, a Sulpician serving the old French-Canadian settlement at

Sandwich. The Lutheran Loyalists along the Upper St. Lawrence were without a regular minister until Johann Wilhelm Samuel Schwerdfeger came from New York State in 1791.[12] Congregationalism was not organized in the Canadas until two generations later, and there is no sure evidence of any Baptist congregations in the St. Lawrence-Great Lakes region until after the division of Quebec into Upper and Lower Canada. It was this failure of Anglicanism and other traditionally parish-oriented churches to provide adequately for the spiritual needs of the settlers that allowed a highly efficient and flexible Methodist circuit organization to win so extensive a following in Upper Canada.

Before the arrival of Methodism from the United States, however, two evangelistic preachers with no authority from any religious body appeared in 1788 in the Bay of Quinte area. One, named Lyons, preached and taught school for a few years; the other, James M'Carty, an Irish follower of Whitefield's Calvinistic revivalism, disappeared under mysterious circumstances after being imprisoned briefly at Kingston on charges of being a vagabond.[13] Major George Neal, who came to Niagara in 1786 as a military settler and began preaching among his neighbours, has been claimed by some historians to be the first Methodist preacher in Upper Canada, but there were among the Loyalist immigrants other Methodists, notably Barbara and Paul Heck and their relatives the Emburys who had been instrumental in founding Methodism among the Anglicans of New York City and now gathered the first Methodist group in the colony from among the Loyalists in Augusta township on the upper St. Lawrence River.

No regular Methodist preacher visited any part of the colony, however, until 1790 when William Losee obtained permission from the New York Conference of the American Methodist Episcopal Church to leave his Lake Champlain circuit and pay a missionary visit to some Loyalist relatives in Canada. Crossing the St. Lawrence near St. Regis, Losee travelled west as far as the Bay of Quinte, preaching at every opportunity. When he returned to the New York Conference in October Losee carried a petition from certain Loyalist settlers for the appointment of a missionary in their area. Bishop Francis Asbury welcomed the invitation and the instrument to spread Methodism and when Losee returned to Canada in 1791 to establish a regular circuit the foundations were laid for the growth of Methodism in Upper Canada and, unwittingly, for the future troubles over the American origin of this missionary work.

There were many causes for the retarded religious development of the Loyalist settlements above Montreal. No doubt the major factor was geographical—the physical remoteness of the widely separated settlements. In the struggle to clear this new land and to wrest therefrom an existence during the first years of settlement, everyday problems took precedence over religion and education. As one of the few educated Loyalists remarked,

"At present the Axe and the Plough are rather to be attended to than Philosophy and the Languages."[14] Given these conditions it is not surprising that an educated ministry and formalized religion held less appeal for practical backwoodsmen than the self-educated revivalist who spoke of salvation in homey terms that the pioneers readily understood. Finally, the European-based churches, particularly the churches of England and Scotland, were singularly lacking in missionary spirit at this time. Missionary funds were not easily obtained from a laity infected by the religious indifferentism of the Enlightenment—in any case charity began at home where the need seemed more apparent. If the pioneer settlers in the western district were going to receive any religious instruction other than that provided by itinerant evangelists, it was obvious that massive support must come from the only body with such resources, namely the British government.

THE SIMCOE YEARS

John Graves Simcoe, veteran of the American Revolutionary War and first lieutenant-governor of the new colony of Upper Canada, had very definite and ambitious plans for the province's development. To complement the English civil institutions the established Church of England would be promoted in every possible way to provide a bulwark of loyalty and orthodoxy against republicanism and dissent. "Every establishment of Church and State that upholds the distinctions of rank, and lessens the undue weight of the democratic influence, ought to be introduced," Simcoe advised the Archbishop of Canterbury when requesting a separate bishopric for his colony.[15] Already the government was adding £50 to the annual salary of £100 paid by the S.P.G. to its missionaries, and provision for endowments in the form of rectory and clergy reserves lands had been made in the Constitutional Act. Simcoe now proposed that the imperial government grant £1000 towards two preparatory schools and a university to be staffed by Anglicans, for which benefits he was sure the settlers would evince their gratitude. Despite Colonial Secretary Henry Dundas's warning that these plans seemed premature for the "infant state" of Upper Canada,[16] Simcoe proceeded to endow his paper system of higher education with 225,000 acres.

Like so many of Simcoe's enthusiasms, his hopes for a full Anglican establishment never became a reality, partly because of his other preoccupations and also because he left the colony after only five years. The Church of England in Canada did advance in later years albeit at a snail's pace, thanks to the arrival of more S.P.G. missionaries and the recruiting of local candidates for its priesthood. In 1792 Robert Addison, the third missionary in Upper Canada, began a thirty-seven-year ministry at Niagara,[17] but a fourth left the colony in 1797 less than a year after arriving and obtaining the glebe lands of Toronto which he later sold for his own profit. George Okill

Stuart, son of John, was ordained by Bishop Mountain in 1800 and stationed at York (Toronto), and two years later Richard Pollard, a former sheriff in the western area of the province, was appointed to serve the lower Thames River region.[18] The most notable addition to the clerical ranks, however, was John Strachan, the young Aberdonian schoolmaster destined to the first bishop in Upper Canada, who had arrived in Kingston in 1800 as a private tutor and founded his famous school at Cornwall when he was ordained and sent there in 1803.[19]

After Strachan no more ordinations were performed until 1812, and the largest number of missionaries in Upper Canada at any time was seven. Few clergy were willing to leave a comfortable situation in England for the rigorous life of the colonies, and Britain's long war with France compounded the difficulty of finding suitable men. Between 1812 and 1818, however, no less than ten more Anglican clergy were added to the roll and another ten were received in 1819 and 1820, so that by the latter year there were twenty-two ministers of the Church of England in the province. Almost half of those who arrived before 1819 left within a short time but the balance of those appointed before 1820 included many younger men whose ministry in the province lasted beyond the midcentury mark.[20]

Few as these clergy were in the early years to serve such an extensive region, it was an undeniable fact that the Anglican laity composed a very small proportion of the population, perhaps as little as 2 per cent.[21] Writing to Simcoe in 1792, Richard Cartwright, the prominent Kingston merchant, had commented, "Of this Church I am myself a Member and am sorry to say that the State of it in this Province is not very flattering. A very small proportion of the Inhabitants of Upper Canada have been educated in this Persuasion and the Emigrants to be expected from the United States will for the most part be Sectaries or Dissenters."[22] Cartwright's prophecy was only too obviously true by 1812—only Americans had come to the province as the wars in Europe delayed British immigration, and the pious expectation of some church leaders that dissenters would gladly join the Church of England because it was supported by government funds had failed to materialize. Too few Anglican missionaries may have been one explanation for the success of dissent, but there were many other factors such as the mobility of sectarian preachers in a frontier society, the strong appeal of their emotional evangelical message and the techniques developed to promote mass religious participation, all of which attracted and held the religiously uncommitted majority in Upper Canada.

In Anglican eyes those most responsible for this situation were the American Methodists, renegades from the Church of England, traitors to their king and uneducated enthusiasts to boot. The remarkable rise of Methodism in Upper Canada had begun with Losee's first year as an itinerant when one hundred and sixty-five joined the Methodist Episcopal Church and the first two Methodist chapels in the Canadas were erected, including the one that still stands at Hay Bay. Losee's glowing report to the New York Conference in 1793 of his successes and prospects brought a second missionary, as Losee returned to the St. Lawrence area where he obtained ninety members. Year after year the number of circuits and members multiplied until in 1798 Upper Canada became a separate district with its own presiding elder. By 1805 the district had eight circuits with ten preachers and almost eighteen hundred members.

This numerical increase in Methodism—over twenty-five hundred members by 1812 with probably four times as many "hearers" or noncommunicants—inevitably necessitated further organizational changes. In 1806 Lower Canada became a separate district, and in 1810 Upper Canada was transferred to the new Genesee Conference centred in western New York. The preachers in Upper Canada, however, were still almost exclusively Americans—not more than seven of the seventy-six missionaries in Canada between 1790 and 1812 were Canadian-born,[23] and their religious sincerity could not in the opinion of their critics atone for their foreign citizenship and lack of formal education. As the probability of war between Britain and the United States grew after 1807 the position of the American-organized and American-staffed Methodist Episcopal Church in the Canadas became increasingly difficult. In 1811 the first visit to Canada of an American bishop, the saintly and revered Asbury, marked ironically an end to this early stage of Methodism in these colonies, for the outbreak of war less than a year later forced the Methodists to begin the process of separation from the American parent body.

THE PATTERN OF RELIGIOUS PLURALISM

Although the tide of immigration from the neighbouring states continued until 1812, when Upper Canada's population had reached an estimated ninety thousand, large areas in the interior remained without churches, schools or other socializing institutions. Nathan Bangs, on a missionary tour of the Thames region in 1804, met teen-agers who had never heard a sermon. Drinking, dancing, gambling and horseracing were the common pastimes, and Sunday was a day for amusement rather than rest. Carrying the bare necessities of their calling in their saddlebags, the itinerant preachers travelled over rough trails to preach in barns, in houses or from tree stumps wherever they could gather an audience. About 1802 they introduced to Upper Canada the American version of the Presbyterian long communion called camp meetings.[24] From a rude platform in a glade or field a team of preachers would lead the crowds, who had come to stay for several days, in prayers and hymns interspersed with emotional sermons calling sinners to repentance. The conversion experience that struck so many listeners was usually accompanied by vocal outbursts and physical contortions which hostile observers denounced as grossly indecorous exhibitionism. Camp meetings, however, drew untold numbers into the Methodist fold and incidentally served a social function by bringing families out of their physcial isolation and into contact with others in what was one of the few community activities practised at the time.

Although other religious bodies in Upper Canada had American connections, or at least American contacts, none but the Methodists faced this political dilemma of divided loyalty. John Stuart continued to correspond with Anglican clergy who had chosen to remain in the United States after the Revolution and he was probably responsible for the close friendship between John Strachan and Bishop Hobart of New York. The handful of Baptist churches in the Bay of Quinte and Niagara regions received fifteen missionaries from three American Baptist associations between 1802 and 1812.[25] Jabez Collver, the second Presbyterian minister in Upper Canada, had been ordained in New Jersey before he settled in Norfolk and organized an independent congregation in 1793, and two years later John Ludwig Broeffle, an American minister of the Dutch Reformed Church, started preaching to German Presbyterians in Stormont and Dundas. Beginning in 1798 the Dutch Reformed Classis (Presbytery) of Albany sent several missionaries into Upper Canada, although only the first arrival, Robert McDowall, remained to accept a call to the Bay of Quinte region where he stayed until his death in 1841. A fourth American Presbyterian, Daniel Ward Eastman, served in the Niagara region from 1802 to 1850. Only one other Presbyterian, William Smart, entered Upper Canada before the war, having been sent by the London Missionary Society to Brockville in 1811.[26] The explanation of the hostility to the Methodists must lie in their very success since they were probably the largest denomination in the province.

One measure of the political status of the various denominations in Upper Canada was their legal right to perform marriages. The first marriage act, passed in 1793, confirmed all previous weddings by magistrates or military officers but limited future legal marriages to those performed by the Church of England, or a magistrate if no Anglican clergyman lived within eighteen miles. Since Stuart, Langhorn and Addison were the only clergy so qualified, the proposal made earlier by Richard Cartwright to empower ministers of all denominations was renewed, particularly by the Baptists and Presbyterians. The result was an amending act of 1798 which extended authority to "Lutherans or Calvinists," the latter term being understood to cover Baptists, Mennonites and Tunkers. This doctrinal restriction and the continuing shortage of clergy in the province put a heavy demand on a few individuals—McDowall and Eastman together performed over four thousand weddings during their pastorates—but the Methodists were excluded because they were American and because they did not meet the theological requirements. No further liberalization of the marriage laws of Upper Canada occurred until 1831.[27]

Despite the government salaries for the Church of England clergy and the generous land endowments of that Church, Upper Canada was developing into a religiously pluralistic society. Individual Quakers, Tunkers, Moravians and Mennonites had come as Loyalists or late Loyalists, but beginning about 1796 and continuing until 1812 a mass migration of Pennsylvania "plain folk"—mostly German-speaking Swiss Mennonites—entered Vaughan and Markham townships and Waterloo County. Aside from the French-Canadian community at Sandwich there were few Roman Catholics in Upper Canada during the Simcoe years but those few, who were Scots, held important government offices. At Simcoe's request Bishop Hubert sent the Irish priest Edmund Burke to Upper Canada in 1794 as a travelling missionary. Burke spent most of his time in the Detroit area but also visited small Catholic groups, mostly soldiers, at Kingston and Niagara, and before his transfer to Halifax in 1801 he made at least one trip to the tiny community of French aristocrat refugees who had settled on Yonge Street under the Count de Puisay in 1798 and built a small church in the vain hope of obtaining a priest.[28]

The condition and prospects of the Catholic Church improved radically after 1804 when Alexander Macdonell, the first Catholic chaplain in the British army since the Reformation and a veteran of the campaigns against the Irish rebels of 1798, brought a large number of Highland Catholics, mostly Macdonells who had served in the now disbanded Glengarry Fencible Regiment, to Glengarry County. The Colonial Office provided 160,000 acres for these men and their families, and a salary of £50 for Macdonell, who reported that Upper Canada had only two wooden and one stone Catholic church when he arrived.[29] By stressing the loyalty and devotion of his flock, Macdonell obtained over a thousand acres of rural and town lots for the future expansion of the Catholic Church in the province. He assumed responsibility for all Catholics in Upper Canada and so impressed his superiors that Bishop Plessis made him vicar general of Upper Canada and proposed to appoint him bishop of the province whenever the diocese of Quebec could be divided.[30]

Settlers from quite a different background were the Delaware Indians, who had been converted to Christianity and pacifism by Moravian missionaries, had fled their ancestral homes during the Seven Years' War and then were forced to abandon their new home in western Pennsylvania to avoid involvement in the American Revolution after ninety men, women and children of one village had been murdered by the rebels in 1782. A decade later, after many more unhappy experiences at the hands of white settlers, the Delawares accepted the offer of asylum in Upper Canada and, led by the seventy-one-year-old missionary David Zeisberger, they settled on the

Thames River twenty miles above the site of Chatham. There a prosperous European-style community emerged, with more than forty houses, outbuildings, two schools, a church, gardens and broad farm fields, and for the next twenty years the refugees lived in peace at Fairfield, which they described as "a garden of the Lord."[31]

THE WAR OF 1812 AND ITS CONSEQUENCES

The War of 1812-14 came as no surprise to Upper Canadians. For four years relations between Britain and the United States had staggered from one crisis to another and Loyalists and their families faced the coming of renewed hostilities by their former enemies with an apathy born of a sense of helplessness. Major-General Isaac Brock, however, as administrator of the province, was not prepared to lose such a valuable colony by default, in spite of the British view that Upper Canada's long frontier was indefensible. Advised by his agents of the American declaration of war three weeks before the news reached him officially, Brock made successful strikes against the enemy posts of Fort Mackinac and Detroit and by his victory at Queenston Heights inspired Upper Canadians to a massive and united effort in their own defence.

Few people could have foreseen the devastation that three years of invasions would inflict on the province from the banks of the St. Lawrence as far as the Detroit River. The churches, too, suffered as armies marched and counter-marched through the countryside and bands of raiders burned towns and farmsteads. The brunt of the damage fell on the Niagara peninsula where church buildings were requisitioned as barracks by the opposing forces and one church, St. Andrew's Presbyterian at Niagara-on-the-Lake, was fired by retreating Americans in 1813 and its minister taken prisoner, as was Addison the S.P.G. missionary at that place.[32] As men were called for military service congregational life was so disrupted that many churches ceased to function. Those denominations with American connections were particularly hard hit because missionaries no longer came from the United States and pastors who were American citizens had to leave the province.

These developments affected particularly the Baptists and Methodists. Several Baptist congregations simply dissolved during the war years,[33] while the Methodists fared only slightly better. In 1812 the Genesee Conference met on the American side of the Niagara River one month after war had been declared. No Canadian preachers attended the conference, however, and as American citizens had already been ordered out of the British colonies the bishop's tidy plan of circuits existed only on paper. Upper Canada still had a few Canadian circuit riders, but Lower Canada had neither hostilities nor Methodist preachers.

Individual clergymen played their part in the war effort by serving as militia chaplains, by comforting the bereaved or, in the case of one Baptist preacher, by carrying supplies for the troops. For Alexander Macdonell and John Strachan the war was a very personal experience that changed the course of their public lives. Macdonell gathered his loyal Highland veterans into the 2nd Glengarry Fencible Regiment and went into action with them. Strachan became involved directly in the war when in April 1813 American forces attacked the tiny capital of York to which Strachan had moved just days after the outbreak of war. As the handful of British troops retreated from York eastward to Kingston in the face of overwhelming numbers of invaders, John Strachan, garrison chaplain, found himself in the unexpected role of negotiating the town's surrender, berating the American commander for allowing looting by his troops, tending the wounded lying in St. James' Church and the hospitals, and caring for the panic-stricken inhabitants. Three months later the Americans were back at York and again Strachan was called upon to treat with the enemy. Greatness had been thrust upon John Strachan by the exigencies of war, and thereafter he knew his destiny was to keep Upper Canada British and Anglican.

Both men were publicly rewarded for their devoted service after the war. Macdonell was recommended to the Colonial Office which doubled his government salary in 1816 and approved his promotion in 1819 to the position of auxiliary bishop for Upper Canada. Strachan was made an honorary member of Upper Canada's executive council in 1815, a full member of that body in 1817, and a legislative councillor in 1820. This last position he compared to that of a bishop in the House of Lords, and one where he believed he could "combat with success the probable opposition" to the Anglican establishment and "by means of my pupils possess a growing influence" over the popularly elected assembly.[34] For both men the War of 1812 had hastened the process of securing positions of power from which they could pursue their shared aims of blocking democratic and republican tendencies, promoting British loyalty, advancing the fortunes of their own churches and making Upper Canada the kind of province Simcoe had dreamed of.

The war also produced changes in the Presbyterian and Methodist communions, which now sought to rid themselves of any taint of Americanism so that they could identify with the province and its people in the new climate of loyalism. The number of Presbyterian clergy in Upper Canada had grown to nine who together with the four ministers in Lower Canada represented five different Presbyterian bodies—the established Church of Scotland and the Associate (Burgher), Antiburger and Relief Synods, and the Dutch Reformed and Presbyterian churches from the United States. In 1817 Easton and three ministers in eastern Upper Canada asked the Associate Synod in Scotland to authorize a Canadian presbytery, but before an answer came three of the petitioners established an independent presbytery to ordain Joseph Johnston, a licensed preacher of the Synod of Ulster and schoolmaster at Cornwall, where he had organized a congregation. The ordination was performed in the name of "the Presbytery of the Canadas"—the fourth petitioner, William Bell of Perth, refused to assist because no reply had come from the Associate Synod. All Presbyterian clergy in the two Canadas were informed of the action and invited to a second meeting of the presbytery. No Church of Scotland minister and no minister west of Brockville answered this call, but Bell, the other three petitioners and Johnston met in Easton's church and adopted "the doctrines, discipline and worship of the Church of Scotland"[35] as their basis of union. Within a week the Presbytery ordained two more licentiates recently arrived from Ireland and Scotland. Thus in 1818, one year after the Synod of Nova Scotia was formed, the first steps were taken to organize Presbyterianism in the Canadas. The results, however, were less promising than the plan—as yet the new presbytery contained only seven of the seventeen Presbyterian clergy in the two colonies.

For Methodism in the Canadas the war produced even more cataclysmic results. The two Canadian districts were largely purged of American preachers—only two or three "of moderate politics, and prudent conduct"[36] remained in the upper province. The vacant Quebec and Montreal stations were supplied in 1815 by three preachers (one a French-speaking missionary) from England but conflict with the American body over jurisdiction in the district soon occurred in Montreal, where the presiding elder from the Genesee Conference closed the chapel to the English missionary. When Bishop Asbury complained of the English intrusion the Missionary Committee in London replied that their missionaries had been invited by the loyal Methodists of Lower Canada. The issue was referred to the American General Conference at Baltimore, "to amicably arrange and settle this business," with William Black (who had just visited Montreal) and another Nova Scotia preacher acting as delegates for the English Conference. The English Conference advised the Baltimore Conference to vacate Quebec and Montreal and to consider in their hearts whether they should not entirely avoid British North America; but the American General Conference refused to abandon any of its twelve circuits in the Canadas after a conference committee reported that the majority of Canadians still wanted American preachers.

The English Conference then proceeded to extend its work field into Upper Canada, creating in 1817 its own district with 166 members and ten preachers spread from Quebec to Kingston; in 1818 it entered two more American areas, the Bay of Quinte stronghold and York. Further protests from two American bishops against this divisive course of the English preachers led the Missionary Society to promise withdrawal from any station "previously occupied by the American brethren." Still the missionaries remained, and in 1819 split the Methodist society in Niagara. Although the American church might have become understandably sceptical about English expressions of "fraternal love," its General Conference of 1819 offered a compromise. The English missionaries should control Lower Canada and the garrison town of Kingston, while an annual conference would be created in Upper Canada.

The English Conference of 1820 accepted the proffered olive branch, advising its missionaries that the needs of the Gospel were stronger than political considerations in Upper Canada.[37] The territorial division effected the following year seemed equitable, but in fact it left Methodism in Upper Canada under a cloud of political suspicion. The connection of Upper Canadian Methodism with the United States was too attractive a weapon for some parties to resist using in their own interests as the spirit of Loyalism dominated the colony of Upper Canada in the post-war decades.

NOTES TO CHAPTER SIX

1. A. H. Young, "The Bethunes," *OH*, XXVII (1931), pp. 553-74.
2. Robert Campbell, *A History of the Scotch Presbyterian Church, St. Gabriel Street, Montreal* (Montreal: Drysdale, 1887), p. 59.
3. William Gregg, *History of the Presbyterian Church in the Dominion of Canada* (Toronto: Presbyterian, 1885), p. 157.
4. Quoted in T. R. Millman, *Jacob Mountain, First Lord Bishop of Quebec* (Toronto: University of Toronto Press, 1947), p. 47. No historical study of the Bentom affair has been made but W. R. Riddell discusses Bentom's legal status in "When a few claimed monopoly of Spiritual Functions," *OH*, XXII (1925), pp. 202-9. William Gregg (*op. cit.*, pp. 153-54) bases his account of the libel case on a memoir by Henry Wilkes who was not born until 1805, and it is possible that the libel case did not in fact happen. Wilkes's account appeared in the *Canadian Independent*, December, 1866.
5. G. F. Playter, *The History of Methodism in Canada* (Toronto: Green, 1862), p. 84.
6. Stuart Ivison and Fred Rosser, *The Baptists in Upper and Lower Canada before 1820* (Toronto: University of Toronto Press, 1956), p. 163.
7. W. D. Powell and John Collins to Lord Dorchester, 18 August 1787. Different parts of this report are quoted in G. R. Craig, *Upper Canada: The Formative Years 1784-1841* (Toronto: McClelland and Stewart, 1963), p. 11, and R. A. Preston, ed., *Kingston before the War of 1812* (Toronto: Champlain Society, 1959), pp. 122-24.
8. G. F. G. Stanley, "John Stuart, Father of the Anglican Church in Upper Canada," *JCCHS*, III (6) (June 1959), pp. 1-13. The expression "Father of the Anglican Church in Upper Canada" was apparently first used by John Strachan.
9. See A. H. Young, "The Revd. John Langhorn, Church of England Missionary, at Fredericksburgh and Ernesttown, 1787-1813," *OH*, XXIII (1926), pp. 523-64, and Preston, *op cit.*, p. 135.
10. See A. H. Young, "The Mission of Cornwall," *OH*, XXV (1929), pp. 481-97.
11. Preston, *op. cit.*, p. 148; A. H. Young, "More Langhorn Letters," *OH*, XXIX (1933), p. 51.
12. E. J. Lajeunesse, ed., *The Windsor Border Region* (Toronto: Champlain Society, 1960), pp. 117-53; C. R. Cronmiller, *A History of the Lutheran Church in Canada* (n.p.; Evangelical Lutheran Synod of Canada, 1961), pp. 88-90.
13. W. S. Herrington, "The Trial of Charles Justin McCarty," *Transactions of the Royal Society of Canada*, 1927, Section II, pp. 63-70; C. B. Sissons, "The Martyrdom of McCarty—Fact or Myth?," *Canadian Journal of Religious Thought*, January-February 1927, pp. 12-18.
14. QUA, Richard Cartwright Letter Book, Vol. I, p. 8.
15. E. A. Cruikshank, ed., *The Correspondence of Lieut. Governor John Graves Simcoe* (5 vols.; Toronto: Ontario Historical Society, 1923-1931), Vol. V, p. 247, J. G. Simcoe to the Archbishop of Canterbury, 30 December 1790.

16. *Ibid.*, Vol. I, p. 179, Henry Dundas to J. G. Simcoe, 12 July 1792.
17. A. H. Young, "The Rev. Robert Addison and St. Mark's Church," *OH*, XIX (1922), pp. 158-70.
18. A. H. Young, "The Rev'd. George Okill Stuart, M.A., LL.D.," *OH*, XXIV (1927), pp. 512-34; A. H. Young, "The Revd. Richard Pollard 1752-1824," *ibid.*, XXV (1929), pp. 455-80; J. J. Talman, "Some Notes on the Clergy of the Church of England in Upper Canada prior to 1840," *Transactions of the Royal Society of Canada*, 1938, Section II, pp. 57-66.
19. Of the several biographies of John Strachan, only the sketch by J. L. H. Henderson, *John Strachan* (Toronto: University of Toronto Press, 1969), is both available and authoritative.
20. J. J. Talman, "Some Notes on the Clergy of the Church of England in Upper Canada prior to 1840," *Transactions of the Royal Society of Canada*, 1938, Section II, pp. 57-66.
21. E. A. Cruikshank, ed., *The Correspondence of the Honourable Peter Russell* (3 vols.; Toronto: Ontario Historical Society, 1932-1936), Vol. II, p. 33.
22. Cruikshank, *Simcoe Correspondence*, Vol. I, p. 235, Richard Cartwright to J. G. Simcoe, 12 October 1792.
23. Goldwin French, *Parsons & Politics* (Toronto: Ryerson, 1962), p. 42.
24. A. E. Kewley, "The Beginning of the Camp Meeting Movement in Upper Canada," *CJT*, X (3) (July 1964), pp. 192-202.
25. Ivison and Rosser, *op. cit.*, p. 61.
26. "Rev. Robert McDowall—Personal Note," *OH*, I (1899), p. 70; H. S. Seaman, "The Rev. William Smart, Presbyterian minister of Elizabethtown," *ibid.*, V (1904), pp.178-86.
27. J. S. Moir, ed., *Church and State in Canada 1627-1867: Basic Documents*, Carleton Library No. 33 (Toronto: McClelland and Stewart, 1967), pp. 140 ff.
28. Brother Alfred [Dooner], *Catholic Pioneers in Upper Canada* (Toronto: Macmillan, 1947), "The Right Rev. Edmund Burke, D.D.," pp. 93-116; "The Windham or 'Oak Ridges' Settlement," pp. 117-39.
29. No biography of Macdonell is generally available. Older works are H. J. Somers, *The Life and Times of the Hon. and Rt. Rev. Alexander Macdonell* (Washington: Catholic University of America, 1931), and W. J. Macdonell, *Reminiscences of the Late Hon. and Right Rev. Alexander Macdonell* (Toronto: Williamson, 1888).
30. *RAPQ*, 1927-28, p. 252, J. O. Plessis to A. Macdonell, 15 March 1807.
31. E. E. Gray, *Wilderness Christians* (Toronto: Macmillan, 1956), particularly Part II.
32. Gregg, *op. cit.*, p. 193.
33. Ivison and Rosser, *op. cit.*, pp. 83, 91, 100, 102, 116, 166.
34. Quoted in G. W. Spragge, "Dr. Strachan's motives for becoming a Legislative Councillor," *CHR*, XIX (4), December 1938, p. 401.
35. Gregg, *op. cit.*, pp. 205 ff.
36. Playter, *op. cit.*, pp. 144 ff.
37. *Ibid.*, pp. 182-85.

SEVEN

A Generation of Unrest

The score of years following the close of the War of 1812-1814 was marked by intense political unrest, economic growth and population expansion in all the British North American colonies. In the wake of the Napoleonic Wars and postwar depression, and in the face of industrialization in England and social unrest in Ireland, a veritable flood of immigrants from the British Isles came to British North America. In Lower Canada the Christian churches reflected many of the stresses and strains of this unsettled generation. Except in the Eastern Townships and Montreal the population was still predominantly French and Roman Catholic in character (only one person in ten was Protestant) yet the reorganization of the Roman Catholic diocese of Quebec proved to be the source, not of strength, but of controversy within the Catholic community.

J.-J. LARTIGUE AND THE BISHOPRIC OF MONTREAL

Plessis' triumphant return from Europe on August 7, 1820, with the new arrangements for subdividing the diocese must have matched that of Briand over half a century earlier and should have allowed the great bishop to enjoy his declining years in peace. Instead, the appointment of Jean-Jacques Lartigue as episcopal agent for the district of Montreal brought a decade and a half of bitter strife within the diocese. The Sulpicians who had sent Lartigue to London to protect their estates from a threat of confiscation by the government now refused to acknowledge his new status and barred him from their house. Their ostensible reason was the Gallican argument that he was not recognized by the government, but the real cause was a deep-seated fear of episcopal interference with the Sulpicians' jurisdiction as seigneurs and parish clergy for the island of Montreal.

Plessis was put in an awkward position by the papal brief that named him "archbishop," an honour which the British government would not acknowledge. His *mandement* announcing Lartigue's new office did not publicize the brief because of the "archbishop" affair, and as long as the brief was not promulgated canonically the Sulpicians refused to recognize Lartigue's authority. Despite Lartigue's charge that Lord Bathurst had broken his word by not ordering Governor Dalhousie to recognize him as bishop in Montreal, a sample of "*English Treachery*"[1] in Lartigue's opinion, Plessis was aware that his diocese had really not been divided but merely partitioned into five districts under auxiliary bishops.

Ostracized by his former brethren, the Sulpicians, Lartigue decided he could serve no useful purpose in Montreal and asked Rome early in 1821 for his demission. In spite of his repeated requests this was not granted and Lartigue remained in his difficult situation, which his outspoken manner did nothing to improve. By 1822 he was quarrelling with Plessis over administration while urging the bishop in the same breath to put pressure on the Colonial Office for some public recognition of himself. In Rome the cardinals were openly siding with the Gallican Sulpicians. Although still unwilling to remain as bishop, Lartigue proceeded in 1823, with the support of only twelve hundred of the ten thousand adult Catholics in Montreal, to begin construction of his own palace and church, St. James, on land given by the Viger family. The unrepentant Sulpicians continued for years to snub the unwelcome bishop on every possible occasion.

The reaction against the papal appointment of Lartigue was symptomatic of a larger philosophical conflict of the age, between Gallican traditions and the new wave of ultramontanism of which Lartigue was probably the first spokesman in Canada. The post-Napoleonic papacy was intent on turning back the tide of liberalism and secularism unleashed by the French Revolution, and the writings of certain French scholars, notably De Maistre, historian and "Prophet of the Past," and the young philosopher-theologian De Lamennais, had already begun to popularize the antisecularist ideals of church supremacy over the state, papal infallibility, religious control of education, passive obedience by all citizens, and Catholicism before patriotism. Typical of the papal leadership given to ultramontanism was Leo XII's condemnation of secret societies, including of course the Freemasons. Lartigue's trip to Europe had introduced him to this militant side of the Catholic revival there, and the opposition of the Gallican-minded Sulpicians to his appointment as bishop made him a confirmed proponent of the Vatican, its rights and powers, although he had as yet few followers in Lower Canada.

Part of Lartigue's difficulties stemmed from the fact that D.-B. Viger and L.-J. Papineau, leaders of the Lower Canadian radical party, were his cousins. Lartigue did not share their anti-government politics—he frequently quarrelled with the Papineau family—but Lord Dalhousie used this relationship as a pretext for ignoring Lartigue. Government salt was rubbed into Lartigue's wounds in 1824 by word that the Colonial Office would recognize Macdonell as independent Bishop of Upper Canada. If there were sufficient reasons for making Macdonell a diocesan, Lartigue commented, "there are ten times as many for having one in the district of Montreal," which now had two hundred and twenty thousand Catholics to Upper Canada's seventeen thousand.[2]

The following year the Roman Catholic Church in British North America suffered an irreparable loss—Plessis died on December 9, 1825. That morning Bernard-Claude Panet, his coadjutor, visited the ailing bishop in his hospital apartment. An hour later Plessis, who was telling his doctor that he had never felt so well, fell back dead. From all sides tributes to the great bishop poured in. "The Church has lost a venerable prelate, the people, an earnest and unwearied guardian of their spiritual welfare, the King has lost a most loyal and faithful subject." Such was Lord Dalhousie's eulogy of Joseph-Octave Plessis.[3]

Panet, now bishop, was an unknown quantity. After twenty years in Rivière-Ouelle as coadjutor, he was just one month away from his seventy-third birthday and in indifferent health when Plessis died. Lartigue had bluntly told Plessis months before that Panet was physically and morally incapable of governing the diocese because of his age and, since Panet had always wanted to renounce his succession, a younger coadjutor should be sought. The forty-four-year-old Lartigue did not suggest himself—but he did ask Plessis to burn this letter.[4] As Bishop of Quebec, however, Panet was a surprising success. His moderation and tact were more required in the coming years than the headstrong actions and sharp words of Lartigue.

As if the troubles with Lartigue were not enough, Panet faced difficulties over the appointment of Joseph Signay, the forty-seven-year-old curé of Quebec, as his coadjutor. Dalhousie readily agreed to the choice, although Signay needed some urging to accept. Panet submitted Signay's name to Rome at once, explaining the reasons for haste—a delay would encourage unworthy people to form cabals, and the British government would be offended if, as the papacy had ordered in 1796, names were submitted to Rome first. The Propaganda, however, insisted on the submission of three names, a procedure that delayed Signay's appointment for a full year and one that Panet warned could never be acceptable to the British government. At some future date the papacy and the government might recognize different men!

At the same time the Montreal issue was reaching crisis proportions in Rome. Robert Gradwell, the Quebec diocesan agent there, accused the Sulpicians of "foul play." "So many intrigues within intrigues, so many falsehoods advanced in confidence and secrecy . . . so many vain suspicions and idle fictions."[5] The slow-moving Roman bureaucracy reached its decision early in 1826—the Sulpicians were to have their authority but Lartigue should keep his church in Montreal. This was less than satisfactory to Lartigue who was still living in hostile territory, unrecognized by the government. Panet appealed for a clearer statement in July, 1826, and was finally told that the Sulpicians must obey Lartigue. But the Sulpicians were not content to let the matter rest. Auguste Roux, their superior, left for New York that summer for his health—and arrived in Rome without his bishop's knowledge. His companion on this secret mission was Jackson John Richards, a former Methodist preacher who had come from Virginia in 1820 to convert the Sulpicians, only to be converted himself. Panet's estimate of Richards as a "great meddler" is supported by Richards' subsequent career.[6]

THE SULPICIAN ESTATES AND OTHER DIOCESAN PROBLEMS

For Roux and Richards the next chapter of the Sulpicians' story began in London (where they sought permission to recruit French Sulpicians) when Bathurst told them the government would test the title of the Sulpician estates in court, a step that Lartigue and Plessis had managed to postpone in 1819. In Rome the two Sulpicians expressed dissatisfaction with the Propaganda's decision in favour of the bishops, but the case was not to be reopened. "The episcopophobia of the Montrealists is looked on with suspicion here," Gradwell reported, "and Propaganda seems to aim at soothing without complying with their irritated feeling."[7] But Roux and Richards were more disturbed by the court decision in Britain that the Sulpicians were not a corporation and therefore had no legal rights. With approval from Rome and intervention by the French ambassador in London, it was agreed that the Sulpicians would be incorporated, would be allowed to receive French priests into their house and would be compensated for the loss of their seigneurial rights. Panet entirely disapproved of this third aspect of the settlement—the Sulpicians were only trustees for the church and could not alienate their rights. He feared if the government got its way in this matter other church rights might be attacked. He would petition the king to have the unwilling Sulpicians retain their property rights whether they wanted to or not. To Lartigue this deal involving the surrender of £10,000 in yearly rents was "spoliation" by the "fanatical and persecuting" government of Lower Canada.[8]

The clergy's petition was despatched in the autumn of 1828 and followed up the next spring by two deputies sent to London and Rome to refute charges that Panet and Lartigue wanted the Sulpician estates for themselves. Panet enjoyed a sweet revenge in 1829 on the "great meddler" by vetoing Roux's nomination of Richards, an unqualified foreigner, for curé of Montreal. In London Panet's deputies got no answer but at Rome the Propaganda saw the implications for church property and revoked its earlier permission for the alienation of the Sulpician properties. Lartigue noted that British interest in the Sulpicians' property was awakened every time they sought to introduce recruits from France. The charge that the French-born Sulpicians had little sympathy for the rest of the church in Canada is supported by the fact that fewer than ten Canadians were admitted to their ranks between 1800 and 1840, and not until 1917 did the Sulpicians acquire a Canadian-born superior.

Although the papacy had defended Lartigue's right to live in Montreal it had refused him the honour of an episcopal throne; its advice to him was—be patient and charitable. Understandably bitter, Lartigue still blamed much of his troubles on Dalhousie's animosity. But in the autumn of 1828 Lartigue decided to demand the erection of Montreal as a separate diocese (like those for Upper Canada and Prince Edward Island-New Brunswick), a project that Panet considered premature even though it had first been mooted in 1781. Sir James Kempt, administrator of Lower Canada, favoured the plan and the Holy See had already agreed, subject to British government approval. Panet's two delegates in 1829 were therefore charged with the added task of presenting a petition to the king. The petition was rejected. In desperation Lartigue insisted that the Holy See must act in spite of the British government or else accept his demission. Rome would do neither and, just when Panet's agent in Rome arranged an interview with the pope in November 1830, Pius VIII died. The accession of Lord Goderich to the Colonial Office in the new Whig government that same month gave hopes for British approval of a Montreal bishopric, but in the political turmoil over the great Reform Bill, Lartigue's project was shelved for another two years.

Bishop Panet had other diocesan problems besides Lartigue and his Montreal bishopric. Late in 1824 the Colonial Office had refused to approve a corporation for Roman Catholic education in Lower Canada, proposing instead to connect those schools with the Royal Institution. Panet was suspicious of the proposal—Lartigue was openly hostile. But the Royal Institution met all Panet's objections by a scheme to establish Roman Catholic and Protestant committees within the institution. To this Panet agreed in 1826 because it would provide money for the parochial schools while leaving them under the church's control. On one point alone he was unsatisfied—the Colonial Office insisted that the Anglican bishop must always be President of the Royal Institution, "by right."[9] Lartigue, however, was still convinced that the whole system was designed to "decatholicize us and anglicize us."[10] Although the plan was not implemented then, a dual system of religious schools did become the basis of the School Act of 1846 which established the pattern of primary and secondary education in the province. Also in the educational field, the activities of Protestant bible societies were disturbing diocesan officials. Lartigue denounced one French school as "a bible school, that is a school of Protestantism and impiety," and had ordered the Sault-St-Louis Indians to turn over to their missionary all Mohawk translations of the Gospel. Only from their mother, the church, might they receive the word of God.[11]

Finally there was the constant problem of the two languages in the diocese, intensified by the Irish immigrants whom Plessis had uncharitably called the "scum of the population."[12] There were now two thousand of them in Quebec, without a priest of their own, and Plessis feared that more would come. In Montreal the Irish seemed more attracted to the Sulpicians than to Lartigue. There was also a growing feeling that somehow these unassimilated English-speaking faithful were less Catholic than the French, but the problems created by their presence were political and economic. Ireland's history made the newcomers radical and anti-British, which most of the hierarchy were not. Unaccustomed to paying tithes at home the immigrants felt no obligation to support the Canadian church financially regardless of what services it provided,[13] and their lack of skills and low standard of living posed a threat to the jobs of French Canadians. All in all, the arrival of the Irish Catholics seemed to militate against Lartigue's ambition for "a powerful and national Church."[14]

RECONCILIATION IN MONTREAL

As Panet celebrated his eightieth birthday, at the beginning of 1832, his duties hung heavy on his shoulders. Late in 1831 he had asked Rome to allow his demission but, despite the precedents of Briand and Hubert, he was refused. Rome would, however, allow Signay to be administrator of the diocese, and four months after he assumed his new duties, in October 1832, Panet was dead. Once again the procedure of appointing a coadjutor caused difficulties with the papacy. The governor, Lord Aylmer, and the Colonial Office were happy to approve Pierre-Flavien Turgeon, but Pope Gregory XVI now requested a list of twenty nominees. Turgeon was at first rejected because "it is said he is *hostile to the Sulpicians*";[15] but Thomas Maguire, one of Panet's delegates to Rome in 1829, made a second trip in 1833 to counteract this latest Sulpician intrigue and obtained Turgeon's appointment in 1834.

At the same time Rome again refused to let Lartigue demit, although they approved a coadjutor, Antoine Tabeau, for him. The Pope now personally established a new procedure for choosing coadjutors—an electoral college of all bishops, coadjutors, suffragans, vicars general and superiors of seminaries would vote secretly and submit the names of the three leading candidates. For the first time since the Quebec chapter disappeared, a corporate system of election was thus established. Lartigue suggested the bilingual Rémi Gaulin as coadjutor for Upper Canada, in hopes of starting a succession of Canadian bishops to re-establish the Quebec discipline in place of Macdonell's Scotch one.[16] A year later, with Gaulin safely installed, Lartigue was urging a similar extension of "Canadian" influence in the Maritimes. But Lartigue was having his own troubles over a coadjutor. Tabeau died in 1835 still unconsecrated, and before a substitute was obtained two unexpected developments led to the fulfilment of Lartigue's main ambition—the erection of a separate diocese of Montreal.

Suddenly, in September 1835, Lartigue's relations with the Sulpicians improved remarkably after their joint participation in a religious festival, and Vincent Quiblier, superior of the Sulpicians, took the lead in having one hundred and twenty-nine priests of the district sign a petition to the pope requesting the erection of Montreal as a bishopric.[17] When Signay delayed sending the petition, saying the government's agreement should be obtained first, Quiblier circulated a second petition to bring pressure on the bishop. But the decisive move came from the new governor, Lord Gosford, who arrived in Lower Canada late in the summer of 1835, armed with extensive powers as a royal commissionary, to investigate the current confrontation between Papineau's French-Canadian reformers and the English-dominated government of the colony. Gosford himself referred the question of a bishopric for Montreal to his royal commission and strongly supported its recommendation to the Colonial Office that Lartigue should receive the long awaited recognition. At the end of May 1836 Rome and London both gave their approval, and by September Lartigue was in possession of his bulls and of the diocese of Montreal. Thus more than fifteen years of bitterness, intrigue, confusion and recriminations within the diocese of Quebec came to an end.

Lartigue was naturally overjoyed—at last his building of the cathedral and seminary was justified. And his cup overflowed when he obtained his long-time secretary and superior of his seminary, thirty-six-year-old Ignace Bourget, "my right arm," as his coadjutor. Planning for Bourget's consecration, Lartigue sounded his fellow bishops on another of his favourite topics—the moulding of the four separate dioceses into an ecclesiastical province under an Archbishop of Quebec. What more opportune time for the laying of concrete plans than their reunion at Bourget's consecration?[18]

The two bishops in the maritime colonies seemed lukewarm to Lartigue's project, and Signay was definitely opposed. Like his two predecessors, Plessis and Panet, the bishop of Quebec was only too conscious of the need for caution when dealing with the Protestant government at London. As it happened only the two coadjutors in the Canadas, Gaulin and Turgeon, came to the consecration, but Bourget, Lartigue's spiritual child, took up the case for the proper establishment of a metropolitan province as intended by Rome when Plessis was prematurely promoted to archbishop in 1819.

On the eve of his consecration Ignace Bourget, the future embodiment of ultramontanism in Canada, stated his faith unequivocally to the Propaganda. Since the day he received holy orders at Lartigue's hands, he had been moulded by the Bishop of Montreal to obey the infallible authority of the church and to reject Gallicanism. Here was an undistorted echo of the ultramontane principles taught by Lartigue as early as 1819.

THE CHURCH OF ROME AND THE REBELLION OF 1837

For a decade the clash between the French-Canadian political radicals and the English-dominated governing clique had steadily increased in violence. Officially the Roman Catholic Church avoided involvement in these political controversies but at two points, the interests of religion and the radical politics of the *patriotes* met with different results. At first the French Canadian popular party supported the bishops against the Sulpicians in opposing the conversion of seigneurial land in Montreal to freehold tenure—the only time when Louis Joseph Papineau and his cousin, Bishop Lartigue, agreed, despite the governor's convictions about their relationship. After 1830, however, when Papineau openly espoused republicanism as his ideal for French Canada, the rift between church and reformers widened immeasurably. Papineau's attempt to broaden and democratize parish government with legislation to allow "notables" (land holders) to vote with church wardens was successfully blocked by the bishops in 1831. By 1834 the clergy had almost unanimously repudiated the radicals, who now talked in the same anti-clerical breath of annexation to the United States and abolition of tithes.

By 1837 Papineau's solid majority in the Lower Canadian Assembly stood in open defiance to the rule of the Colonial Office. Lord Gosford's attempts at reconciliation had been undone in May by the passing at Westminster of Lord John Russell's Ten Resolutions, which authorized the governor to spend taxes with the legislature's consent. At public meetings Papineau denounced the "foul stain" of Russell's resolutions in language that incited rebellion. In the face of this seditious movement centred in his diocese, Lartigue could no longer keep silent. His sermon at Bourget's consecration late in July urged the assembly of one hundred and fifty priests to warn their flocks that rebellion against legitimate authority was always wrong and to refuse absolution to seditionists.

The reaction of the radicals against Lartigue's "illiberalism" was instant and violent—"The self-styled Patriotes newspapers have come down on me in a body." Lartigue remarked to Signay, "but they'll soon weary of it."[19] In fact the course of rebellion may have been hastened rather than stayed by Lartigue's advice. More demonstrations followed until, on October 23 at St-Charles in the Richelieu Valley, Papineau himself tried to stop the tide he had raised, only to be told by his lieutenants that the time had come to melt spoons into bullets. The following day Lartigue issued a *mandement* obviously prepared before this meeting, to be read from every pulpit in his diocese, stating that the Catholic faith demanded civil obedience. Perhaps the *mandement* was his answer to the twelve hundred *patriotes* who had demonstrated opposite his cathedral at vespers on the preceding Sunday, but it aroused such hostility that Lartigue retired to the Montreal Hôtel-Dieu incognito. Outside Montreal the popular agitation against Lartigue was so vocal that he suspended the publication of the *mandement* "for reasons of prudence."[20]

Apparently it was too late to exert moral pressure on the rebels. Fighting began on November 17 in the Richelieu Valley. The next day Lartigue was prepared to flee to Quebec if necessary, "for the people are very excited against me."[21] The rebellion south of Montreal was soon crushed at St-Denis and at St-Charles, whose curé was imprisoned for three months for his imprudent but not treasonable remarks. Weeks later fighting broke out north of Montreal, at St-Eustache where the church and presbytery were burned in revenge, said Lartigue, by a "gang of Orangemen,"[22] and at St-Benoit where sacrileges occurred in the church and the curé fled to the woods. Only two priests actually joined in the rebellion which was itself restricted to seven of the province's twenty-one counties. But when the tragic events ended in utter defeat for the rebels the church demanded penance before readmitting them to the sacraments. *Patriotes* who had died in arms against their queen were denied church burial. Both Signay and Lartigue felt the culprits had been "more blind than blamable"[23] in allowing themselves to be misled by schemers who, Lartigue charged, were mostly Protestants.

Before the fighting began, the priests in the Richelieu Valley had protested that the *mandement* seemed to give the church's unqualified approval to every government action. As Canadians and as leaders of French-Canadian society, they felt obliged to speak out against government policy, while affirming at the same time their continued loyalty. Gosford agreed to support their petition to the queen, but before the signatures were collected the events at St-Denis and St-Charles dictated a change of approach by the Roman Catholic Church. Gosford had failed to find a solution to Lower Canada's problems but his efforts had not been entirely unappreciated. Signay had found him "a sincere friend of the clergy" who went in a body to pay their respects and present an address of loyalty before his departure in the spring of 1838. Lartigue repeatedly urged him as their friend to do all in his power to block a reunion of the provinces, which the bishop was sure would cause the separation of the colonies from the mother country. And Lartigue was personally indebted most to Gosford, "next to God,"[24] for the later incorporation of his diocese.

Towards the new governor, Lord Durham, the clergy were distinctly more reserved. It was an open secret that Durham and his royal commission investigating the rebellions would recommend a reunion of the two Canadas to Anglicize the French population. When Durham asked the bishops to announce his proclamation on taking over the government of Lower Canada, Lartigue indignantly refused to be used as a government mouthpiece. His *mandement* against rebellion had been issued voluntarily, uninfluenced by the government. "I am then ultimately convinced," he told Durham, "that the service of the Queen would gain much by leaving the Catholic clergy to act independent of the civil power."[25]

With the constitution of Lower Canada suspended the Catholic clergy was again pushed into the role of spokesman for French Canada as it had been immediately after the Conquest. Proclaiming the separation of Catholic church from Protestant state, the clergy did not hesitate to oppose a union which threatened to destroy the French-Canadian people and their church. Union, however, came despite these protests, though Lartigue did not live to see its consummation. On April 19, 1840, as the Union Bill was before the imperial parliament for its second reading, Lartigue died in Montreal. In many ways his passing marked the end of an era. After the years of difficulty his diocese had just been securely established as the province of Lower Canada was about to disappear. The church had healed its own divisions and was about to expand the scope of its work through the introduction of new groups such as the Christian Brothers, the Oblates and the revived Society of Jesus. In the years ahead, Lartigue's dream of a metropolitan see would become a reality, and the religious life of the church would be quickened by renewed devotional fervour.

A NEW ANGLICAN BISHOP OF QUEBEC

Four weeks before Bishop Plessis returned in 1820 from his epoch-making trip to Europe, Bishop Mountain landed in Quebec after two and a half years in England. His journey had certainly been less profitable than Plessis'. It was now obvious that the Church of Rome had been the victor in the rivalry for practical establishment. Mountain had not been allowed to surrender his bishopric—instead his salary was raised by £600—nor had his request for the erection of an Upper Canadian diocese been accepted. His only achievements had been the conversion of commissaries into archdeacons—a mark of respectability rather than power—and the despatch of seven more clergymen overseas to the diocese.

Mountain's remaining five years of life were marked by steady if modest expansion of the Anglican Church in Lower Canada. Between 1820 and his death eleven churches served by six clergymen were established in Lower Canada, and fourteen priests ordained for the diocese of Quebec. In 1820/21 Mountain conducted his last episcopal tour, visiting the whole diocese except the Gaspé. Much of the diocesan administration was now performed by Archdeacon George Jehosaphat Mountain, the bishop's son, who was himself destined to become Bishop of Quebec in 1837, and by Charles James Stewart, appointed travelling superintendent of missions in 1819. Stewart preceded Mountain's tour of 1820 by a few months with an eighteen-hundred-mile visit to the missions in both Canadas. From 1815 to 1817 Stewart had been in England where he solicited funds to support church extension in the three thousand square miles of the Eastern Townships which had only three clergymen in 1816. By 1820 over £2500 had been collected from which some eleven Anglican churches in Lower Canada as well as several in Upper Canada were aided. An additional £2000 was given by the S.P.G. in 1820, and as a result of a second trip to England in 1823 Stewart raised another £2500 for this worthwhile undertaking. But despite the herculean efforts of these self-sacrificing men the Church of England still grew but slowly in Lower Canada.

As Bishop Mountain's health declined, the problem of a successor came to the fore. When he again asked for release from his episcopal duties, Stewart, who was in England, applied for the position with Mountain's approval, as he had done in 1818. The Colonial Office, however, were now prepared to divide the diocese and make Stewart bishop in Upper Canada. But before these arrangements were complete Mountain died, in June 1825, and Stewart became second bishop almost automatically, to the disappointment of G. J. Mountain and John Strachan who had been casting covetous eyes on the mitre for Quebec.

In his thirty-two years as bishop Jacob Mountain had encountered insuperable obstacles in Lower Canada and general apathy in Britain to his plans for a great colonial establishment. If Mountain failed to adapt sufficiently to colonial conditions, if he relied too much on precedence and too little on cordial personal relations, it is still doubtful if many men could have accomplished more in that period when the functions and organization of the Church of England were disrupted for almost a quarter century by wars with France, with Napoleon and with the United States of America.

Mountain's successor, Charles James Stewart, third son of the seventh Earl of Galloway, had proven his ability and his devotion in the eighteen years since accepting the mission of St-Armand in 1807. Just fifty years old when he became bishop, Stewart was a confirmed bachelor, well connected in Britain and respected by all his diocesan clergy. Most important, Stewart grasped more clearly than Mountain the differences between North America and Europe. Without abandoning the legal position of his church as the state religion, he was prepared and even anxious to see justice done to other Christian denominations residing in the egalitarian society of the British colonies.[26] During his episcopate the restrictions on other Protestant clergy regarding marriages were removed as one step in the growth of religious equality.

Stewart was consecrated in London on New Year's Day, 1826. His diocese, stretching from the Gaspé to Sault Ste Marie, contained fifty parishes and missions (with as many clergy) and sixty-three churches. To Mountain's two archdeaconries of Quebec and York, a third, Kingston, was now added. In due course Stewart succeeded to Mountain's positions in the legislative and executive councils of Lower Canada, where he was a fairly regular attendant. In his first three years Stewart toured all parts of his diocese except its eastern and western extremities, and during his visit to Upper Canada in 1828 met Bishop Inglis, son of the first bishop of Nova Scotia, and their mutual friend, Bishop Hobart of New York. The most active area of the diocese was Upper Canada where Stewart opened new missions to serve the large number of immigrants now reaching that province. Beginning in 1830 Stewart organized a group of catechists to assist in missions that were too large for a single missionary. That same year he founded a Sunday school society to provide Christian education for the young.

The physical extent of Stewart's diocese was so great that he again sought its division when he was in England in 1831—and again the Colonial Office took no action. Although he continued to urge division, the most that he could obtain was the consecration of G. J. Mountain as his suffragan in 1836, under the title of Bishop of Montreal. Mountain's appointment came none too soon, for Stewart's health was failing so rapidly that Mountain took over practical control of the diocese late in 1836, less than a year before Stewart's death. To meet the need for closer episcopal supervision in Upper Canada, Stewart spent three winters at York (or Toronto, as it became in 1834). As a further means of knitting together the scattered servants of the Church he promoted a church periodical in 1827, but it disappeared in a very few years after infrequent appearances.

NEW CHALLENGES TO ANGLICAN ESTABLISHMENT

In this generation of unrest Stewart's two major problems both involved church-state relations, particularly in financial matters. The Church of Scotland's claim to be coestablished in the empire, and therefore entitled to share in the Clergy Reserves, had first been raised in Upper Canada after the War of 1812-14. The protracted battle of the Church of England to retain its monopoly of the reserves was fought mainly in the upper province, but as Anglican bishop in both colonies Stewart was inevitably involved. In 1823 he had been Mountain's emissary bearing to England the clergy's rebuttal to the Presbyterian demands for a share of the reserves' funds. There he had joined John Strachan in 1824 in a successful bid to prevent one half of the Upper Canadian reserves being sold to the newly formed Canada Company. Two years later the Reformers in the Upper Canadian assembly wanted to end the Clergy Reserves controversy by secularizing the lands. With rare insight Stewart pointed out to Lord Bathurst that it was the reserves, not the church, that were under fire. "It is because the church is protected by the State, and has the character of an Establishment, that the leaders of the popular party make her an object of their present attack."[27]

As a result of Stewart's suggestions the Clergy Reserves Sales Act of 1827 established a new policy. The Clergy Corporation would be allowed to sell half of the lands which previously could only be rented. Still the Church of Scotland was demanding a share, and Stewart replied charitably that if his church was making "an unjust claim, and grasping at more than is fairly ours," he would renounce "our pretentions." In both provinces, but especially the upper, the Clergy Reserves continued to be the cause of political wrangling and religious discord but, because no agreement on the Clergy Reserves problem could be found in the colonies, the British government had decided by 1831 that the only solution was to reinvest the lands in the crown. The necessary colonial bill to amend the relevant sections of the Constitutional Act failed to pass the Lower Canadian assembly because of a misunderstanding and in Upper Canada a pro-Anglican majority in a new assembly refused to discuss reinvestment. In Lower Canada some three hundred thousand acres were sold in the decade after the Sales Act, but the invested capital was returning less than £1000. Despite all its efforts the Church of Scotland in Lower Canada got only a pittance from public funds until 1836, when it was granted £500 from the reserves monies, in line with the new policy in Upper Canada of aiding all the larger denominations, including the Roman Catholics.

Stewart's second problem concerned government grants to his diocese. The Clergy Reserves had been intended to supply the church's material needs but until these lands could produce a sufficient revenue the imperial parliament gave annual grants as a temporary stop-gap. In the years 1825-31 the S.P.G. was granted some £15,000 annually for distribution in the diocese of Quebec, but by the latter date the new Whig government seemed convinced that the time had arrived for the Church of England in British North America to stand on its own financial legs. In December 1831 the S.P.G. was informed that the grants would be decreased annually until finally eliminated in 1835, leaving the colonial church to depend henceforth on colonial resources. This decision, like the proposed reinvestment of the reserves, was evidence of the growing anticolonialism fostered in the mother country by the free trade movement that had been gaining strength since the end of the Napoleonic Wars.

The income from the Clergy Reserves was still incapable of supporting the church in the Canadas and, when it became apparent that the colonial clergy would suffer if the parliamentary grants ended, the Colonial Office relented so far as to promise 85 per cent of the current salaries for the life of the incumbents—the deficit and salaries for new clergy became the responsibility of the S.P.G. and the diocese. Behind the colonial church's financial problems lay the refusal of Anglican settlers to give voluntarily to the support of their church—religion had been "free" at home, why should it not be free in every British colony? Here was another obvious weakness of a church-state connection in the democratic atmosphere of North America. Anglicanism in the Canadas continued to pay a high price for its status as a privileged or semi-established church.

With G. J. Mountain installed as suffragan, Stewart returned to England where he died in July 1837. Under his guiding hand the diocese had grown in strength and the clergy in number, the Clergy Reserves preserved almost intact in the face of a vigorous opposition, and continuing financial support secured, albeit on a reduced scale. Through a decade of hostile feelings Stewart had faithfully served his church while exhibiting the most charitable sentiments towards other Christian denominations. His successor continued to hold the double bishopric of Quebec and Montreal, administering it as a single diocese. But Lord Durham's mission, in the wake of the 1837 rebellion, was soon to cast a clear and cold light on the position of the Church of England in the Canadas and to challenge some of its most cherished assumptions about its own role in colonial life.

NOTES TO CHAPTER SEVEN

1. *RAPQ*, 1941-2, pp. 364-65, J.-J. Lartigue to J.-O. Plessis, 21 April 1821.
2. *Ibid.*, pp. 458, 462-63, J.-J. Lartigue to Dr. Poynter, 1 April 1825.
3. *Ibid.*, 1933-4, p. 264, Lord Dalhousie to B.-C. Panet, 9 December 1825.
4. *Ibid.*, 1941-2, p. 459, J.-J. Lartigue to J.-O. Plessis, 23 April 1825.
5. *Ibid.*, 1933-4, p. 271, Robert Gradwell to J.-O. Plessis, 10 January 1826.
6. *Ibid.*, p. 292, B.-C. Panet to J.-J. Lartigue, 27 May 1826. For an account of Richards' colourful and quixotic career, see J. R. Danaher, "The Reverend Jackson Richards, Missionary to the Sulpicians," *CCHAR*, 1943-4, pp. 49-54.
7. *RAPQ*, 1933-4, p. 338, Robert Gradwell to B.-C. Panet, 27 February 1827.
8. *Ibid.*, 1942-3, pp. 27, 26, J.-J. Lartigue to Cardinal Capellari, 15 August 1828 and same to Dr. Robert Gradwell, 31 July 1828.
9. *Ibid.*, 1933-4, p. 331, Lord Dalhousie to B.-C. Panet, 26 January 1827.
10. *Ibid.*, 1942-3, p. 24, J.-J. Lartigue to D.-B. Viger, 22 June 1828.
11. *Ibid.*, 1941-2, pp. 428, 464, J.-J. Lartigue to J.-O. Plessis, 21 October 1823, Pastoral Letter to the Iroquois of Sault-St-Louis, 30 July 1825.
12. G. L. Nute, ed., *Documents Relating to Northwest Missions 1815-1827* (St. Paul: Minnesota Historical Society, 1942), p. 398, J.-O. Plessis to J.-N. Provencher, 6 April 1823.
13. OA, Macdonell Papers, Vol. I, pp. 79-80, A. Macdonell to J.-J. Lartigue, 7 April 1821.
14. *RAPQ*, 1941-2, p. 482, J.-J. Lartigue to B.-C. Panet, 3 May 1826.
15. *Ibid.*, 1936-7, p. 184, Nicolas Wiseman to Joseph Signay, 24 April 1833.
16. *Ibid.*, 1942-3, p. 162, J.-J. Lartigue to Joseph Signay, 13 October 1832. Lartigue had similar plans for French control in the Maritimes, see *ibid.*, 1943-4, pp. 251, 298.
17. Lucien Lemieux, *L'établissement de la première Province ecclésiastique au Canada 1783-1844* (Montreal: Fides, 1967), p. 375.
18. For a complete account of the events leading up to the creation of the ecclesiastical province, see Lemieux, *op. cit.*, pp. 432 *ff.*
19. *RAPQ*, 1944-5, p. 247, J.-J. Lartigue to Joseph Signay, 29 July 1837.
20. *Ibid.*, 1945-6, p. 143, Ignace Bourget to J. Marcoux, 2 November 1837.
21. *Ibid.*, p. 259, J.-J. Lartigue to Joseph Signay, 18 November 1837.
22. *Ibid.*, 1944-5, p. 263, J.-J. Lartigue to Joseph Signay, 19 December 1837.
23. *Ibid.*, 1938-9, pp. 238-39, Joseph Signay to Lord Gosford, 9 February 1838.
24. *Ibid.*, 1945-6, p. 78, J.-J. Lartigue to Lord Gosford, 16 September 1838.
25. *Ibid.*, p. 65, J.-J. Lartigue to Charles Buller, 9 June 1838.
26. T. R. Millman, *The Life of the Right Reverend, The Honourable Charles James Stewart* (London: Huron College, 1953), p. 167.
27. *Ibid.*, pp. 72-73.

EIGHT

The Struggle for Religious Equality

With the conclusion in 1815 of Britain's quarter-century of wars with France, and Napoleon's recent ally, the United States, a great migration began to flood across the Atlantic from the British Isles to the New World, spurred on by the social dislocation and political unrest that disturbed Britain as it entered the great age of the Industrial Revolution. Individually or as groups, a large proportion of the 125,000 immigrants who left Britain during the next decade settled in Upper Canada, the colony so recently purged of American sympathizers in the crucible of war. The religious affiliation of the newcomers cannot be ascertained but certainly a high proportion were nominal members of the churches of England and Scotland. Once again however, as in the Loyalist period, immigration proceeded more rapidly than the provisions of religious facilities, and many of these newest arrivals were attracted to those denominations that were able to fill the spiritual vacuum of the frontier. Since most immigrants became farmers—the population of York as late as 1830 was only 2,800 when Upper Canada's was over 230,000—the Methodists with their flexible system of circuit-riders held a distinct advantage over those churches that tied themselves rigidly to the static European concept of parish organizations.

THE BEGINNINGS OF CANADIANIZATION

The basic challenge to all the churches was to Canadianize—to provide services in the Canadas adapted to Canadian conditions. John Strachan had early and clearly seen the need for a "native ministry" of Canadian-born men, or at least of Britishers able and willing to accommodate themselves to a highly fluid society of homey but enterprising individualists, and this belief may account for Strachan's opinion that the scholarly Jacob Mountain was ill-suited to be a bishop in the new world.[1] In 1812 Strachan had proposed to train ordinands for the Church of Upper Canada if the S.P.G. would provide scholarships. This plan was implemented in 1815 and maintained for twelve years, and several young men were recruited by this means. More clergy arrived from England in addition to the twenty acquired in 1819 and 1820, but there were never enough to meet the task at hand. By the 1830s, however, a new source of Anglican clergymen appeared as troubles in Ireland caused the migration of well-to-do members of the Anglo-Irish squirarchy who were joined by several Church of Ireland clergy, most of whom were strongly evangelical graduates of Trinity College, Dublin.

Bishop Mountain's declining health—he made his last visitation in 1820—led to speculation and intrigues about the future administration of the diocese. Although Mountain was anxious to resign he rejected the offer of a small pension, and the Archbishop of Canterbury opposed the appointment of any auxiliary bishops.[2] Charles Stewart, who had been functioning very effectively as travelling missionary in the Canadas since 1821, had actually been considered by Mountain as a possible successor in 1807, and Stewart had recommended himself for the post in 1818. The ambitious John Strachan, who was striving to make Anglican influence predominant in every aspect of Upper Canadian life, pressed the Bishop of London in 1824 to support a division of the diocese and his elevation to Bishop of Upper Canada where admittedly the Church of England was strongest. Mountain's own preference for next bishop was his son, George Jehosaphat, but by the spring of 1825 he was willing to accept a divided diocese with Stewart as bishop of the upper province. Before the bishop could return home on leave, or Stewart be consecrated, Jacob Mountain died and the plan for division was abandoned as Charles James Stewart became second Bishop of Quebec and Strachan was made Archdeacon of York.

Because of its connection with the state, the Church of England was unable, even if it had been willing, to assume a more Canadian appearance. Other denominations however, for a variety of motives but with varying degrees of success, deliberately sought to identify with a provincial society that was both Canadian and British. The independent Presbytery of the Canadas, organized in 1818, grew so quickly that a synod of three presbyteries in Upper Canada and one in Lower was formed in 1819. When the synod met in 1820, however, only nine clergy attended and seven were from Upper Canada. Annual meetings were held for the next four years but the distances to be travelled were so great that attendance was always scanty and in 1825 the synod formally dissolved, surviving only as the United Presbytery of Upper Canada.

One reason for the synod's demise and for its lack of heirs in the lower province was the growing strength of the Church of Scotland which had boycotted the synod from its beginning. In 1818 there were three Church of Scotland ministers in Lower Canada but nine in Upper. Despite secessions from both Montreal congregations the Church of Scotland in Lower Canada showed no disposition towards independence from the mother church—all its ministers were imported from Scotland and most Presbyterians in that province inclined towards the conservative and ethnocentric Kirk, a tendency reinforced by the formation in 1825 of the Glasgow Colonial Society with Lord Dalhousie, Governor of Lower Canada, as its patron. In the Canadas the society's help in obtaining ministers was warmly welcomed by adherents of the Church of Scotland, and the society's annual income of only £500 was husbanded so carefully that in the six years after its first missionary came to the Canadas in 1829 over forty ordained clergy were sent to the colonies each with a free outfit, passage and £50 per annum for the first three years in the field.[3] Because of the rapid growth of Upper Canada's population and the Catholic preponderance in Lower Canada, few missionaries settled in the lower province and there their work was confined to the two urban centres, Montreal and Quebec.

Another Presbyterian body, the Associate Church of America, had entered Upper Canada almost by accident in 1822 as a result of a request from Stamford for a missionary to baptize a child. Liberal, revivalistic and loosely organized, the Associate Church concentrated its efforts in the Niagara Peninsula where extensive Presbyterian settlements already existed and organized several congregations which eventually formed the Associate Presbytery of Stamford (Niagara) as an offshoot of the Presbytery of Albany.[4]

The Roman Catholic Church too achieved a larger measure of identification with Upper Canada after the War of 1812 when the loyalty of Bishop Macdonell and his Highland Catholics had been proven once again. The elevation of Macdonell in 1824 as titular Bishop for Upper Canada (with a government salary of £400) indicated the degree of cultural separation from the French-Canadian church, and Macdonell's appointment to the legislative council in 1831 marked his political recognition. There were virtually no English Roman Catholics in British North America for the simple reason that Roman Catholicism had been virtually extirpated in England by the Reformation; but Macdonell's diocese, like those in the other colonies, now began to receive sizable numbers of Irish who introduced new traditions and attitudes that were difficult to assimilate into the Canadian church.

The Irish brought a strong liberal and anti-English political outlook, a reputation for individualism and violence, and their own priests who caused Macdonell untold grief by their independent and undisciplined behaviour. Macdonell charged that the Irish priests, several of whom he had educated in his own home at his own expense when he himself could not afford a servant or a horse, had harmed religion, and he cited the case of one who pawned his vestments to get liquor and gave the church ornaments to children for toys.[5] Nevertheless, on the strength of his increased flock, Macdonell repeatedly urged the imperial and provincial governments to give him and his diocese more money, including the salaries for three priests and four teachers promised him in 1816, and a share of the Protestant Clergy Reserves. "Be assured my Lord," he advised Plessis, "whatever they will grant the Catholics of Canada will be from fear and not from love";[6] but publicly he stressed always the strong loyalty and conservatism of the church in his diocese.

The most successful denomination in the effort to Canadianize in Upper Canada was the Methodists, although ironically their achievement of complete autonomy in 1828 was the result of their American origins. The concordat of 1820 which saved Upper Canadian Methodists from English Conference tutelage spurred demands for separation from the American church whose presence in Upper Canada had been the excuse for the post-war "invasion" by the English missionaries. Agitation for separation, by a declaration of independence if necessary, centred in the Loyalist-settled Bay of Quinte region, which was reportedly "all ablaze for separation,"[7] and was led by the Reverend Henry Ryan, said to have been a converted American pugilist. To cool down the Canadians the American General Conference sent a bishop to visit in 1824 but the first positive step towards autonomy was permitted that year when a Canadian Conference was created for the thirty-two preachers and 6100 members. The first meeting of the Canada Conference repeated the request to the American parent body for independence, arguing that the war had revived anti-American "asperity and prejudice" in Upper Canada, that the provincial government had aided the recent English missionary incursion because of the Canadian connection with the American body, and that in the event of another war with the United States church administration would be "extremely hazardous if not totally impracticable."[8]

Although the subject was not mentioned in 1824, the Canada Conference had the previous year begun a successful mission to the Mohawk Indians on the Grand River, the nucleus of extensive future mission work in the province, and the good will of the local government would be necessary if this outreach to the king's "red children" was to continue. In quick succession missions to the Indian bands on Lake Simcoe, Rice Lake, the Credit River and three other locations were added to the list by 1828, when the Canadian Petition was accepted by the American General Conference and the independence of the Methodist Episcopal Church in Canada thereby recognized. By that date too Henry Ryan and one other preacher, encouraged by certain Loyalists, had already formed the miniscule Canadian Wesleyan Methodist Church of two hundred members. Ryan's action, however, was of little historical significance compared to the row over loyalty and religious equality in Upper Canada which had broken out in the spring of 1826.

THE CLERGY RESERVES CONTROVERSY—THE OPENING PHASE

Given the assumption that a Christian state must have an established church, the generous endowment of the Church of England with one-seventh of the land naturally aroused no opposition when the Constitutional Act was passed in Britain and attracted little attention in Upper Canada during the next quarter century. Coincident with the end of the War of 1812-14, however, the Clergy Reserves became increasingly a source of religious and political controversy in the province, symbolizing the many-faced church-state controversy which bedevilled the years from 1820 to 1840.

As successive townships were surveyed, Clergy Reserves lots were interspersed on a chequered plan among crown and school reserves and lots available for sale. In 1803 a system of leasing the Clergy Reserves was instituted to provide the Church of England with a regular income in lieu of legalized collection of the tithe, which even Simcoe had agreed would not be "palatable to the people."[9] Land, however, was the one resource that Upper Canada had in abundance, and the lavish gifts of land to Loyalists and others, and the low price to those who wished to purchase, meant that few settlers were willing to rent these reserves. As late as 1811 only four hundred acres were under lease and government officers showed little initiative in collecting rents or ousting squatters who stripped the lots of their prime timber and then moved on to repeat the process elsewhere in the province.

Controversy over the Clergy Reserves arose first as an incidental result of the reaction by certain land speculators against the Colonial Office's new policy of curbing previous free-wheeling disposal of lands in the province. Robert Gourlay, a voluble and demagogic Scot related to two of the largest speculators, incited popular opposition to this policy and to the existence of the reserves by circulating questionnaires and holding public grievance meetings. In 1819 Gourlay was banished from Upper Canada on a legal technicality, largely through the efforts of Strachan who warned Bishop Mountain that recent assembly resolutions attacking the reserves would become an annual clamour.[10] Public interest in the Clergy Reserves was further aroused in 1819 when the Niagara Presbyterian congregation, whose church had been burned by the Americans during the war, petitioned Lieutenant-Governor Sir Peregrine Maitland for an annual grant of £100 from the Clergy Reserves to help in rebuilding their church and finding a minister. Their request was considered in England by the Law Officers of the Crown who reported that the Protestant Clergy Reserves funds could be given to the Church of Scotland as an established church of the United Kingdom, but not to dissenters.[11] Maitland chose not to inform anyone in Upper Canada of this interpretation except Anglican members of his executive council, and the Church of Scotland in the Canadas subsequently mounted a campaign to share with the Church of England in the Clergy Reserves as a coestablishment, unaware that the principle had already been conceded.

As a member of that executive council Strachan was sensitive to the Kirk's threat to the Anglican monopoly of the Clergy Reserves and in the broader sense its challenge to the establishment principle. To protect the interests of the Church of England and incidentally to improve the management of the reserves lands, Strachan obtained in 1819 a charter for a Clergy Corporation of Upper Canada suggested by Mountain and modelled on his corporation for the lower province. The creation of the corporation, which assumed full control of the reserves, served unwittingly to focus public attention even more sharply on the Anglican monopoly, on the preferred, if not truly established, status of that church, and on its close interconnection with the state epitomized by Strachan's own double career as churchman and politician. On the other hand the Clergy Corporation proved no more effective at administering the reserves than the government had been. At least one potential cause of opposition to Anglican paramountcy was removed by a provincial act of 1822 declaring the tithe illegal in Upper Canada, a step urged by Strachan as early as 1816.[12]

Although the Church of Scotland was one of the smaller Protestant denominations in Upper Canada and without formal organization, its members were still pressing for some public aid even if the Clergy Reserves, as they had now been told, were intended exclusively for the Church of England. William Morris, a wealthy merchant at Perth and member of the assembly, was the effective spokesman for the Kirk who in 1823 obtained from the assembly a resolution favouring government "support and maintenance" for Church of Scotland clergy on the grounds that the conquest of Canada had been a British rather than an English victory.[13] The Clergy Corporation countered the Kirk's request for aid with a defence of the Anglican position based on the exclusive interpretation of "Protestant Clergy" and on an ecclesiastical chart which indicated that except for Methodists and Church of Scotland adherents, Upper Canadians were either Anglican or favourable to the Church of England. Lieutenant-Governor Maitland supported the corporation by advising the Colonial Office that any aid given to non-Anglicans should be for specific congregations, not to denominations, to ensure that dissent did not prosper "at the expense of the Church of England."[14]

After due consideration the Colonial Office informed the General Assembly of the Church of Scotland in 1825 that it accepted the principle of support for that church in the colonies—but regretted that no funds were available at the moment. To earlier complaints from the Canadians that the mother church showed little interest in supporting its claims and was reluctant to acknowledge any connection between the church at home and the church in the colonies, the General Assembly replied that the colonial church would have to organize itself before it could expect recognition from either the state or the parent religious body. Such organization was obviously difficult to arrange in the Canadas, but the formation in 1825 of the Glasgow Colonial Society, modelled on the S.P.G., was evidence of the awakened interest of the Church of Scotland in its brethren overseas and a warning that the campaign for endowment and coestablishment in the colonies would henceforth be pushed with greater strength and unity.[15]

When Strachan returned to Britain in 1824 for the first time since his arrival in Canada, he carried with him a proposal by Maitland to sell the reserves to enable the Church of England to support "two hundred or 300 clergymen" who "would infuse into the population a tone and feeling entirely English, and acquiring by degrees the direction of education. . . ."[16] This proposal fitted well the Colonial Office's desire to promote emigration to British North America through land development companies. Accordingly the Canada Company was incorporated in 1826 and offered a block purchase of the Crown and Clergy Reserves. The Church of England in Upper Canada soon had second thoughts about such a deal and, convinced that the church could get a better price by selling the reserves privately, Strachan, the Clergy Corporation and Maitland successfully thwarted this land transfer. An imperial act permitting the Governor-in-Council to sell up to one hundred thousand acres of the reserves per year was passed, but because of the obstruction by friends of the Church of Scotland the arrangement fell short of the clergy control that Strachan had hoped for.

In Upper Canada William Morris was attacking the Church of England monopoly of the reserves ever more violently and this quarrel between the two "national" churches encouraged demands of a new kind from a third group of Upper Canadians, whose representatives in the assembly informed the king that the lands "ought not to be enjoyed by any one denomination . . . but . . . should be devoted to the advancement of the Christian Religion generally . . . or . . . applied to the purposes of education."[17] Strachan was now forced to defend his church's endowment on two fronts—against the Church of Scotland's demands to share as a coestablishment, and against the growing group of voluntarists who wanted to end all church-state connections in the province. The Clergy Reserves soon became but one thread woven into the tapestry of religious conflict in Upper Canada after 1826.

REFORM *VERSUS* LOYALTY

On Sunday, 3 July 1825, John Strachan delivered a sermon in St. James' Church, York, to mark the death of Jacob Mountain. In somewhat fulsome terms he praised the virtues and abilities of the late bishop, but he did not stop there. Strachan went on to make a strong plea for greater government support to the established church—"a Christian nation without a religious establishment is a contradiction." "What can fifty-three clergymen do, scattered over a country of greater extent than Great Britain? . . . the religious teachers of the other denominations of Christians, a very few respectable ministers of the Church of Scotland excepted, come almost universally from the republican states of America." "Uneducated itinerant preachers . . . leaving their steady employment, betake themselves to preaching the gospel from idleness, or a zeal without knowledge, by which they are induced without any preparation to teach what they do not know, and which from pride they disdain to learn."[18] Members of the congregation congratulated Strachan on his sermon and there the matter might have rested had Strachan not decided to publish his text as a pamphlet the following spring.

When a printed copy of the sermon came into Methodist hands a champion to defend the loyalty, learning and intelligence of the Methodist preachers arose in the person of Egerton Ryerson, a twenty-three-year-old circuit rider whose devastating rebuttal to Strachan was published by William Lyon Mackenzie as support for his own vendetta against the provincial government and its Anglican mentor.[19] Ryerson began by expressing admiration for the Anglican form of Christianity, but denied that Christ ever intended a union of His church with any state. If the Church of England was a minority religion in Upper Canada, Strachan should look for causes inside the church. Then, after refuting Strachan's "ungenerous, unfounded and false" accusations of ignorance, Ryerson came to the sorest point of the famous sermon, the charge of disloyalty. Ryerson's family had been Anglican Loyalists before Strachan even heard of Upper Canada, and two of Ryerson's older brothers had served against the Americans in the recent war, one being permanently maimed at Black Rock. Ryerson pointed out that all but eight of the Methodist preachers in the province were British subjects born and educated, and of the other eight six were naturalized citizens.

Although this rebuttal caused a sensation in Upper Canada, Strachan did not deign to reply—he was preparing for a second trip to England, in connection with the Clergy Reserves business and a university for Upper Canada. In the course of his seventeen-month sojourn in Britain Strachan obtained a charter for King's College at York and its endowment with over 225,000 acres. The fact that the college presidency was attached to the office of Archdeacon of York and that professors and college council members must be Anglican seemed natural in an English context, and for its day the charter was surprisingly liberal since it admitted dissenters as students. Such an exclusive institution, however, would never satisfy the dissenting majority in Upper Canada and its charter came under immediate and sustained attack from the opponents of church establishment.

In connection with the proposed sale of the Clergy Reserves Strachan prepared a long letter to the Colonial Office demonstrating that "Protestant Clergy" could only mean Anglican, and to this he appended an Ecclesiastical Chart of the Province of Upper Canada.[20] The chart was intended to destroy statistically the Church of Scotland's claims to a share of the reserves, but again Strachan repeated that dissenting clergy (he excepted only seven) were Americans and that the Methodists were "subject to the orders of the [American] Conference." Strachan returned to Canada confident that he had proved to the Colonial Office that the Church of England was not merely the most respectable but also the most numerous body of Christians in the colony. Instead he soon encountered a whirlwind of denunciation from all sides when his letter was published in Britain and copies broadcast in Canada. The blatant inaccuracies of his chart and the exclusive nature of his college charter united all denominations against him, and his attempted self-defence in a speech to his colleagues in the legislative council—"I feel proudly conscious that I deserve the friendship and esteem of all honourable men, and the approbation of the whole Province"[21]—merely fanned the flames of opposition. Petitions to the assembly signed by almost 5,700 persons defended the loyalty of the Methodists, denied that "the tendency of the population is towards the Church of England," and charged that the principle of King's College charter was inconsistent with "our civil and religious rights and privileges."[22]

A committee of the assembly investigating these complaints called fifty-two witnesses—Strachan at first refused to appear or explain his statements—and concluded that the Church of England "has always had, in this Province, peculiar privileges," that although the Church of England was one of the smaller denominations in Upper Canada its members were as capable of supporting its clergy as other denominations were theirs, that the insinuations against the Methodists were unfounded and slanderous, and that the university charter was "sectarian" and "objectionable."[23] The gist of this report was then sent as an Address of the Assembly to the King, while in the public press the attack continued as Ryerson published eight widely reprinted letters denying that the Church of England was or had any right to be the established religion of Upper Canada.[24] Although other contemporary developments in the Canadas might seem to deny it, the truth was that from this time forward Strachan and the establishment principle were on the defensive against an aroused provincial society bent on establishing complete religious equality.

In 1828 Strachan's strong ally, the opinionated Lieutenant-Governor Maitland, was replaced by Sir John Colborne, a man of more liberal inclinations and more practical ideas—and less likely to submit to Strachan's domination of the political scene. Almost immediately Colborne stopped Strachan's university plans by diverting funds to a preparatory school, Upper Canada College. In 1829 the Methodist Episcopal Church took the first steps towards creating a rival school on Christian but nonsectarian principles, Upper Canada Academy, the future Victoria University. King's had been intended as the cope-stone of a provincial system of Anglican-controlled schools which Strachan promoted by school acts of 1807, 1816 and 1820, and which

Maitland had fostered by appointing Strachan president of the General Board of Education in 1823. In subsequent years it had been a common and justified complaint that with Strachan holding the educational purse-strings the staff and curriculum of the three hundred common and ten district grammar schools were Anglican.[25] Almost annually in the late twenties and early thirties bills to liberalize the school system by taking it out of the hands of a single church were rejected by the legislative council where Strachan's influence was supreme over that loose grouping of similarly-minded individuals called "the Family Compact."

Also in 1829 opponents of church establishment acquired an effective voice in the new Methodist weekly, the *Christian Guardian*, edited by Egerton Ryerson. Clergy Reserves were still the central issue of the church-state controversy, and on behalf of all voluntarists the *Guardian* consistently rejected the claims of the Church of Scotland to coestablishment as strongly as it deprecated the existing Anglican monopoly. "The constitution of a Church and State Establishment is not suited to the atmosphere of Canada. Such a monster, whether with one, two, or three heads, must very soon share the fate in this country, which he has lately met with in France."[26] Government grants to the Roman Catholics and Church of Scotland brought charges by the *Guardian* that the executive council was "buying off" opposition to the reserves. When the Methodist Conference of 1831 presented a counter-petition to one from the Anglican clergy which defended their monopoly of the reserves, Colborne replied that the Methodist preachers meddled in politics, gave "absurd advice" to the Indians,[27] were ignorant and by implication American, a statement that seems in retrospect quite out of character for Colborne.

Colborne was chastized by the Colonial Office for these insulting comments to the conference, but behind the scenes government measures were already afoot by 1832 to break the Methodists' strength by reintroducing the English Methodist missionaries who had early regretted the concordat of 1820 which restricted them to Lower Canada. The excuse for their return was the Canadians' supposed inability to finance their extensive Indian missions, but the reason was direct encouragement by the provincial and imperial governments to promote "sound British principles" in Upper Canada.[28] The response of the Canadians to this renewed challenge was both unexpected and disarming—they proposed to the English Conference a union in which the Canadians would accept an English president, the English Discipline, and direct English control of the sensitive Indian missions. Egerton Ryerson was sent to England to complete the union arrangements, but while there he was conscripted by Mackenzie to cooperate with certain British radical politicians in presenting petitions against a recent proposal to reinvest the reserves in the crown (which would then provide for the churches of England and Scotland separately). Some provision for the latter church seemed certain since it had organized as a Canadian Synod in 1831 and was negotiating for a union with the smaller United (Secession) Synod formed the same year. As for the Church of England the imperial government believed the income from the reserves was enough to replace the £15,000 annual grant to the S.P.G. which was to end in 1834.[29]

Ryerson managed to enlighten the colonial secretary regarding the true state of religious affairs in Upper Canada, where some minor progress towards religious equality had been made in 1831 with the extension to all clergy of the right to perform marriages and with the successful revolt that same year against the practice of appointing only Anglican chaplains to the House of Assembly.[30] Ryerson and Mackenzie each seemed to have achieved some success in England for his own particular goal, respectively religious equality and civil liberty, but their meeting in England had unwittingly clarified the vast differences between the two men. Ryerson was repelled by the irreligion of Mackenzie's friends such as Joseph Hume, and their radicalism was tantamount to treasonable republicanism in the eyes of Egerton Ryerson, Loyalist, conservative and monarchist. The publication of such sentiments by Ryerson in the *Guardian* under the title "Impressions Made By Our Late Visit to England" provoked a hysterical outburst by Mackenzie: "The *Christian Guardian* . . . has gone over to the enemy"; Reformers had been "duped by a jesuit in the garb of a methodist preacher"; "The Americans have their Arnold and the Canadians have their Ryerson."[31] Ryerson's reply showed the depth of the chasm between the search for religious equality and the promoting of political radicalism. Regarding the Clergy Reserves he admitted they sought the same end, secularization—"but that we have ever supported a measure, or given publicity to any document from Mr. Mackenzie, or any other political man in Upper Canada, on any other grounds than this, we totally deny. . . ."[32] Ryerson could not have been aware when he printed his "Observations" on radical politics that Mackenzie was mourning the death that week of his infant son, Joseph Hume.

REACTION AND REBELLION

Of more importance in the struggle for religious equality than Ryerson's denunciation of radicalism were the results of the union of English and Canadians into the Wesleyan Methodist Church. One of the first fruits was the formation of a new body under the old title, Methodist Episcopal Church, composed of those suspicious of the political purposes of union. Although Ryerson was elected editor of the *Christian Guardian* for 1833-4, the tone of that paper became deliberately conservative, to the point of refusing to discuss the Clergy Reserves question. On the general election in the autumn of 1834, which returned a Reform majority to the assembly, the *Guardian* commented merely, "We stand independently of party," but not "neutral on what relates to the *connexion between* this Colony and the Parent State."[33]

Where the Methodists had been twice divided in the space of seven years, the trend among Presbyterians was towards union under the Church of Scotland, except for a new but short-lived Niagara Presbytery which emerged by 1837. The nucleus of this presbytery was several preachers supported by the American Home Missionary Society who introduced revivalistic preaching and the use of Isaac Watts's hymns, two practices which, conjoined with their origins in the United States, made them suspect to all Presbyterians of the British tradition.[34] Other denominations entered the province in the mid-thirties, including the Mormons, the Primitive Methodists, the Methodist New Connexion and another Wesleyan offshoot, the Bible Christians. The Lutherans, who had been without any regular supply of pastors, now received a number of clergy from the United States and elsewhere, but a minority of both laity and clergy were attracted into the Church of England, giving rise to several disputes over the ownership of church property.[35]

This trend towards greater religious pluralism seemed to be matched by an increasingly complex political situation in the colony after 1834. Under pressure from the Colonial Office Strachan retired from the executive council. The majority in the assembly produced its omnibus Seventh Grievance Report while Mackenzie attacked the Wesleyan Methodists, aided and abetted by William O'Grady, a quixotic Irish priest who had been ousted from the church after he rejected Bishop Macdonell's authority over his Toronto parish. The violent language of the radicals in both Canadas had, however, estranged political moderates, and in Upper Canada the replacement of Colborne by the unpredictable Sir Francis Bond Head was followed by a series of confusing events. Head appointed three moderate Reformers to his executive council but accepted their resignations just two weeks later because they had tried to give him unsolicited advice. Then, taking advantage of the assembly majority's obstructionist tactics, he seized the political initiative by calling an election in May 1836. Head simplified the issue of his election to a choice between republicanism and the British connection—"Will you argue with your own bread and butter?"[36] This appeal to moderation and Upper Canadian loyalism carried the day as Mackenzie and most reformers of all shades went down to defeat at the hands of the voters. The issue apparently was not influenced by the revelation a few weeks earlier that Colborne had in the last hours of his administration signed patents erecting forty-four Anglican rectories in Upper Canada and endowing them with four hundred acres each.

Regarding these rectories the *Guardian*, formerly the mouthpiece of opposition to religious privileges, expressed "extreme regret" at an obviously unpopular move, but defended the lieutenant-governor's prerogative right to such action.[37] Ephraim Evans, the new editor of the *Guardian*, and brother of James, the famous missionary to the West, and a supporter of the English Wesleyans' deferential attitude towards establishment and the "national church," insisted weakly that Methodists believed in religious liberty but would never for party purposes betray their "loyalty to the British Crown."

Even the Methodist stand in favour of using the Clergy Reserves for education was weakened by Evans's admission in the *Guardian* of December 14, 1836, that division of the reserves among "*all Protestant Churches*" was the next best solution. The election made strange religious bed-fellows, as Bishop Macdonell combined forces with the Orange Order against the radicals,[38] and the *Christian Guardian* was never more political despite all its protests of neutrality. In the opinion of many the Canadian Methodists had been corrupted by the £600 government grant for Indian missions that came as a bonus with union to the English Conference, whose missionnaries in Canada got an additional £900 from the government. Neither the Church of Scotland nor the Church of Rome, however, had been bought off so easily, for Macdonell was again petitioning for a share of the Protestant Reserves and William Morris went to England in 1837 as the spokesman of the Kirk to press its case for coestablishment.

By the summer of 1837 it seemed that drastic changes in the relations of church and state could be expected soon from the Whig-Liberal government in Britain. The question of Colborne's rectory patents had been referred to the Law Officers of the Crown who advised that the documents were "not valid and lawful Acts."[39] Some division of the Clergy Reserves seemed certain, probably along the lines of the "semi-voluntary" plan used in New South Wales whereby the government gave grants to all denominations in proportion to the amounts that each church raised by its own exertions. Such a scheme was the antithesis of separation of church and state, but it was also the antithesis of monopolistic establishment which seemed so unpopular in Upper Canada that almost any other solution was beginning to look attractive.

Even while the future of the rectories and reserves was under discussion the rebellions of 1837 broke out. An observer could see the slow drift of events in Lower Canada towards armed confrontation, but Mackenzie's call to revolt in the upper province was totally unexpected and almost as unanimously condemned. Mackenzie's attempt to convert his personal frustrations into popular grievances was quickly suppressed with the help of many whose desire for improvements did not encompass treason. Church establishment and its related practical issues were undoubtedly a cause of popular complaint but even in Mackenzie's wild rhetoric they were of secondary importance to his political and economic objectives.

The comic opera rebellion in Upper Canada had, however, tragic results as two of Mackenzie's fellow rebels were hanged and others were sent to the penal colony of Tasmania. The immediate reaction of all the churches to the rebellion was an outburst of expressions of loyalty, but when loyalist victory was followed by loyalist persecution, moderation found its voice once more. William Harvard, the English-appointed president of the Canadian Wesleyan Methodist Conference, had initiated a purge of suspected rebel sympathizers among the fifteen thousand Wesleyan Methodists which produced only two culprits, one of whom was an old woman. This witch-hunt was denounced by Egerton Ryerson in a five-thousand-word letter to the *Guardian* entitled "What is Christian Loyalty?"[40] When the annual conference met in June 1838, Ryerson was chosen editor of the *Guardian* in place of Evans as a mark of approval by his Canadian brethren for the policies he had pursued in the past and would revive in the future, against the Clergy Reserves and against the rectories which had now been declared legal! Already new hope for a peaceful settlement of Upper Canada's problems, civil and religious, was being felt by supporters of loyal reform—in the closing days of May 1838 Lord Durham had reached Canada as Her Majesty's High Commissioner to investigate the recent troubles and recommend measures of redress.

DURHAM'S REPORT AND THE CLERGY RESERVES SETTLEMENT

Lord Durham's investigation of the Canadian rebellions lasted only five months and of that time less than two weeks was spent in Upper Canada. Nevertheless he received submissions from many church bodies in the upper province and his famous Report, published in February 1839, had considerable to say regarding religion. The concentration of political and economic power in the hands of members of the Church of England had been a source of popular dissatisfaction and the monopoly of the rectories and reserves by a single denomination which, by the most generous juggling of statistics could not possibly include one-third of the population, was an example of the "exclusive privileges" that could "endanger the loss of the Colony." The loyal Catholics, Durham believed, had been excluded from sharing in the government and patronage and insulted by the government's toleration of the Orange Order, a society whose ends were more political than religious. "The greatest practical question, however, . . . is that of the clergy reserves. The prompt and satisfactory decision of this question is essential to the pacification of Canada. . . ."[41] Durham had high praise for the "voluntary principle" but he was content merely to recommend the repeal of all past legislation relating to the contentious reserves without offering any specific details for a settlement.

While the imperial parliament was considering Durham's Report and its major provision—a legislative union of the Canadas to swamp the French and rectify the mistake made in 1791 of dividing the natural economic unity of the St. Lawrence-Great Lakes basin—the latest lieutenant-governor of Upper Canada, Sir George Arthur, pushed ahead in the provincial legislature with the Colonial Office's plan of applying the New South Wales semi-voluntary scheme to the Clergy Reserves. A bill for this purpose was rejected by the assembly by thirty-seven votes to six and a chaotic episode followed with all sorts of resolutions on the Clergy Reserves until in desperation both houses agreed to sell the reserves and use the money for religious purposes. The final vote was carried by a majority of only one, at a late hour in the night preceding prorogation.[42]

In the legislative council only Strachan and one other had opposed the division of the reserves as spoliation of the national church. Strachan left the debate "chop fallen" according to a fellow councillor,[43] but Strachan now had the chance to plead his case in England. At age sixty-one he had at last achieved his ambition of becoming the first Anglican Bishop of Toronto, and because the provision of a diocesan endowment depended on the Clergy Reserves settlement, he was anxious to make the most advantageous arrangement possible. He still believed that the larger denominations could be bought off with sops so that his church could retain at least half of the reserves money, and it was while he was still in England in the autumn of 1839 that he first made contact with John Henry Newman, leading figure in the Oxford Movement which was publicly opposing state interference in the affairs of the church.

Two separate developments offered Strachan a small ray of hope that the Clergy Reserves, or at least the bulk of them, might be saved for the Church of England. Poulett Thomson (later named Lord Sydenham), the new governor of the Canadas, announced that the provincial Clergy Reserves act had been disallowed in Britain and a new bill must be passed. At the same time the Methodist union of 1833 was obviously disintegrating as the English Wesleyans attacked Ryerson and the *Guardian* for being hostile to the established Church of England. Thomson's Clergy Reserves bill, however, offered a quarter of the reserves funds each to the Church of England and the Church of Scotland, with the rest for any denominations who applied on the semi-voluntary principle.

With the aid of Ryerson ("my high Priest")[44] and Morris, Thomson gathered enough support to pass his bill and the scene of battle then shifted to the imperial parliament where the bishops in the House of Lords forced the Whig government to seek a legal opinion on this latest settlement. To the surprise of all and the delight of Strachan the Law Officers advised that only the imperial parliament could alter the terms of the Clergy Reserves which had been created by the imperial Constitutional Act. The upshot of pressure from the Archbishop of Canterbury was an imperial statute that gave the Church of England (20 per cent of the Upper Canadian population) 42 per cent of the reserves, the Church of Scotland (almost 20 per cent of the population) 21 per cent of the Reserves, and left the remaining 38 per cent to be divided at some future date among other denominations.

A "final settlement" of the long-standing Clergy Reserves question had apparently been achieved. The four largest denominations had been provided for, because the annual grants to the Methodists and Roman Catholics would henceforth be paid from the reserves funds too. There was deep irony in the fact that the Methodists, so long the champions of voluntarism, now joined the ranks of a pluralistic Protestant establishment, as in fact did the Church of Rome! If no one was really satisfied with this settlement at least the strife-weary majority in Upper Canada would accept it for the sake of religious peace. The only practical problem remaining was, which of the rival Wesleyan bodies, Canadian or English, should get the Methodist share? The English Conference had dissolved their union in October 1840, and were, according to Ryerson, using grants from Canadian funds "in a hostile crusade against the Methodist Church in Canada."[45] The Solomon-like decision of the Colonial Office was to suspend grants to both groups until such time as they composed their differences, a bitter and empty reward for the Canadians who had sacrificed their voluntarist reputation and even their unity in the struggle for religious equality.

NOTES TO CHAPTER EIGHT

1. T. R. Millman, *Jacob Mountain, First Lord Bishop of Quebec, A Study in Church and State, 1793-1825* (Toronto: University of Toronto Press, 1947), pp. 144 ff.
2. For an account of the complex manoeuvres regarding the bishopric of Quebec see Millman, *op. cit.*, pp. 258-63.
3. No history of the Society's operations in Canada is available, but copies of its correspondence are in UCA.
4. William Gregg, *History of the Presbyterian Church in the Dominion of Canada* (Toronto: Presbyterian, 1885), pp. 552-56.
5. OA, Macdonell Papers, A. Macdonell to J.-O. Plessis, 17 November 1821.
6. *Ibid.*, A. Macdonell to B.-C. Panet, 3 September 1827.
7. Quoted in G. F. Playter, *The History of Methodism in Canada* (Toronto: Green, 1862), p. 235.
8. *Ibid.*, p. 241.
9. J. S. Moir, ed., *Church and State in Canada 1627-1867: Basic Documents*, Carleton Library No. 33 (Toronto: McClelland and Stewart, 1967), p. 151.
10. *Ibid.*, p. 160. See also J. L. H. Henderson, *John Strachan: Documents and Opinions*, Carleton Library No. 44 (Toronto: McClelland and Stewart, 1969), pp. 66-70, and Toronto Reference Library, Scadding Collection, Strachan Papers, John Strachan to Bishop Mountain, 12 May 1817.
11. Moir, *op. cit.*, pp. 161-62.
12. *Ibid.*, p. 152; Toronto Reference Library, Scadding Collection, Strachan Papers, John Strachan to Bishop Mountain, 19 March 1816.
13. Moir, *op. cit.*, p. 164.
14. *Ibid.*, p. 167.
15. PAC, Q Series, Vol. 176, pp. 75-82, Lord Dalhousie to Lord Bathurst, 24 March 1826.
16. Moir, *op. cit.*, p. 167.

17. *Ibid.*, p. 169.
18. Henderson, *op. cit.*, pp. 87-94.
19. For a full account of Ryerson's exchange with Strachan, see C. B. Sissons, *Egerton Ryerson, His Life and Letters* (2 vols.; Toronto: Clarke, Irwin, 1937, 1947), Vol. I, chap. 2.
20. This letter and chart have been frequently reprinted. An abridged version can be found in Henderson, *op. cit.*, 95-99. The full text is in A. G. Doughty and Norah Story, *Documents relating to the Constitutional History of Canada 1819-1828* (Ottawa: King's Printer, 1935), pp. 370 ff.
21. Quoted in Sissons, *op. cit.*, Vol. I, p. 83.
22. Quoted, along with many other relevant documents, in Egerton Ryerson, *Canadian Methodism; Its Epochs and Characteristics* (Toronto: Briggs, 1882), pp. 170 ff.
23. *Ibid.*, pp. 203 ff.
24. See Sissons, *op. cit.*, Vol. I, pp. 85 ff.
25. G. W. Spragge, "John Strachan's Contribution to Education 1800-1823," *CHR*, XXII (2) (June 1941), pp. 147-58.
26. *Christian Guardian*, 16 October 1830.
27. Sissons, *op. cit.*, Vol. I, pp. 145 ff.
28. PAC, Q Series, Vol. 204, pp. 496-99, Richard Watson, Wesleyan Missionary Society, to Lord Goderich, 22 November 1832.
29. Millman, *op. cit.*, pp. 114 ff., for an analysis of the financing of the Church of England in the Canadas.
30. Moir, *op. cit.*, pp. 148-49, 155 ff.
31. Quoted in Sissons, *op. cit.*, Vol. I, pp. 198-99. See also William Kilbourn, *The Firebrand: William Lyon Mackenzie and the Rebellion in Upper Canada* (Toronto: Clarke, Irwin, 1964), p. 95.
32. *Christian Guardian*, 6 November 1833.
33. *Ibid.*, 21 January 1835.
34. John Banks, "American Presbyterians in the Niagara Peninsula 1800-1840," *OH*, LVII(3) (September 1965), pp. 135-40.
35. Two cases may be found in J. R. McCartney, "Sectarian Strife in Dundas County: A Lutheran-Episcopalian Land Endowment Controversy, 1784-1846," *OH*, LIV(2) (June 1962), and V. P. Mayerhoffer, *Twelve Years a Roman Catholic Priest* (Toronto: Rowsell & Ellis, 1861).
36. Kilbourn, *op. cit.*, 139.
37. *Christian Guardian*, 14 December 1836.
38. W. B. Kerr, "When Orange and Green United 1832-9; the Alliance of Macdonell and Gowan," *OH*, XXXIV(1942), pp. 34-42.
39. Moir, *op. cit.*, pp. 202 ff.
40. See Sissons, *op. cit.*, Vol. I, pp. 454 ff.
41. C. P. Lucas, ed., *Lord Durham's Report* (3 vols., Oxford: Clarendon, 1912), Vol. II, pp. 173, 176, 177, 180-181. For a useful abbreviation of the Report see G. M. Craig, ed., *Lord Durham's Report*, Carleton Library No. 1 (Toronto: McClelland and Stewart, 1963).
42. For the political history of this period of the Reserves see J. S. Moir, *Church and State in Canada West: Three Studies in Denominationalism and Nationalism* (Toronto: University of Toronto Press, 1959), chap. 2.
43. QUA, Morris Papers, J. Crooks to William Morris, 7 May 1839.
44. Paul Knaplund, ed., *Letter from Lord Sydenham Governor-General of Canada, 1839-1841 to Lord John Russell* (London: Allen & Unwin, 1931), p. 95.
45. Sissons, *op. cit.*, Vol. I, p. 569.

NINE

The Flowering of the Maritime Colonies

The beginning of the new century brought the renewal of the Napoleonic Wars, in 1803, which in turn produced dramatic changes in the economic and social structure of the Maritime colonies. During the war years smuggling, timber trade and fisheries produced wealth in the colonies such as they had not known before, and wealth eroded many of the aristocratic tendencies of the post-Loyalist generation that had been especially evident in New Brunswick. The War of 1812 served simply to confirm these changes, since the hostilities created even greater profits for the Atlantic colonies without the destruction wrought in the Canadian sister provinces. During the first three decades of the new century the population of all the colonies increased despite the blighting effects of the wars on immigration. For Nova Scotia at least, where the number of inhabitants grew from eighty thousand to over one hundred and twenty, the very nature of society altered as Scottish immigrants now outnumbered the American element which had predominated for almost half a century.

The mood of the Maritimes became one of self-confidence and self-awareness, confirming the inherent particularism of their geographic and political separateness. These factors were reflected to a lesser degree in the experience of several of the Christian denominations, who in the early decades of the new century began to identify themselves more with colonial life than with their transatlantic mother churches. The major difference between the religious and the secular scene was the emphasis of the former on regional instead of parochial or provincial loyalties and organization, an emphasis that made it possible for at least some of the denominations to develop within a larger context and in more dynamic forms.

Just as these decades are remembered as the great Age of Reform in Britain, the same period in the colonies was similarly marked by radical changes in politics, economics and society. Some religious changes in the colonies paralleled those in Britain—such as the emancipation of the Roman Catholics and the granting of a large measure of equality to dissenters in such matters as marriage laws. This trend towards religious equality had in fact begun in British North America before the Age of Reform in Britain, but one other development in the Mother Country hastened the total process. By the late 1820s public opinion there was largely convinced that the colonies had reached a stage of maturity where they could justly be expected to take a larger share of responsibility for their own development and so relieve the British taxpayer of the heavy burden of expense so long incurred on behalf of the overseas empire.

PROBLEMS OF A "PRIMITIVE BISHOPRICK"

Charles Inglis's desire to make the Church of England attractive to dissenters, or at least to live in harmony with other denominations through a policy of toleration and equitable treatment, was frustrated by external forces over which he had little or no control. Immediately after the granting of a charter to King's College a commission in England established regulations for the colonial college based on the religiously exclusive statutes of Oxford University. All faculty of King's must be Anglican, and all students must subscribe to the Thirty-nine Articles and attend no religious service other than those of the Church of England. This reactionary move, so far from the concept of a nonsectarian college envisaged by the Nova Scotian Assembly and by Inglis himself, naturally created distrust of King's on the part of non-Anglicans. At least the College's problems were not financial ones. When war with the United States threatened in 1808 Lieutenant-Governor Sir George Prevost convinced the assembly to levy a four-penny-per-gallon surtax on liquors to pay for equipping the militia. This "Arms Fund" grew to over £20,000 but when war did not come Prevost obtained Council's permission in 1811 to spend a quarter of the sum on King's College, half on Anglican churches and schools and the rest on public projects for the enjoyment of all citizens. Thus the established church and its college received a magnificent windfall created by thirsty Nova Scotians.[1]

In his later years Inglis was particularly anxious to promote the career of his only surviving son, John, a graduate of King's College. In 1796 the bishop moved to a country estate near Annapolis, apparently in the belief that Windsor would become the provincial capital, and when John was ordained in 1801 he was made his father's commissary and five years later was despatched to England in search of the creation of an archdeaconry for Nova Scotia. The first attacks of a serious illness in 1806 led Charles to urge on the Archbishop of Canterbury John's qualifications to be his successor as bishop, and after the bishop suffered a stroke in 1812 he again pressed the archbishop to appoint John his suffragan or coadjutor, even invoking the support of his friend the Duke of Kent in this family cause.[2] But when Charles Inglis died in February, 1816, in his eighty-second year, the episcopal succession passed to Robert Stanser, rector of Saint Paul's since 1791, thanks to the support of Governor Sherbrooke, the Nova Scotian Assembly and the Archbishop of Canterbury for Stanser's candidacy.[3] Stanser had gone to England for a rest in 1815 and he was still there at the time of his appointment as bishop. Although he returned to Nova Scotia near the end of 1816 and held a visitation of his clergy, he sailed for Britain late in 1817, never to see his diocese again. In Stanser's absence John Inglis was commissary as well as rector of St. Paul's at the capital.

Stanser had attended only four meetings of the King's College board of governors and now the lack of direct church representation had serious repercussions on that institution. Attempts by the board to liberalize the college's rules against dissenters were blocked by the home government which was now spending over $30,000 annually on the diocese and was intent on promoting the established religion as a bulwark of loyalty in the colonies as well as at home. In reaction against such official intransigence Lieutenant-Governor the Earl of Dalhousie, pillar of the Church of Scotland, founded the college named in his honour, as a nondenominational institution. King's, to which John Inglis was at last elected a governor in 1821, had begun construction of a stone building using customs monies collected at the port of Castine, Maine, during its occupation by the British in the recent war. Despite this investment, various parties were urging the removal of King's to Halifax and its union with Dalhousie College. Ultimately the legalistic protest of Chief Justice S. S. Blowers against any change of status carried the day in 1824, and King's continued as a separate Anglican college at Windsor, cut off from the mainstream of Nova Scotian cultural growth.

The combination of Charles Inglis's lengthy illness and Stanser's absence meant that effectively the diocese had no bishop for seventeen years. After 1823 the governor insisted on treating Stanser as absent without leave from duties for which he was being paid £1,000 annually.[4] When Colonial Secretary Lord Bathurst asked for the bishop's resignation Stanser replied that he was too poor to absorb the monetary loss and too weak to survive the climate of Nova Scotia. A solution of this problem of the absentee diocesan was only achieved after Earl Bathurst obtained for him a pension of £800 paid by Nova Scotia, New Brunswick and the S.P.G.,[5] thus clearing the way for the appointment of John Inglis who received an increased bishop's salary and a seat in the legislative council.

Inglis was consecrated third bishop of the diocese of Nova Scotia (which still included New Brunswick, Prince Edward Island, Newfoundland and Bermuda) in England in March 1825, and by June he was back in Halifax, immersing himself in the many problems of his long neglected diocese. During the first year of his episcopate Inglis visited throughout Nova Scotia, New Brunswick, Prince Edward Island and Bermuda, but his hope of reaching Newfoundland too was frustrated. Except for the obvious need for more clergy in his vast diocese, the condition of the church was generally satisfactory to the bishop. If only the church were placed on a more dependable financial basis it could attract more clergymen.

To this end Bathurst directed the governors of Nova Scotia and New Brunswick in 1825 to examine the possibility of creating Clergy Reserves on the pattern of the Upper Canadian Clergy Reserves. Sir Howard Douglas, governor of New Brunswick favoured this proposal, but he also recommended that the Church of Scotland be endowed wherever a kirk had been built. The following year Bathurst wrote Nova Scotia's governor, Sir James Kempt, confidentially and in more detail, regarding the state of the diocese. Although the Anglican clergy were supported by the S.P.G., Bathurst pointed out that since 1816 the society's funds came largely from a parliamentary grant, which meant that the British taxpayers were carrying the burden of the church's expenses in the colonies. Since these colonies were now past the pioneering stage the church should be supported locally. The imperial government were therefore prepared to order the colonies to reserve a seventh of all future land grants for the church's use to compensate for the loss of the imperial grant. Both Kempt and Inglis were convinced that such reserved lands would be valueless for many years, and that Bathurst's plan would only create religious controversy in Nova Scotia, and Douglas soon saw the impossibility of promoting such an unpopular measure in New Brunswick.[6] Six months later Bathurst and the Tory government of Britain was replaced by the Whigs whose program called for political and religious reform both at home and in the colonies.

The same strain of religious exclusivism was echoed in the midst of agitation against the Anglican legal monopoly over marriages. Quaker, Catholic and Church of Scotland marriages were valid if both parties belonged to the same parish, but repeated attempts by other denominations, and especially by the Baptists, to have all clergy licensed to marry were successfully blocked for three decades by the Inglises, father and son, because the establishment principle seemed to be threatened. By the late 1820s, however, the issue was again being agitated by dissenters although Inglis was hopeful that the Religious Congregations Act recently passed in Nova Scotia would be disallowed in Britain, since it gave "every sect now existing a sort of establishment."[7]

Reviewing the progress of his diocese in 1827, Bishop Inglis reported that to the total of one hundred and one churches (thirty-six in Nova Scotia, twenty-nine in New Brunswick, twenty-five in Newfoundland, nine in Bermuda and two in Prince Edward Island) he had added sixty-two more in the past two years, had travelled ten thousand miles on visitations and had confirmed more than six thousand seven hundred. For each colony he had now appointed an archdeacon, hoping this would provide more local initiative and supervision in the affairs of the church, yet, as he admitted, for lack of Anglican churches in some regions large numbers had joined the dissenters and Romanists.[8]

Unfortunately for Inglis's ambitions, the tide was running against the establishment principle on both sides of the Atlantic. Political equality for Roman Catholics in the colonies, already requested by a thousand Catholics and passed into law by the Nova Scotian Assembly in 1827, was confirmed by Britain's acceptance of Catholic emancipation in 1829. The parliamentary grant to the S.P.G. was terminated in the early 1830s by the reforming Whig government of Lord Grey, and Inglis was forced to curtail his plans for church extension. Henceforth the S.P.G. would not support any new missions, and the society's aid would be withdrawn from any old mission congregations which did not show a disposition to help themselves. Voluntary offerings in Nova Scotia amounted to only £10 per church each year, and one clergyman had been forced to sell his library to survive.[9] In New Brunswick the government was selling crown lands without making any provision for the church; in Prince Edward Island the Presbyterians had arranged the nationalization of Clergy Reserves without compensating the Church of England; and in Nova Scotia even the small endowments that the church had received were exciting jealousy among other denominations. Finally, to add to Inglis's immediate concerns, King's College, his father's creation and his alma mater, was again being threatened with absorption by its secular rival, Dalhousie University.

PRESBYTERIAN UNION AND A NEW INTRUSION

After its founding in 1786 the Burgher Presbytery of Truro, which had gained only two ministers in the decade, added only four more preachers in the next score of years. Even less progress had been made by the Church of Scotland whose sole clergyman in 1800 in all the Maritime colonies was Archibald Gray at Halifax. Symptomatic of the Kirk's attitude towards its members abroad was the General Assembly's reply to a petition from Shelburne for a minister. After two years' delay the assembly refused any help to the colonists but approved of "the loyalty and attachment to this country and to the Church of Scotland expressed by the petitioners, and of their design of building a house for public worship," and encouraged them "to persevere in prosecuting their pious purpose. . . ."[10] In contrast to the lack of progress recorded by the Church of Scotland and the Burgher Presbytery of Truro, the Pictou Antiburgher presbytery expanded rapidly after the opening of the nineteenth century. Ten more ministers arrived from Scotland between 1803 and 1817, of whom one went to Prince Edward Island, was ordained in DesBrisay's Anglican church but, dying within three years, was replaced by Edward Pidgeon, originally sent to the Bay of Chaleur by the

London Missionary Society, who thus became the second Presbyterian minister in the Island's history.

The most notable of these new arrivals was Thomas McCulloch, whose boundless energy, penchant for polemical writing and traditional Scottish concern for education quickly brought him into the centre stage of provincial affairs after his induction to the Pictou congregation in 1804. As a newcomer to North America McCulloch was immediately aware of the two dominant characteristics of Scottish Presbyterians in the colonies—their intense attachment to their denomination and their deep loyalty to Britain, both heightened by the atavistic sense of exile that afflicts Scots in all ages.[11] When Robert Stanser became embroiled in 1807 in a pamphlet war with the Roman Catholic vicar general, Edmund Burke, over the relative merits of Catholicism and Protestantism, McCulloch gratuitously rushed to Stanser's aid with two weighty volumes, entitled *Popery Condemned* and *Popery Again Condemned*! McCulloch also sought the establishment of a Protestant college for all who rejected the Anglican exclusiveness of King's, but this dream was frustrated by the government until 1817 when he converted the school that he had begun in his own home about 1804 into the renowned Pictou Academy.

Important as McCulloch's role was in the development of Presbyterianism in the Maritimes, it is still the figure of James MacGregor that holds the attraction of human interest in those years. He could never refuse a call to visit no matter how distant the mission field. Typical of his many journeys into the interior were his trip up the Saint John River in 1805 and his six weeks' tour of Prince Edward Island the following year. On the Nashwaak River above Fredericton he encountered Highland Loyalist settlers living in depressed conditions who had been left to "stray like sheep in the wilderness."[12] The £7 collected in appreciation of his services MacGregor gave to a poor widow to replace her lost cow. Since an adequate supply of ministers of the word seemed impossible MacGregor founded a Bible Society to provide tracts and copies of Holy Scripture in Gaelic, there being "but only three or four full copies of the Bible" among all the inhabitants of Pictou.[13] Such poverty of body and spirit soon disappeared, at least in MacGregor's home area of Pictou, thanks to the insatiable demand for forest products during the Napoleonic Wars; but the preacher was left to lament that affluence only encouraged sin. "The great demand for timber has in a manner caused us to lay aside farming, our most innocent, and in the long run our most profitable earthly employment, and give up ourselves to the felling, squaring, hauling, rafting, and selling of timber to the ships, and the squandering of money. Once in a day I could not have believed that all the vices of the world would have done so much damage in Pictou, as I have seen drunkenness alone do within these few years."[14]

Because the three Presbyterian groups remained dependent on their mother churches for clergymen and some financial support, ncessity became the mother of several inventive techniques for the two secessionist presbyteries, Burgher and Antiburgher. They developed a form of limited itineracy to reach their scattered flocks, whereas the Church of Scotland still showed no interest in British North America—the establishment of a presbytery was not even suggested. Presbyterianism in the Maritime colonies had also shown other evidences of a flexible approach to North American conditions as in its adoption of the practice of the long communion—services extending over several days to accommodate worshippers who gathered from distant points —that was the later inspiration for American Methodist camp meetings.

With the passing of the years, however, denominational prejudices brought from the old country declined among Presbyterians to the point that an organic union of all three churches was possible. The Synod of Nova Scotia, formed in 1817, comprised twenty-nine congregations in three presbyteries—Truro, Pictou and Halifax—served by nineteen ministers. Fourteen of the synod's ministers came from the secession bodies, three from the Kirk, and two had English Congregationalist origins. A few individual clergy did not join the synod for various reasons. Comingo, now ninety-four years old and the first and only Presbyterian ordained in the Lower Provinces, remained separated at Lunenburg, while the Halifax Dissenting congregation vetoed Gray's desire to join. Two recently arrived Presbyterian ministers—one each in Nova Scotia and New Brunswick—remained unconnected with the synod, and Prince Edward Island was again without a Presbyterian clergyman at this time.

This union of Burgher, Antiburgher and Church of Scotland Presbyterians was a bold and imaginative step. The synod's purpose was simple—to gather Presbyterians of all persuasions into a single body in the Maritime colonies—and this action of creating an autonomous and indigenous religious organization was based on the premise that the differences which separated Presbyterians in the Old World had no "practical importance" in the New.[15] To a confirmed Antiburgher friend in Scotland MacGregor justified a union which in his early days he opposed for denominational reasons. "The way in which congregations are formed is somewhat as follows: Providence brings into one neighbourhood, say a dozen of families from the low country of Scotland, two dozen from the Highlands, a dozen from Ireland, a dozen from the United States, a dozen from Canada, a dozen born in the Province, with a few more from England, Wales, Denmark, Germany, & c. Here are different denominations, and different opinions, all uniting to get and maintain a minister, for no one party is able to maintain one. They lived some time, perhaps long, without one, and many of them without a Bible or any religious book. . . . Every one knows that he cannot get a minister of his own sort, therefore, rather than want, every one agrees to take a good minister of any kind."[16]

The Synod of Nova Scotia, the largest Protestant church in the Maritimes, had forty-two thousand adherents in an estimated population of one hundred and sixty thousand in the three colonies. This large number of Presbyterians was more a tribute to the steady faith of the Scotch settlers and their self-sacrificing ministers than to any care or encouragement extended by the mother churches in Scotland. One motive for union had been the commonly-felt need for a native ministry. Thus, three years after McCulloch's school was transformed into Pictou Academy in 1817 theological studies were added to the curriculum through the establishment of an affiliated college. The academy was open to all denominations, and its students, dressed in red gowns after the model of Glasgow University, attracted mingled admiration and disapproval.[17] Its early success encouraged the formation of a Domestic Missionary Society to support church extension, particularly in Cape Breton and New Brunswick which were notably short of clergy. Of the twenty-five clergy on the roll of Synod in 1822 (including the fourth Presbytery, Prince Edward Island, formed the previous year) only two ministers were in New Brunswick and only one on Cape Breton. Other institutions which developed under the mantle of the synod included a Sabbath School Society begun at Pictou in 1823 which soon had seventy-seven affiliated schools.

One serious problem facing the Synod of Nova Scotia was its legal inability to perform marriages until the mid-1830s when all denominations were granted equal rights in the wake of insistent demands from the dissenting denominations. The older issue of bilingualism—preaching in English and Gaelic—had apparently been solved by the selection of clergy and by the gradual decrease in the number of Scottish Presbyterians who insisted, either from necessity or prejudice, on having services performed in Gaelic.

Some measure of the development of the Presbyterian church and of the colonies in the decade following the War of 1812 can be found in two incidents in the last years of that indomitable preacher and traveller, James MacGregor. After thirty-three years of service in the Maritimes he was given a gig so that he could take advantage of the much improved roads of the region. Three years later it was possible for the first time to reduce the pastoral duties of the sixty-six-year-old minister to a single church because the supply of clergymen was sufficient to meet the demands of a laity conditioned by previous shortages to accept and appreciate church services however infrequent.[18]

Only one minister had not joined the synod in 1817 from the Church of Scotland. In time this presence of the Church of Scotland might have disappeared had it not been for the intervention of the Glasgow Colonial Society and some strange beliefs among recent immigrants to Pictou. Members of this Pictou group, mostly adherents of the Church of Scotland, complained that synod ministers refused to cope with witches who were bothering the settlers, and so they obtained from Scotland a Church of Scotland clergyman who would tackle this problem. Other ministers of the Kirk followed, and this intrusive element in the territory of the synod of Nova Scotia received support from the Glasgow Colonial Society after 1825. Despite protests against the divisive effects of creating a rival Presbyterian body in the colonies, the Society continued to send what McCulloch described as "wayfaring men"[19] into the region until, in 1833, ten Church of Scotland ministers formed their own synod. The complaint of the Synod of Nova Scotia was that the society's missionaries entered areas already served by the synod in competition with the synod clergy, while other areas were left destitute of religion.

Certain characteristics of Presbyterianism in the Maritime colonies that had begun to appear at the time of the American Revolution were reinforced during the post-1812 War period. Few Presbyterians had been among the Loyalists and most of the later Presbyterian immigrants had come directly from Scotland. Thus later Presbyterianism in the Maritime colonies was untouched by the elements of revivalism which were prominent in the American Presbyterian church, and their whole orientation was towards Scotland. The intrusion of the Church of Scotland encouraged this tendency because that body claimed to be more ancient, more loyal and more legitimate than any of the secession churches that had sprung from her in the eighteenth century. Furthermore, Moderatism, though weakening in the nineteenth century, was still a powerful force in the Church of Scotland and an effective counterweight against any strain of evangelicalism such as the Great Awakening had evoked in America. Therefore Presbyterianism in the British North America, and especially in the Maritimes, was characterized by conservatism and a certain ethnic exclusivism, tempered by an active interest in Presbyterian ecumenism.

LIGHT AND SHADOWS IN THE CATHOLIC CHURCH

Although it was not readily apparent at the beginning of the new century, a period of expansion for Roman Catholicism in the Maritime colonies had begun in which new organizational patterns reflected the church's awakened concern for a flock too long neglected. By 1800 the church in that region contained three diverse and distinct national strands, each with peculiar traditions and special demands for spiritual attention. Of the original Acadian population most were to be found in three localities—along the upper Saint John River and east coast of New Brunswick, in Prince Edward Island where they were virtually the whole of the church membership and half the Island's population, and at the southern corner of Cape Breton. The bulk of the Irish Catholics still resided in Halifax, while the Scottish ones were largely grouped on Cape Breton and around Antigonish. The flow of Highlanders to the latter centre was resumed in 1801 with the arrival of another destitute and disease-ridden party, but the main focus of Scottish Catholic settlement thereafter was on Cape Breton Island, which was politically independent of Nova Scotia until 1820.

A landmark in this new era was the visit of Bishop Denaut in 1803, the first confirmation tour of the region since Saint-Vallier's in 1695. Denaut's trip took in Nova Scotia, Cape Breton, Prince Edward Island and New Brunswick, and at every stop hundreds of confirmations were performed. At Arichat alone Denaut confirmed 1162—virtually the whole population including "infants at the breast."[20] Another episcopal tour of the lower provinces, by Plessis in 1812, gave that bishop an opportunity to assess both the gains and the shortcomings of the church. During this seventeen-week visitation Plessis spent three weeks on Prince Edward Island alone where he found the churches sadly devoid of church furnishings—one had no missal, another used a tin cup for a chalice. At St. Andrew's dogs ran loose in the church. No Scotch church on the Island, or in Cape Breton or Nova Scotia, possessed a monstrance. But the Bishop's most frequent complaints were against the plunging necklines affected by the Scotch women and the Scotch Catholics' custom of falling on the floor and literally crawling to the altar rail during the mass.[21]

One result of Plessis' revealing tour was his proposal to transfer the lower provinces to the jurisdiction of Newfoundland. A generation earlier Hubert had recommended a division of the Quebec diocese but the only action taken in the intervening years had been the appointment in 1801 of Edmund Burke, formerly professor in the Quebec seminary and vicar general of the Upper Canadian missions, as superintending priest.[22] Just when conditions in the Maritimes demanded closer supervision and the church seemed ripe for a reorganization, the turmoil of the Napoleonic Wars again prevented any papal action because the pope had been Napoleon's prisoner since 1809. Plessis again broached the subject of division after the pope was freed in 1814, but in the meantime, Burke made an unauthorized visit to Rome. Burke presented to the Cardinals of the Propaganda a depressing picture of the church's condition in the Atlantic colonies—no monastery, no nunnery and no Roman Catholic school existed; the seven thousand Catholics on Cape Breton were served by a single priest.

Burke had made his point at Rome and returned to North America with a letter asking Plessis' approval of him as a vicar apostolic in the lower provinces. Plessis made the desired appointment in 1817 although he strongly resented Burke's independent action.[23] Burke's authority was limited to the colony of Nova Scotia but the reorganization of the Church in British North America was further advanced in 1817 when Angus Bernard MacEachern was made Plessis' suffragan in Prince Edward Island and two years later was promoted to the missionary episcopacy to rule Prince Edward Island and

Cape Breton. Although these appointments were intended to strengthen the Roman Catholic Church in the Maritimes by decentralizing the administration of the massive diocese of Quebec, the results were initially less than satisfactory. Burke died two years after his appointment and, since his coadjutor refused to serve, the care of the district devolved on Burke's twenty-two-year-old nephew William Carroll, who had been ordained only six months earlier.[24] Despite Carroll's sincere efforts to be a faithful caretaker he met with opposition and disappointment at every turn. Burke's church building at Halifax was suspended and the seminary he had formed of Carroll and four other students dissolved at his death.

For several years no successor could be found for the post of vicar apostolic, and funds that Burke had collected for diocesan development were soon exhausted. Older priests apparently resented the young Carroll, and the arrival in 1822 of Gaelic-speaking Father William Fraser with some three hundred Highland immigrants at Antigonish, where four of Fraser's brothers had settled, was the occasion for a local "revolt" by the Scotch against their Irish priest. Fraser's prestige was further enhanced when he became the protegé of MacEachern, and hence it came as no surprise when Fraser was appointed as Burke's successor six and a half years after the latter's death.[25] Carroll, who had served without reward or recognition, thereupon withdrew immediately to Saint John, New Brunswick.

In part, the Church's difficulties in the Maritimes had been caused by rivalry between the Irish and the Scots, which explains why MacEachern rather than Burke had been given charge of Cape Breton. Instead of residing in Halifax, where the Irish predominated, Bishop Fraser insisted on living with his fellow Scots at Antigonish, leaving the Irish Catholics of Halifax as well as much of the administration in the hands of an Irish vicar general. The second district, comprising Prince Edward Island, Cape Breton and New Brunswick, progressed more peacefully under the pious direction of MacEachern. In 1825 he received a government salary of £50 annually in recognition of his loyalty and services, and in 1829 he was promoted to Bishop of Charlottetown.[26] But MacEachern seemed to find difficulty in delegating work and in his relations with the senior bishopric of Quebec. His request for priests from Quebec to serve the half dozen Acadian parishes on the Island was rejected by Bishop Signay who explained that Quebec itself was short of priests and in any case Canadians did not want to move to the Maritimes where they would feel isolated.[27] Bishops Panet and Signay both complained that MacEachern did not answer letters although he corresponded regularly with Rome. MacEachern believed that Plessis had prevented Fraser from becoming MacEachern's coadjutor, and when MacEachern died in 1835 at the age of seventy-six he still had not chosen a successor.

Aside from this development of two dioceses to serve the church in the Maritime region, the most important change was the political emancipation of Roman Catholics. Catholics, who had been able to vote in Nova Scotia since 1789 and in New Brunswick since 1810, elected to the Nova Scotian legislature in 1822 one of their number who was seated with the approval of the Colonial Office after he had taken the oath of loyalty only. Encouraged by this disavowal of the Test and Corporation Acts, the legislature proceeded to pass a provincial act abolishing all remaining Catholic disabilities, but before it became law Catholic emancipation was accepted by Britain in 1829 and automatically extended to all parts of the empire.[28] The major remaining problem of the church was the chronic shortage of priests which occasionally had necessitated the employment of unsuitable men. That problem was still present in the 1830s but could be remedied in the future by the establishment of local seminaries and colleges. Nevertheless among the laity, who were predominantly from the lower economic classes, the patterns of Catholic life had by now become firmly fixed. If the average Catholic in the Maritimes was afflicted with grinding poverty, he was already noted for his fervent piety and his abiding loyalty to Britain.

AUTONOMY *VERSUS* DEPENDENCE—CONTRASTING BAPTIST AND METHODIST REACTIONS

Although "New Lightism" had provided religious inspiration for Baptists in Nova Scotia and New Brunswick it failed in itself to create any continuing organization. Thus it became the task of the Baptist "fathers" like John Payzant, the Mannings and T. H. Chipman to create an institutional structure to fill this vacuum. At their invitation six pastors and delegates from six churches met at Cornwallis in 1798 to lay the foundations of the "Baptist and Congregational Association." A second meeting, in 1799, adopted a "Plan of Association" modelled on the constitution of an American group, the Danbury Association of New England. The dominant Baptist element at the meeting then proceeded to formulate rules which, by excluding all who practised infant baptism, made it simply "the Nova Scotia Baptist Association."

Six churches accepted these rules in 1800, but two refused because the association contained churches that still accepted open communion with unimmersed Congregationalists and New Lights. The tide within the Baptist fellowship, both in the British colonies and in the United States, was running strongly towards closed communion in the strictest sense. This doctrinal issue with its very practical application in a church's constitution would have disappeared when the last unimmersed members died, but in church after church it was now pushed to the critical stage with unhappy results. The association reached a firm decision in 1809 to "withdraw fellowship from all the churches who admit unbaptized persons to what is called occasional communion."[29]

This statement caused an immediate decrease in the number of Baptists and the withdrawal of four churches from the association. Membership fell to less than five hundred in the twelve Nova Scotia and six New Brunswick churches, but the doctrinal purge soon effected its own cure. The association's stand had ended a protracted controversy and thereafter the number of churches grew so rapidly that a separate New Brunswick Association could be established in 1827, although no church existed in Prince Edward Island until that year. The association fulfilled well its functions of coordinating pastoral calls, settling disputes and enforcing discipline, yet there remained a reluctance to interfere with congregational autonomy. Even such association practices as ordaining and granting licences to preach were soon abandoned in favour of congregational regulation.

Cooperation at the association level went far to overcoming the inherent weakness of Baptist congregational autonomy. In 1814 a Missionary Society was formed to meet the ever-growing demand for preachers, and Maritime-wide organizations soon appeared in connection with Sunday schools and American-inspired temperance societies. Some churches had formed Sunday schools as early as 1820 and a decade later the *Missionary Magazine* carried a regular section for younger readers. Although drunkenness was considered a sin by all Christian denominations, moderate indulgence had always been tolerated even among Baptists. The excessive use of alcohol, particularly distilled spirits, became so common in colonial society that the reaction against it went to unprecedented lengths to control social behaviour. Temperance was soon equated with total abstinence, and one of the first temperance societies formed in the Maritimes prohibited its members from even doing business with merchants who sold strong drink. The temperance movement, though not primarily denominational, found its strongest advocates among Baptists and Methodists, and particularly among the former who viewed abstinence as only one of many urgently needed and interrelated moral reforms. Edward Manning, pastor at Cornwallis, made a practice of delivering a temperance sermon at every wedding. To critics of his zeal Manning retorted cheerfully, "As I am disposed, in cases of emergency, to go to the forepart of the battle, I get pretty well bespattered."[30] The success of the temperance movement in reducing the sale and consumption of alcoholic beverages wrought a marked social and economic improvement in colonial society, and not a few devout Baptists urged that teetotalism be made a prerequisite for church membership.

The growth of the association between 1810 and 1827 was noteworthy because the increase of pastors and members came by conversion rather than by immigration. By the latter year New Brunswick had fifteen pastors, twenty-eight churches and over thirteen hundred members, and Nova Scotia had seventeen pastors, twenty-nine churches and seventeen hundred members. In both colonies the number of adherents was four times larger than actual church membership. The church buildings, however, were still generally rough and poorly furnished, and not infrequently barns were used as places of worship. Such rude surroundings did not dampen the enthusiasm of the faithful who were prepared to travel several miles by foot or cart to attend day-long services composed of alternate three-hour devotional sessions and half-hour intermissions. Of all the Christian denominations represented in the Maritime colonies, the Baptist fellowship, by its physical growth and by its firm support of Baptist "principles," reflected most completely the flowering of that region in the first three decades of the nineteenth century.

Unlike the Baptists, the Methodists seemed either unwilling or unable to accept more responsibility locally and thus were burdened by constricting habits and attitudes of dependence inherited from their mission beginnings. The increased Anglican hostility towards Methodist dissenters noted in the 1790s had been based on the exclusivist ideal of church establishment rather than on any feeling of anti-Americanism, but the hostility may have influenced William Black's decision at the turn of the century to look for preachers in England instead of in the United States. The loss of American support was partly redressed in 1800 by the arrival of four English missionaries, one of whom was assigned to the schooner *Polly*, Robert Barry's mission ship that made a seagoing circuit of the southern ports of Nova Scotia. All the Methodist preachers uniformly decried the sins of a pleasure-seeking world and consciously avoided any political involvement in current issues so that in 1804 Black could report proudly to the Missionary Committee in London that the Methodists of the Maritimes were "esteemed by those in authority for their quiet and orderly lives, good morals and strict loyalty."[31]

Such self-satisfaction could not hide the fact that Methodism in the region lacked a certain dynamism, that respectability and social acceptance were not bringing large increases in numbers. It was 1803 before a society was formed in Fredericton, and the following year the conference had a total of only nine hundred members. Perhaps some of this absence of initiative stemmed from the peculiar hybrid circuit-parish system that had evolved locally, and from the deferential attitude towards the state church of England. By 1810 the conference had only eleven hundred and fifty members, a small return for a quarter-century of devoted labour in a field where the other Christian churches had made such progress that they had already passed from the pioneer era into an age of institutional maturity and sophistication.

Black's retirement as chairman of the Nova Scotia District in 1812 was symbolic of this condition of Methodism in the Maritime colonies. As the work in the colonies came increasingly into the hands of English missionaries, their rigid and authoritarian insistence on English Methodist practices and their generally conservative approach to religion kept Methodism in the Maritimes psychologically as well as institutionally a mission church. By

1823 more than half of the eighteen preachers were men who had come to the colonies since 1812, and only two were native Nova Scotians. The War of 1812-14 produced no crises for Methodism in the Maritimes comparable to the strains of divided loyalty felt in the Canadas, and two postwar developments went even further towards confirming this mission status. The organization in England of the Wesleyan Missionary Society in 1817 resulted in more effective centralized control of the district, and at the same time the wave of immigration from Britain (which roughly doubled the population of each colony) reinforced the strongly English elements in the membership, thus delaying still further any process of Canadianization.

The needs of a geographically and demographically expanding population of the district were not met until 1826 when its twenty-two hundred members and twenty-five clergy were separated into two districts—Nova Scotia, which included Prince Edward Island, and New Brunswick, which took in the Annapolis region of Nova Scotia. During the next decade Methodism in the Maritimes was marked by a successful search for respectability in conformity with the improved social status already achieved by the mother church in England. Revival meetings had already been forbidden in 1820 because they caused "enthusiastick [*sic*] excesses."[32] Methodism's evangelical message was now muted by a more conventional outward appearance of decency and order in public worship. Confrontations between Methodists and Anglicans ceased, and William Temple, secretary of the new Nova Scotia District, boasted of Methodism's "sincere esteem for the venerable Establishment of our country."[33] There was little dynamic in the Missionary Society's rule that refused aid to any mission costing more than £50 per annum, nor was there much encouragement for the development of a native ministry when local volunteers were officially classed as "assistants" to the English missionaries and barred from sharing in the missionary pension fund. The society's answer to all colonial complaints was the advice to cultivate humility. Thus local conditions and official English Methodist policy combined to prevent Wesley's followers from sharing in the flowering of the Maritime colonies.

NOTES TO CHAPTER NINE

1. See D. C. Harvey, "A Documentary Study of the Origin and Distribution of the Arms Fund," *Bulletin of the Public Archives of Nova Scotia*, No. 9, Halifax, 1947.
2. R. V. Harris, *Charles Inglis, Missionary, Loyalist, Bishop (1734-1816)* (Toronto: General Board of Religious Education, 1937), p. 135.
3. PAC, Nova Scotia "A", Vol. 149, pp. 135-36, Sir J. C. Sherbrooke to Lord Bathurst, 18 April 1816. The archbishop felt that although John Inglis had more talent than Stanser, he was still young enough to succeed him.
4. PAC, Nova Scotia "A", Vol. 164, p. 87, Sir James Kempt to Lord Bathurst, 16 December 1823.
5. C. H. Mockridge, *The Bishops of the Church of England in Canada and Newfoundland* (Toronto: Brown, 1896), p. 41.

6. J. S. Moir, *Church and State in Canada 1627-1867: Basic Documents,* Carleton Library No. 33 (Toronto: McClelland and Stewart, 1967), p. 54.
7. *Ibid.,* pp. 61-63.
8. PAC, Report, 1913, p. 271, John Inglis to ?, 26 November 1827.
9. PAC, C.O. 217, Vol. 154, pp. 125 ff.
10. Quoted in William Gregg, *History of the Presbyterian Church in the Dominion of Canada* (Toronto: Presbyterian, 1885), pp. 128-29.
11. William McCulloch, *Life of Thomas McCulloch, D.D., Pictou* (Truro, 1920), pp. 33, 35.
12. George Patterson, *Memoir of the Rev. James MacGregor, D.D.* (Edinburgh: Oliphant, 1859), p. 347.
13. *Ibid.,* p. 380.
14. *Ibid.,* p. 370.
15. *Ibid.,* p. 409.
16. *Ibid.,* p. 457.
17. PAC, Dalhousie Papers, transcripts, Vol. 5, pt. 1, Wallace to Lord Dalhousie, 6 June 1822.
18. Patterson, *op. cit.,* p. 476.
19. *Ibid.,* p. 487.
20. A. A. Johnston, *A History of the Catholic Church in Eastern Nova Scotia,* Vol. I, 1611-1827 (Antigonish: St. Francis Xavier University Press, 1960), p. 204, quoting François Lejamtel to J.-O. Plessis, 2 May 1811.
21. *Ibid.,* 230-32, Extensive portions of Plessis' Journal are translated and reproduced in this volume, pp. 228-59.
22. See Brother Alfred (Dooner), *Catholic Pioneers in Upper Canada* (Toronto: Macmillan, 1947), pp. 93-116.
23. Johnston, *op. cit.,* p. 349.
24. *Ibid.,* pp. 426-28.
25. See A. A. Johnston, "The Right Reverend William Fraser, Second Vicar Apostolic of Nova Scotia, First Bishop of Halifax and First Bishop of Arichat," *CCHAR,* 1935-36, pp. 23-30.
26. See Emmet J. Mullaly, "A Sketch of the Life and Times of the Right Reverend Angus Bernard MacEachern, the First Bishop of the Diocese of Charlottetown," *CCHAR,* 1945-46, pp. 71-106.
27. *RAPQ,* 1936-7, p. 135, J. Signay to A. B. McEachern, 2 November 1832.
28. Moir, *op. cit.,* pp. 64-67.
29. Quoted in G. E. Levy, *The Baptists of the Maritime Provinces 1753-1946* (Saint John: Barnes-Hopkins, 1946), p. 78.
30. Quoted in W. H. Elgee, *The Social Teachings of the Canadian Churches, Protestant, The early Period, before 1850* (Toronto: Ryerson, 1964), p. 144.
31. Quoted in Goldwin French, *Parsons & Politics* (Toronto: Ryerson, 1962), p. 38.
32. *Ibid.,* p. 65.
33. *Ibid.,* p. 62.

TEN

The Golden Age of the Atlantic Colonies

In Britain the Age of Reform—the 1830s and 1840s—was marked by liberalization in politics, the flowering of machine-age technology and the victory of free trade over mercantilism or protectionism in economics. All these developments had repercussions affecting both secular and religious life in British North America. The thrust of events was towards self-government and self-reliance, and for the colonial churches this meant greater autonomy and greater dependence on the voluntary support of the faithful to replace government aid. Just as Britain's adoption of free trade in the mid-forties threw the colonies on their own economic resources, so the mission status which characterized their early religious life had ended by the time of Confederation as the religious bodies were forced, reluctantly in some cases, to accept more responsibility for their future development.

Two major religious forces in Britain furthered this trend towards Canadianization, although their impact in British North America was at first more confusing than clarifying. In England the Oxford Movement, or Tractarianism, appeared in the thirties, insisting that the church was an entity distinct from the state, which should cease its Erastian interference with religious life. At the same time Thomas Chalmers voiced the same criticism against civil control over the Church of Scotland and led in the disruption of the Kirk and the creation of the Free Church of Scotland in 1843.

Fortunately for the churches in the Atlantic colonies the organizational period of their life was well under way by the 1840s and they were better prepared to face these challenges of the new age. Bishoprics, synods, conferences and associations were already established, along with all their auxiliary bodies and interests, from schools and colleges to temperance societies and pension plans. Thus in the generation preceding Confederation the churches were able to consolidate their physical structures while a sophisticated and affluent society found the time and resources which the pioneer period had denied them to assess their aims and ideals. Paradoxically in this golden age, interdenominational conflict arose between the churches in those Maritime colonies which had for so long been a model of moderation and harmony.

GROWTH OF THE ANGLICAN AND ROMAN CATHOLIC CHURCHES

In Britain during the 1820s advocates of industrialism and free trade charged that colonies brought no material advantages to the mother country, were a burden to the British taxpayers and in case of war, as in 1812-14, a liability to the empire. This anticolonial sentiment affected religion, since Parliament wished to eliminate or at least drastically reduce such commitments as the £8000 spent annually on the Anglican diocese of Nova Scotia. In part this policy of retrenchment also reflected changed priorities in religion as the growing enthusiasm for the mission of saving non-white, non-British peoples both inside and outside the empire diverted mission funds to new objectives and new fields. When the imperial parliament did reduce its support of the colonial church in 1834, Bishop Inglis met the financial crisis with a bold innovation that paved the way for eventual independence. In 1836 he formed Church Societies of clergy and laymen in each of his four archdeaconries.[1] The purposes were many but could be summarized as self-help: to aid Sunday schools, establish divinity scholarships, promote church construction, provide missionaries to neglected areas, supply books and tracts and publicize "the interests and merits" of the Church of England. The success of Inglis's church societies was so immediate that similar groups were instituted in the other British North American dioceses.

During the next decade a structural reorganization of the Church of England in the Atlantic colonies led to further and unexpected steps towards autonomy. Newfoundland and Bermuda were separated as a diocese in 1839 and from the western portion of the diocese of Nova Scotia another was created in 1845 to serve the eighty parishes and thirty clergy in the province of New Brunswick with the scholarly John Medley, an exponent of Tractarianism,[2] as Bishop of Fredericton. Symptomatic of the changed relationship between church and state stemming from the more liberal and secular ideology of the Age of Reform was the New Brunswick Legislative Council's protest against Medley's membership in that body as "highly objectionable and inexpedient."[3] Medley wisely never attended council, and the political character of Anglican bishops henceforth disappeared. In Nova Scotia another High Churchman, Hibbert Binney, became bishop after John Inglis died in 1850. Although born in Cape Breton in 1819 of a clergyman's family, Binney had been educated at Oxford and was only thirty-two when he returned to his native province in 1851. His high church views on church and state, probably acquired during his student days at Oxford when John Henry Newman's influence was dominant, were balanced by a "broad and statesmanlike" attitude towards church administration that gained him the respect of his clergy.[4]

The granting of political self-government to the colonies in the late 1840s emphasized the need for self-government of the colonial church as well. Despite fears of the Colonial Office that giving too much power to the bishops would replace the Church of England's unity with a host of independant Anglican communions, an imperial Act of 1856 permitted the creation of colonial synods but prohibited them from imposing temporal penalties or altering their relation to the See of Canterbury. In the early 1860s, however, the famous Colenso case completed the process of separation. J. W. Colenso, Bishop of Natal, who had been excommunicated for heretical biblical criticism, appealed to the Judicial Committee of the Privy Council in Great Britain, which ruled that the letters patent of a metropolitan or bishop did not authorize bishops' courts. Not only were the proceedings against Colenso void but the powers of all colonial bishops were now in doubt. Separation of church and state was henceforth to be the rule throughout the empire and the gist of this policy was embodied in a Colonial Office directive to all governors in 1864—"Where there is a responsible local government the crown should not interfere in ecclesiastical matters."[5]

Like the Church of England, the Roman Catholic Church felt the need for further decentralization because the population of the region had doubled between 1815 and 1840. Fraser, who had refused to live among the Irish of Halifax, was made titular bishop of that city in 1842 and given a coadjutor in the person of the able and energetic Irishman William Walsh. Fraser, however, had not been consulted about this appointment, and the fact that the two men were not on speaking terms was circumvented only in 1844 by translating Fraser to a new bishopric, Arichat, comprising Antigonish and Cape Breton, and making Walsh bishop of Halifax, thus effectively separating the Irish and Scottish elements. In 1842 the decision had also been taken to separate New Brunswick from Prince Edward Island. Bernard Donald McDonald, a native of the Island, had succeeded MacEachern in 1837, and in 1843 William Dollard, an Irishman who had come to Canada in 1816, was consecrated first Bishop of New Brunswick.[6]

By 1850 the three Maritime colonies possessed no less than four bishops, an ever-growing number of clergy and a large, loyal and devout Roman Catholic population. Educational and church facilities were now expanding rapidly as the church shared in the affluence flowing into the colonies from the export of timber, fish and agricultural products. Fraser's most lasting achievement during a seventeen-year episcopate had been the founding in 1841 of St. Mary's College, ironically in Halifax, while Colin Francis Mackinnon, a native Nova Scotian who replaced Fraser on his death in 1851, opened a seminary at Arichat which, by the time it was chartered as St. Francis Xavier University in 1866, had become a fertile source of much needed priests for the whole Maritime region. In 1852 Walsh was raised to the dignity of Archbishop of Halifax, Thomas L. Connolly became bishop in New Brunswick under the new title of "Fredericton."[7] Seven years later, when Connolly was translated to Halifax as successor to Walsh, his successor in Fredericton was John Sweeny, a thirty-eight-year-old Irishman. A third young Irishman, James Rogers aged thirty-three, was appointed bishop over the new see of Chatham in 1860, with only seven priests and three nuns; and on Prince Edward Island McDonald had been succeeded at his death in 1859 by another native Islander, Peter MacIntyre, whose diocese had thirty-nine thousand Roman Catholics but only fourteen priests.[8]

The decision to form Chatham, the second diocese in New Brunswick (where one third of the population was Roman Catholic), was due in part to the church's growing interest in the Acadians in the northern part of the province. The Acadians lacked any outward evidence of a sense of identity until Abbé F.-X.-S. Lafrance, parish priest of Memramcook from 1852, founded his *petit séminaire* which soon became the nucleus of an Acadian intellectual resurgence.[9] A decade later his successor, Camille Lefebvre, who spoke no English and had no classical education, opened St. Joseph's College on the foundations laid by the *petit séminaire*. Previously no school in the province had taught in French, but here the instruction of pupils in their native tongue provided the needed stimulus for the revival of Acadian culture.

This organizational expansion of the Roman Catholic Church was marked by the ascendancy of Irish bishops in all the dioceses except those on Prince Edward Island and Cape Breton. Even in New Brunswick where the Acadians numbered almost half of all Roman Catholics the bishops were Irish. This Irish influence in the church was both liberalizing and dynamic. The interest of the church became identified most frequently with provincial reform parties and its relations with most of the other Christian denominations were on the whole good in the pre-Confederation era. The Roman Catholic Church in the Maritimes shared in the general "renewal" of the faith in the midcentury period, as new orders, both male and female, were established to provide a wide variety of church work, and the increased piety and affluence of the laity was seen in the new, handsome and well-filled churches of the provinces.

Until midcentury Roman Catholics in the Maritimes enjoyed relatively happy relations with members of other Christian churches, but the creation of a Roman Catholic hierarchy in England in 1850 sparked a deeply emotional reaction by the national church against so-called "papal aggression"—the return of a foreign jurisdiction which had been expelled by the religious nationalism of Henry VIII—that sent shock waves across the Atlantic. In Nova Scotia, the only eastern colony where the hostility of the two religious traditions produced serious disputes, the conflict began in the mid-fifties in reaction to Joseph Howe's attempts at Boston to recruit Irish navvies for service in the Crimean War. Soon after, when Irish Roman Catholic labourers on the Windsor Railway attacked some Protestants who had ridiculed transubstantiation, Howe as chairman of the railway board prosecuted the rioters and then declared publicly that Protestants had a right "to laugh at what we believe to be absurd."[10] This statement united Catholic sentiment against the Reform government of Nova Scotia and caused its defeat in March 1858, for which Howe blamed Archbishop Walsh. Howe viewed these events as a defeat for British justice and a victory for "religion by the bludgeon" and for the Church of Rome.[11]

Walsh's successor, Connolly, avoided political interference, and entered the public arena in 1865 only to defend the Confederation scheme and to denounce the Irish Fenian Brotherhood for trying to foment trouble in the colonies.[12] In the public press Connolly upheld the imperial connection, Nova Scotian traditions of loyalty and the bright promise of Canadian confederation. Similarly Bishop MacKinnon of Arichat expressed his support for British North American union in the face of Fenian threats, though his pastoral letter on the subject reflected the reservations of most Nova Scotians and New Brunswickers about a strong central government. Bishop MacIntyre of Prince Edward Island, who had been involved in a politico-religious controversy over his planned St. Dunstan's College, was one of the few bishops who did not support the Confederation plan, but then neither did most of his fellow Islanders.

DISRUPTION AND UNION AMONG THE PRESBYTERIANS

In the late 1820s the Maritime colonies had witnessed the disruptive intrusion of the Church of Scotland's missionaries backed by the Glasgow Colonial Society, and in 1833 the formation of its two presbyteries of Nova Scotia and New Brunswick in competition with the older indigenous (Secession) Synod of Nova Scotia. When Church of Scotland membership in New Brunswick doubled in the next two years a synod of two presbyteries, St. John and Miramichi, was created, but after this initial burst of activity the work of the Church of Scotland in that province was virtually static for lack of local ministerial candidates. Nevertheless this newly established synod proceeded in 1836 to seek a union of all Presbyterians in the eastern provinces, to which the Synod of Nova Scotia responded with surprising charity, considering that the Church of Scotland had been the unwelcome intruder who had prevented unity just a decade earlier. On the strength of a pro-union resolution passed in 1838 by the older Synod of Nova Scotia, negotiations proceeded with the Church of Scotland Synod which offered to receive all members of the Synod of Nova Scotia into the fold of the Church of Scotland on terms of equality. This proposal, so far removed from an organic union of the two bodies and from the ecumenical spirit which had produced the great union of 1817, was rejected by the older synod.

Union discussions were virtually ended by the internal troubles of the Church of Scotland that were driving it towards its great Disruption. The Kirk Synod in Nova Scotia had already adopted unanimously a resolution of support for Thomas Chalmers' position, so that when the Free Church of Scotland was established in 1843 the synod repudiated its tenuous connection with the parent body and adopted the ambiguous title of "the Synod of Nova Scotia adhering to the Westminster Standards." Only four ministers of the former Church of Scotland Synod refused to join this Free Church body and two of the four departed almost immediately for Scotland. For the next decade no court of the Church of Scotland existed in Nova Scotia, but in New Brunswick the results of Scotland's Disruption were exactly the reverse. There only three ministers withdrew their connection with the Auld Kirk.

In Nova Scotia the Free Church soon proved itself a dynamic force as it grew more rapidly than the older Presbyterian Church and launched a wide variety of enterprises. In 1845, its first year of life, the synod discussed plans for a theological college to train a native ministry and the following year resolved to establish academies at Halifax and Saint John to prepare students for theology and other careers. By January of 1848 the Halifax Academy was open and soon Presbyterians outside the Free Church were offering support towards a theological college. By November the college was operating with three professors, though only half of the expected funds had been received. Despite the large number of clergy who had left the Church of Scotland, by 1850 the Free Church was in need of fifteen ministers and thirty missionaries, thus underlining the purpose of the seminary and the remarkable growth of that church.[13]

Union negotiations between the Presbyterian Church of Nova Scotia and the Church of Scotland had been in progress at the time of the latter's Disruption, but the virtual disappearance of the Church of Scotland from Nova Scotia directed attention to the newly formed Free Church. In Scotland and in Nova Scotia the Free Church had no objection to church establishment, provided the state which paid the piper did not attempt to call the tune as well. By contrast the Presbyterian Church of Nova Scotia, sprung from Secessionist background in 1817, was both voluntarist and anti-establishmentarian—complete separation of church and state was its ideal. Faced with this ideological gulf the two bodies in Nova Scotia suspended negotiations in 1850.

Ultimately the basis of union rejected a decade earlier was accepted by both churches in 1860, and the statement of the uniting bodies suggests that increased anti-Catholic feeling in the 1850s had done much to hasten union. "Completely independent of foreign jurisdiction and interference," the new church was to be a testimony against "Popish, Socinian, Arminian, Erastian and other heresies."[14] As a "free institute under the law to Jesus," it repudiated civil enforcement of faith as contrary to the laws of Christ, the spirit of the Gospel, the rights of conscience and the liberties of man. In 1860 this voluntarist Synod of the Lower Provinces (including Newfoundland and Bermuda), contained forty-five ministers of the old Presbyterian Church of Nova Scotia and thirty-five from the Free Church, as well as four ordained missionaries and a professor, and represented over fifty thousand members and adherents. The smaller Synod of the Free Church in New Brunswick joined the Synod of the Lower Provinces in 1866, adding eighteen more ministers to the roll, one third of them graduates of the Free Church College at Halifax. Now only three Presbyterian bodies remained outside the union —the two-minister Presbytery of the Reformed Presbyterian Synod of Ireland, and the New Brunswick and Nova Scotia-Prince Edward Island Synods of the Church of Scotland. These last two united in 1868, preparing the way in the Maritime region for the union of all Canadian Presbyterians in 1875 as response to the challenge of political union from sea to sea.

Even before the union of 1860 the Free Church in Nova Scotia had shown an interest in foreign missions by printing the letters from India of the famous Alexander Duff and by sending a Greek missionary to Constantinople in 1858. More important for the history of Canadian missions, however, was the action of the Presbyterian Church of Nova Scotia in despatching John Geddie to the New Hebrides. Geddie, his wife and another missionary reached the New Hebrides in 1848, where they were assisted by seven native teachers paid by the London Missionary Society. Besides preaching and teaching Geddie's work encompassed medical practice, with some startling results. Mrs. Geddie noted in 1853 that hygienic habits taught by the missionaries were producing a population explosion in the New Hebrides.[15]

The Geddies were joined in 1852 by a missionary from the Reformed Presbyterian Church of Scotland. Five years later three more missionaries arrived, but one was murdered on Erromanga in 1861 by natives who blamed them for a measles epidemic. The other two established a station on Tanna in 1859 but the early death of one and deteriorating relations with the natives forced the survivor and his wife to return to Geddie's station at Aneityum, where both died in 1860. Volunteers who came forward to replace the fallen included a brother of the first martyr, who suffered the same fate in 1872. After eighteen years in the island mission Geddie toured all the British North American colonies in 1864 to encourage support for his work, which included translating the Bible into the native language. Death came to Geddie in Australia in 1872, a quarter-century after he undertook this Canadian pioneer mission abroad. His monument in Aneityum reads, "When he landed in 1848, there were no Christians here, and when he left, in 1872, there were no heathens."[16]

THE GOLDEN AGE OF BAPTIST MISSIONS

The developments which were to make the Baptist fellowship the most dynamic religious force in the Maritimes during the three decades before Confederation had been inaugurated by the formation of the two provincial associations in the mid-1820s. The New Brunswick Association began in 1833 the practice of coopting several pastors for a few weeks each year to visit churches which lacked pastors, and poorer regions where congregations still had not been organized. Subsequently the province was divided into five missionary districts, each administered by a board of directors answerable to the annual meetings of the association. The number of New Brunswick churches grew to thirty-seven by 1845 and membership rose to over four thousand, while in Nova Scotia sixty-six churches and fifty-six hundred members were reported in 1838, and twelve years later one hundred and eleven churches and more than ten thousand members, a rate of increase even more remarkable than that of the New Brunswick Association.

A recurrent problem among smaller and more remote churches where pastors were lacking was the incursions of non-Baptist itinerant ministers or less frequently of Free Will Baptists who, unlike the Association or Regular Baptists, were not committed to Calvinism. The early adoption of closed communion as an association rule had left a residue of open communion or Free Will Baptists outside of the Regular Baptist organization. By 1832 six New Brunswick Free Baptist churches who shared two pastors formed a "General Conference" and in 1834 a similar conference was established in Nova Scotia. The Nova Scotia Conference soon received recruits from the American-oriented anti-Calvinistic Christian Baptists and from these elements the loosely organized Free Christian Baptist Conference was formed in 1837, although the two provincial conferences failed to establish a workable union for another decade.[17]

Union of the Regular Nova Scotia and New Brunswick Associations into a Convention had been advocated by the Nova Scotia Association in 1844. The timing of this proposal proved opportune—popular support for the convention idea was so widespread that by 1845 a joint committee of the associations was appointed to formulate a basis of union which was adopted by both associations in the summer of 1846. The Convention's purpose was not to replace the associations but to coordinate their work and exploit the wider possibilities of the larger geographic area. In 1846 the New Brunswick Association had divided in two, and a similar "swarming" brought the division of the Nova Scotia Association into three associations in 1850. The Convention played its part in promoting matters of common interest to all the associations by establishing boards or committees. Five such boards existed at various times, including Colportage, Sunday Schools and Domestic Missions.

The beginning of home and foreign mission work by the churches of British North America reflected the great missionary awakening of Victorian Britain, but it also must be viewed as one more indication that the pioneer life was giving way to a mature and settled society in the colonies enjoying a degree of affluence that could support such outreach of religious activity. In 1853 the two New Brunswick Baptist associations gave their support to a newly created Home Missionary Society, and four years later a similar society was organized in Nova Scotia. Both proved to be effective instruments of outreach. The only section of the Maritimes that did not share in this advance of home mission work was Prince Edward Island where as late as 1852 there were only eight churches. Not until 1845 was a Baptist church built in Charlottetown, and other congregations had existed for years without chapels. Part of the difficulty in Prince Edward Island was lack of numbers, for nearly half the population were Roman Catholic, but another factor was a difference in traditions between Baptists of the mainland and those of the Island, the latter being mainly Scots who insisted on expelling any member who married outside the fellowship.

Interest in French missions had been awakened in the Convention by the visit in 1846 of Dr. J. M. Cramp, president of the Montreal Baptist College, who came as fraternal delegate from Canada to describe the Grande Ligne Mission. Maritime efforts at French evangelization produced, however, fewer results than those in Lower Canada. Work was conducted for several years among the Acadians of Nova Scotia and New Brunswick under the auspices of the Western Association of Nova Scotia, but the only French Baptist church formed was in Yarmouth County.[18] A mission to Gaelic-speaking Roman Catholics on Cape Breton also had little success and after a decade was abandoned in 1866.

The most important and successful of all the domestic missions aided by Maritime Baptists was that to the Micmac Indians. Silas T. Rand, largely self-taught in classic and modern languages and master of three Indian tongues, was appointed by the Nova Scotia Association in 1845 to evangelize the Micmac tribe. When Rand discovered that other Protestant bodies were interested in his project he founded the interdenominational Micmac Missionary Society in 1850. Until his death in 1889 Rand itinerated throughout the Maritimes wherever the Micmacs were to be found but probably his most enduring achievement was his translations of the Bible and other works into the Micmac language using his own phonetic system for writing Micmac.[19]

The impetus to foreign missions was provided by the Nova Scotia Association in 1838 when it proposed to unite its efforts with those of the Baptists in the other two colonies. The response from the New Brunswick Association was immediate and enthusiastic, and committees were established to coordinate their work. Previously mission funds had been forwarded to the

American Baptist Missionary Board but now the money was used to support a young New Brunswick preacher, Richard Burpee, who spent five years in India before returning home in 1850 because of ill-health.[20] No small part of this missionary interest was due to the appearance in 1837 of *The Christian Messenger* replacing the *Baptist Missionary Magazine* which in 1828 had been the first Baptist publication in British North America.

Throughout the score of years preceding Confederation the boards of the Convention continued to suffer from the vagaries of local initiative and from lack of a centralized system of support. The congregational-based Union Societies, older in fact than the Convention itself, were slow to accept the need for budgeting on a denominational scale. This was the price paid for the Baptist tradition and practice of congregational autonomy, although the general economic depression at the end of the 1850s accentuated such problems. Nevertheless the formation of the Convention in 1846 did inaugurate a new age for the Baptist fellowship in the Maritime colonies, reducing to some extent both the virtues and hindrances of extreme Baptist independence and individualism. In obvious and in subtle ways the fellowship in the Maritimes assumed some of the administrative structure and mental attitudes of its more intensely organized sister denominations during the generation before Confederation. Despite financial difficulties the first generation of the Convention's life had been one of physical expansion and institutional sophistication. Between 1850 and 1870 one hundred and thirty-two names were added to its roll of ministers, one hundred and six churches formed or renewed, and one hundred and thirty church buildings erected. By 1867 Baptist educational and home mission undertakings were on a solid if limited foundation, and interest in foreign missions was reaching a new peak. The tomorrow of Confederation held great promise for the Baptist fellowship in Canada's Maritime provinces.[21]

THE BLIGHT OF DEPENDENCE

Although Congregationalism had disappeared in the Maritime colonies by 1800 because of Henry Alline's preaching of the "New Light," it lingered in the region as a tradition. At least four churches later claimed a continuous existence during the next sixty years but their membership must have been quite small until new life was breathed into that denomination in the early 1840s. Congregationalists settling in the two Canadas after the Napoleonic Wars had received financial support from the London Missionary Society, and by 1842, when the energetic Montreal preacher Henry Wilkes toured New Brunswick and Nova Scotia, the Society was supporting no less than thirty ministers in Canada. Wilkes visited several former Congregational churches, including Mather's chapel in Halifax, most of which were Presbyterian in all but name.[22] His efforts led to a brief reawakening of Congregationalism in the two colonies, as several new churches were begun thanks to the financial aid of the London Missionary Society and a handful of missionaries sent from Britain and the Congregational College in Canada.

For a decade Congregationalism gained ground slowly, but in the late 1850s a steady loss of members to the Presbyterians resulted from divisions within particular Congregational churches. Local support for Chebogue, the oldest Congregational church in the lower provinces, declined until the minister resigned in despair. Membership of Yarmouth church fell to twenty-five and the remnant displayed little religious vitality. The Congregational Union of Nova Scotia and New Brunswick was forced to rely on the Congregational College in Canada for ministers and on the Congregational Missionary Society for money. The distribution of missionary and educational funds became such a bone of denominational contention that many churches left the union. In 1860 the union contained about sixteen churches—two years later only ten churches were reported.[23] The seeds sown by Wilkes had indeed fallen on stony ground.

As early as the 1820s it had become obvious that Methodism's outreach in the Maritimes was suffering from tensions between colonists and the Missionary Society, from a shortage of preachers and funds, and from the attraction of other denominations, especially the more vocally evangelical. One response was the introduction to New Brunswick in 1836 of "protracted meetings"—four-day revivalistic sessions carried on in the controlled environment of a chapel rather than in the unlimited spaces common to camp meetings. By all accounts these protracted meetings proved to be a successful renewal technique and they were soon employed in both districts. Other signs of a stirring of local initiative included an abortive attempt to found a Methodist journal and the belated decision to establish a denominational academy following the example of other churches. By the late 1830s the Missionary Society was beginning to promote the very idea of local self-reliance which it had so successfully repressed for a generation.[24] A proposal of 1839 to reunite the two Maritime districts met with indifference and even some resistance—the society's interference in previous years had taught the virtues of dependence only too well—but persistent pressure was applied for several years until in 1847 agreement was reached to form a conference of the two districts.

From 1847 to 1855 the London Missionary Committee pressed the Methodists of the eastern colonies to accept more responsibility for "the work." But their reluctance to proceed at anything more than a leisurely pace was reinforced by the recurrent dislocations in the regional economy and by the tide of emigration that flowed almost as fast as immigration to the same colonies. The stimulation of a new periodical, *The Wesleyan*, and the decision of the Missionary Committee to divide the Nova Scotia District and impose self-sufficiency on the older missions were needed to bring the three districts of Nova Scotia and New Brunswick to relinquish their comfortable mission status. Even this step was taken with reluctance as endangering the connection with the ties with Britain. But the way was now open, if only slightly, for the committee to force self-government on the Methodists of the Maritimes, and the committee's senior secretary, the able and diplomatic John Beecham, was assigned the task of on-the-spot negotiations in 1855.

With Beecham's guidance the Conference of Eastern British America was established "under the sanction of the British Conference." The new conference, which included Bermuda, had seventy-nine ministers, thirteen thousand members, and an estimated sixty thousand adherents. "Untrammelled action led to a new sense of responsibility," commented a contemporary.[25] True an impetus to expand home missions and circuit boundaries followed, with the number of ministers more than doubling by 1867, but this growth was not accompanied by a similar increase in adherents because Methodism was still unwilling to adapt to local conditions. The expression "untrammelled action" is misleading since the affiliated Conference remained under English control in many important ways. The parent body retained a veto over the nomination of a president and over all conference legislation, and Wesley's English Discipline was rigidly enforced. Nevertheless this new if limited status carried some advantages. All missionaries were guaranteed pension benefits and an annual grant from the Missionary Society was promised, subject, however, to its gradual reduction and ultimate elimination. One important step towards self-government was the provision that all missionary funds collected by the Conference would be retained for its own use, although the Missionary Society's grant would be reduced by an equal amount.

In retrospect the new arrangements of 1855 seem conservative in the extreme. Moreover Methodism in the Maritimes meant exclusively English-style Wesleyan Methodism—the evangelical Primitive and New Connexion churches never entered the field as rivals, as they did in the Canadas, and as late as the Methodist union of 1883 only a few Bible Christian churches were to be found, all in Prince Edward Island. But the Wesleyan Methodists remained relatively few in number—perhaps only 10 per cent of the region's population—and forty years of tutelage under the Missionary Committee had developed habits of dependence that were now confirmed by the controls frequently exercised by the English Conference. Methodism in the Maritime colonies had to wait until the union of 1874 before it attained autonomy.

"THE COLLEGE QUESTION"

In the Maritime colonies, and especially in Nova Scotia, the interest of the churches in higher education became a cause of denominational friction and political clashes in the 1830s and 1840s. Three factors—Anglican exclusiveness, denominational rivalry, and the trend from confessional towards secular higher education—met in conflict in Nova Scotia at the very time that Joseph Howe was starting his campaign for responsible government. Inevitably political and religious issues became intertwined.

Unlike King's College, McCulloch's Academy at Pictou imposed no religious tests on its students, but like King's its location was poor in relation to areas of settlement and its enrolment consequently never large. In any case, the Presbyterians looked to Dalhousie's proposed college to provide a liberal higher education with the Academy remaining essentially a seminary. This attitude towards higher education was shared by the other denominations, Anglicans excepted, but conflict between the legislative council and the assembly of Nova Scotia delayed the opening of Dalhousie even though its buildings had been started in 1820. When the college did open in 1838 McCulloch was made principal and two other Presbyterian ministers were appointed as the professors. This development destroyed Pictou Academy, yet Dalhousie seemed to many to be little more than Pictou transferred to Halifax, and the long delay in starting teaching caused a further loss of public interest in the project of a provincial college. In addition Dalhousie faced the competition of two rival institutions because King's still existed separately and the Baptists had now established Horton Academy.

Every attempt to unite Dalhousie and King's had been frustrated by the influence of Bishop John Inglis and Brenton Halliburton, Chief Justice of Nova Scotia, until their retirement from the Dalhousie board. Presbyterian support for Dalhousie was assured because all the professors were Presbyterian, and the Baptists were willing to suppress Horton Academy if E. A. Crawley, pastor of Granville Street Church, was made professor of classics. When Crawley was not hired Horton Academy was retained and converted into Acadia College.[26] Instead of a single provincial institution, Nova Scotia now had three denominational ones. Howe opposed this proliferation of denominational colleges, and when Acadia found itself in financial trouble in 1843, he brought the question of public aid to such colleges before the provincial assembly. The friends of Acadia were, he said, grasping and intolerant: "If we are to have a pope, I would as soon have one in Rome as at Horton. . . ."[27] Sectarian colleges, he claimed, were the enemies of religion and tranquillity. "The People must have One College, as they have one Supreme Court; one Province Building; one Penitentiary; and if others want more, let them maintain them at their own expense." Howe's stand on the "College Question" destroyed his coalition government with J. W. Johnston, a prominent Baptist and defender of independence for Acadia College.

Assured now of continued aid from Johnston's new Conservative government, Baptists raised $9,000 for Acadia, whose first buildings had been erected by volunteer labour and gifts of material.[28] Economic recession and unwise investments, however, drastically reduced the college's fortunes and enrolment during the next few years. The other colleges encountered equally serious problems, though often of a different kind. Pictou Academy virtually collapsed after McCulloch left for Dalhousie; Dalhousie suspended teaching for six years after McCulloch's death in 1843, and despite government aid King's College at Windsor continued to decline.

Although the Nova Scotia Baptist Education Society surrendered control of Acadia in 1850 to a board of governors responsible to the Convention, Acadia was still harried by financial problems, and public appeals for funds were resented because Acadia received provincial government grants. The decision not to spend government money on Acadia answered some critics but did nothing to solve the financial dilemma, and the unwise investment of part of the college endowment compounded this difficulty. The faltering college got a new lease on academic life when Dr. J. M. Cramp arrived from Montreal to become president in 1851. To Acadia he brought not only enthusiasm but a breadth of knowledge in the humanities, science and theology that ranks him high in the annals of Canadian scholarship.[29] The Convention's supervision of Acadia brought other permanent benefits too, as the college was put on a sound financial basis before Confederation.

The Presbyterians did not develop their own arts college but relied on the accessibility of publicly-supported Dalhousie. When the union of the two Presbyterian churches in 1860 gave the new body more educational facilities than needed, the synod merged the two seminaries and two academies at Halifax and Truro respectively, Halifax continuing the theological work and Truro the preparatory, until 1863 when Dalhousie began a more effective college operation and Truro Academy became superfluous. In sharp contrast to the experience of the Presbyterians and other denominations was the Methodist experiment in higher education. As early as 1828 the Nova Scotia District Meeting had proposed a Methodist school to serve all the Maritime colonies and in 1839 a wealthy Methodist, Charles Frederick Allison, purchased property at Sackville, New Brunswick, close to the Nova Scotian border, and gave over £4,000 for a building.[30] Sackville Wesleyan Academy (now Mount Allison University) opened in 1843 with only seven students, but the concentration of effort in a single institution, centrally located and generously supported by private persons, ensured its success.

In New Brunswick King's College had been opened to students of all denominations but it retained an aura of Anglicanism and received so few students that the provincial government appointed an investigating commission in 1854. The commission, of which Egerton Ryerson was a member, recommended that the institution become the provincial university with a modernized curriculum including sciences and modern languages. Although the government did suspend its grant to King's College, the commission's recommendations were not implemented until 1860, when the teaching of theology and religious tests for both faculty and students were prohibited at the new liberal and secularized University of New Brunswick. The same trend towards secular control of all educational facilities had been virtually completed in Prince Edward Island by the 1850s when the province took over the Anglican elementary schools, and the process ended in 1860 with clergy prohibited from being professors in the new Prince of Wales College at Charlottetown.

BROADENING HORIZONS IN NEWFOUNDLAND

Despite the increase in Newfoundland's population after 1760, it was not until 1817 that Newfoundland got a resident governor. Seven years later political agitation on the Island forced the imperial parliament to recognize its oldest overseas possession as a British colony and its inhabitants as legal colonists rather than unwelcome squatters, and finally in 1832 representative government was granted.

Although Roman Catholics comprised about half of Newfoundland's population in the first decades of the nineteenth century, the Catholic church was still starved for priests and funds. Thomas Scallan, third vicar apostolic to the Island and Labrador, had only seven priests when he assumed his duties in 1817 and only ten at his death twelve years later.[31] His successor, Michael Anthony Fleming, another Irish Franciscan, undertook a massive reorganization and expansion of the church's work by dividing Newfoundland into regular missions, obtained more priests from Ireland and introduced two orders of nuns to perform charitable and educational work.

The proportion of Roman Catholics declined slowly until by 1850 they were no longer an absolute majority, but their numbers nevertheless justified the organization of a regular diocese. In 1847 Fleming became titular Bishop of Newfoundland with John Thomas Mullock, another Irish Franciscan, as his coadjutor. A major undertaking for the new diocese was the construction of a cathedral at St. John's, one of the first churches dedicated to the newly declared dogma of the immaculate conception. When the cathedral was finally consecrated in 1855, three bishops from the other colonies assisted at the ceremonies, indicating the new importance of Newfoundland. One year later the diocese was divided as John Dalton became Bishop of Harbour Grace, a jurisdiction that included the whole Labrador coast.

The Church of England, with a third of the total population, was next in size to the Roman Catholic Church. In 1827 John Inglis made the first episcopal visitation to the nine clergy there, travelling five thousand miles, consecrating eighteen churches and confirming almost two thousand four hundred members.

Anglican church work received new impetus with the appointment as first Bishop of Newfoundland of Aubrey George Spencer, an Evangelical who had served there as a missionary for two years. Spencer found only eight clergymen in that part of his diocese—Bermuda formed the other half—but in four years he started a theological seminary, built more than twenty churches, collected funds for a cathedral and increased his clergy to twenty-seven, each of whom depended on the S.P.G. for his salary, as indeed did the bishop himself. Spencer's work carried him to the religiously destitute parts of Newfoundland and to the Labrador coast on visitations often conducted in open boats and frequently in inclement weather. "The missionary in Newfoundland," he commented, ". . . must have strength of constitution to support him under a climate as rigorous as that of Iceland; a stomach insensible to the attacks of sea-sickness; pedestrian powers beyond those of an Irish gossoon, and the ability to rest occasionally on the bed of a fisherman or the hard boards in a woodman's tilt."[32] Spencer had the will but not the constitution for such labours and failing health forced his retirement in 1843.

His successor, Edward Feild, had the physique of an athlete and the living habits of a Spartan. Feild found thirty missionaries in the colony, and the application of his energy and enthusiasm soon put new life into all aspects of the Church's endeavours. Like his contemporaries of every denomination on the island, Feild was shocked by the widespread religious ignorance. On one tour aboard his mission ship, the *Hawk*, he encountered one hundred and thirty-four nominal Anglicans in three remote settlements who had never seen a clergyman.[33] For this shortage of clergy the obvious antidote of lay readers was impossible because of illiteracy. At Greenspond, where an Anglican teacher had laboured for many years, Feild noted in 1856 that two hundred and eighty-five of three hundred and thirty-four persons married in the previous seven years had marked the register with an X. On one of his earliest tours he met a semi-literate lay couple who performed marriages and baptisms for their neighbours, his wife conducting baptisms because this service required more reading than the husband could master.[34] The energetic bishop extended Spencer's tiny theological college, built a cathedral at St. John's in 1850 and founded an orphanage after the cholera epidemic of 1854. But Newfoundland was only part of his diocese—distant Bermuda must also be served. Short of priests, engrossed in educational and charitable works, dependent on the financial aid of the S.P.G., faced with a far-flung diocese that could only be served by a sailor-bishop, Feild laboured alone until he obtained the aid of a coadjutor in 1867.

Methodism was the smallest of the three major denominations, accounting for about one sixth of the population, but two other Protestant denominations were also represented. The Church of Scotland and Congregationalism each claimed about five hundred adherents, but the support of each was limited to St. John's where the only Congregational meeting house had been built in 1789. The Church of Scotland congregation was not formed until 1842 and, insignificant as this Presbyterian presence was, the Disruption of the mother Church of Scotland was echoed in the St. John's congregation by conflict that finally led to the building of a Free Church in 1850.

The organization of Newfoundland as a Methodist missionary district in 1815 had seemed to augur well for that denomination's future in the colony, since the next year the number of missionaries doubled and five new circuits were added, all in the heavily populated southeast corner of the Island. But almost as suddenly this expansion of Methodism came to an end. A quarter of a century later there were still only twelve circuits in the District which remained in every sense a mission. The main reason for this static condition was the necessary dependence on England for preachers and teachers—the Methodists of Newfoundland did not, and probably for lack of educational facilities could not, produce leaders of their own. Sunday schools (with twelve hundred children and some adults enrolled in 1825) provided most Methodists with their only formal education. The absence of roads, the preoccupation of the Islanders with the fisheries, and the ubiquitous sabbath-breaking and use of strong drink were also discouragements to the missionaries. One Methodist visiting the outports in the early 1840s found half the adults of one village drunk when he arrived.[35]

The long period of Methodist inactivity in Newfoundland had begun to lift in 1841 when mission work was extended westward as far as Cape Ray and northeast to Cape John. Four years later the Labrador mission, abandoned in 1834, was reopened successfully and permanently.[36] By 1855, when the Eastern British American Conference was formed, the number of Methodists on the Island had grown to two thousand six hundred, an increase of 100 per cent over the previous quarter century, with probably another twelve thousand counted as "hearers." Methodism was by now firmly rooted for all time on the rocky shores of Newfoundland.

Newfoundland, like other British North American colonies, experienced increased anti-Roman Catholic feeling after the "papal aggression" controversy, but its denominational school system may have played a part in keeping Protestant and Catholic at a safe if not respectable distance. After 1833 the S.P.G. reduced its financial support for Anglican teachers on the Island and finally in 1858 withdrew entirely from the education field there. This reduced support had caused Bishop Feild to complain as early as 1849 that the Church of England was being "jostled out of her rights" by Roman Catholics and dissenters.[37] To add to the bishop's difficulties, the Newfoundland School Society, founded in the 1820s by the merchant Samuel Codner, would work only with evangelical churchmen[38]—and Feild was not considered an evangelical although he denied having any high church sympathies. Bishop Feild's insistence that his church be treated separately by the government, like the Roman Catholic Church, provoked the Methodists to petition the legislature in 1851 against any division of the Protestant school grant; but separate Methodist schools were given a share of the provincial grant after 1852.[39] Thus was created Newfoundland's system of state-supported denominational schools that is unique in Canada.

At the beginning of the 1850s Newfoundland Liberals demanded responsible government for their island and a political struggle ensued in which parties were largely divided along denominational lines. Roman Catholics were nearly all Liberals—Protestants by contrast, were not so solidly Conservative. In the decisive election of 1855 every Roman Catholic riding returned Liberals while most Protestant areas returned Conservatives. Victory for the Liberals and for responsible government depended on the results in predominantly Anglican Harbour Grace and two constituencies where Roman Catholics, Anglicans and Methodists were fairly balanced in numbers. This lesson in the politics of religion was not lost on P. F. Little, Newfoundland's first Roman Catholic premier, who included two Protestants in his cabinet.

A decade later Newfoundland sent two "Fathers of Confederation" to Charlottetown—one Protestant, F. T. B. Carter, the other, Ambrose Shea, a Roman Catholic. Momentarily Newfoundland seemed to be facing westward, away from Britain and towards confederation with the rest of British North America. When Carter became premier in 1865 he tried to broaden support for the Confederation movement by including Shea and another Roman Catholic Liberal in his cabinet. This coalition won an indecisive election on the Confederation issue in 1865. But Confederation was not to be for Newfoundland in the nineteenth century—the economic and social ties with the mother country proved too strong. The landing of the Transatlantic submarine cable at Heart's Content in 1866 turned Newfoundland's bonds of sentiment to bonds of steel. Britain now was unbelievably close, Canada more distant than ever, and Newfoundland's history, both secular and religious, continued to be little more than a footnote to Canada's for another four generations.

NOTES TO CHAPTER TEN

1. M. R. Kingsford, "Church Societies," *JCCHS*, VII, 1965, pp. 3-34.
2. L. N. Harding, "John, By Divine Permission—John Medley and the Church in New Brunswick," *JCCHS*, VII (4) (December 1966), pp. 76-87; E. R. Fairweather, "A Tractarian Patriarch: John Medley of Fredericton," *CJT*, VI(1) (January 1960), pp. 14-24.
3. J. S. Moir, *Church and State in Canada 1627-1827: Basic Documents*, Carleton Library No. 33 (Toronto: McClelland and Stewart, 1967), p. 69.
4. J. C. Dent, *The Canadian Portrait Gallery* (4 vols.; Toronto: Magurn, 1880-1), Vol. III, p. 200.
5. PAC, Nova Scotia Despatches, Vol. 108, pp. 97-101, printed circular from the Duke of Newcastle, 11 February 1864.
6. See W. J. Osborne, "The Right Rev. William Dollard, D.D., First Bishop of New Brunswick," *CCHAR*, 1941-2, pp. 23-28.
7. See F. J. Wilson, "The Most Rev. Thomas L. Connolly, Archbishop of Halifax," *CCHAR*, 1943-4, pp. 55-62, and N. F. Davin, *The Irishman in Canada* (Toronto: Maclear, 1877), pp. 637-39.

8. See A. L. McFadden, "The Rt. Rev. James Rogers, D.D., First Bishop of Chatham, N.B.," *CCHAR*, 1947-8, pp. 53-58, and Lawrence Landrigan, "Peter MacIntyre, Bishop of Charlottetown, P.E.I.," *CCHAR*, 1953, pp. 81-92.

9. See Antoine Bernard, *Histoire de la Survivance Acadienne 1755-1935* (Montreal: Les Clercs de Saint-Viateur, 1935), pp. 125-44.

10. J. M. Beck, *Joseph Howe: Voice of Nova Scotia*, Carleton Library No. 20 (Toronto: McClelland and Stewart, 1964), p. 144.

11. *Ibid.*, p. 145.

12. F. J. Wilson, *op. cit.*

13. *Presbyterian Witness*, 8 January, 26 February, 21 October, 4 November 1848, 13 August 1850.

14. William Gregg, *Short History of the Presbyterian Church in the Dominion of Canada* (Toronto: Poole, 1900), pp. 95-96.

15. *Missionary Register*, November 1853. On the early development of the mission see *ibid.*, January 1850 and September 1852, and George Patterson, *Missionary Life Among the Cannibals: Being the Life of the Rev. John Geddie, D.D.* (Toronto: Campbell, 1882).

16. Patterson, *op. cit.*, pp. 508.

17. See E. R. Fitch, *The Baptists of Canada* (Toronto: Standard, 1911), pp. 68-70, 90-92, and G. E. Levy, *The Baptists of the Maritime Provinces 1753-1946* (Saint John: Barnes-Hopkins, 1946), pp. 237-42.

18. T. A. Higgins, *The Life of John Mockett Cramp, D.D. 1796-1881* (Montreal: Drysdale, 1887), pp. 123, 127; and Levy, *op. cit.*, p. 164.

19. Levy, *op. cit.*, pp. 167-70; *Presbyterian Witness*, 17 and 24 November 1849, 4 May 1850.

20. Levy, *op. cit.*, pp. 156-58.

21. *Ibid.*, pp. 163, 181-83, 185.

22. E. B. Eddy, "Henry Wilkes," UCA, *The Bulletin*, 1962, pp. 18-19; *Canadian Independent*, November 1862.

23. *Canadian Independent*, November 1860, November 1862.

24. Goldwin French, *Parsons & Politics* (Toronto: Ryerson, 1962), pp. 196-97.

25. John Lathern, "Historical Sketch of Methodism in the Eastern Provinces," in *Centennial of Canadian Methodism* (Toronto: Briggs, 1891), p. 48.

26. R. S. Longley, *Acadia University, 1838-1938* (Wolfville, 1939), pp. 28-29.

27. Beck, *op. cit.*, pp. 93-94.

28. Longley, *op. cit.*, p. 46, 60.

29. Higgins, *op. cit.*, chap. X *et passim.*

30. D. W. Johnson, *History of Methodism in Eastern British America* (Sackville: Tribune, 1926), p. 365; William Wilson, *Newfoundland and its Missionaries* (Cambridge, Mass., 1866), p. 361.

31. P. J. Kennedy, "The Church in Newfoundland," *CCHAR*, 1952, pp. 37-48.

32. C. H. Mockridge, *The Bishops of the Church of England in Canada and Newfoundland* (Toronto: Brown, 1896), p. 99.

33. H. W. Tucker, *Memoir of the Life and Episcopate of Edward Feild, D.D., Bishop of Newfoundland 1844-1876* (London 1877), p. 25.

34. Quoted in F. W. Rowe, *The History of Education in Newfoundland* (Toronto: Ryerson, 1952), pp. 23-24.

35. UCA, Diary of William Marshall.

36. William Wilson, *op. cit.*, pp. 400-01, 406.

37. Quoted in Rowe, *op. cit.*, p. 46.

38. D. W. Prowse, *A History of Newfoundland* (London: Macmillan, 1895): Supplement, "A History of the Churches in Newfoundland," p. 6. By 1830 the Society was operating almost thirty schools with 3000 adults and children in day and Sunday schools.

39. Frederick Jones, "Religion, Education and Politics in Newfoundland 1836-1875," *JCCHS*, XII (4) (December 1970), pp. 63-76.

ELEVEN

The False Calm of Union

The reunion of the Canadas had no direct significance for the religious scene but the concurrent settlement of the Clergy Reserves issue allayed for a time the religious strife that had bedevilled Upper Canada. That settlement had satisfied virtually no one except its authors, the British government, yet at least few people seemed desirous of reopening the vexing question in the immediate future. After more than a decade of denominational controversy, political unrest, and finally armed rebellion, exhaustion seemed to have overtaken the two troubled colonies. The decade which followed was notable both in secular and religious life for the spirit of rebuilding and consolidation which was both welcome and necessary. Compared to the troubled 1830s the forties were a period of religious calm disturbed only by quarreling over the Anglican control of King's College and its endowment. In retrospect, however, the forties were a false calm before the most bitter period of religious strife in the history of Canada.

ANGLICAN ADVANCES

The creation of the Anglican diocese of Toronto allowed Bishop Mountain to concentrate his attention on the demographically smaller diocese of Quebec, and throughout the first decade of the union his primary concern was education. Two groups—the Newfoundland and British North America Schools Society and the Colonial Church Society—were foremost in establishing Anglican schools, all with a strongly evangelical and anti-Tractarian bias. Mountain had resigned as principal of McGill College (which functioned only as a medical faculty) and supported the establishment of Bishop's College at Lennoxville. All diocesan theological training was carried on at Bishop's after McGill's three-year-old Arts faculty ceased to teach divinity in 1846. A second interest of Mountain during these years was missionary work in the West where he cooperated with the S.P.G. and the Church Missionary

Society in finding missionaries. He personally visited the vast region by canoe from Montreal on a historic journey in 1844.

In Upper Canada John Strachan threw himself into the organization of the new diocese with his accustomed energy. The settlement of the Clergy Reserves question and the exclusion of Strachan and Mountain from the Legislative Council of the United Canadas had gone far towards reducing the political image of the Church of England. In 1840 Strachan traversed the whole of his jurisdiction even to Sault Ste Marie, confirming nearly two thousand; thereafter he visited one-third of his diocese annually. As part of his long-held ambition to Canadianize the Church he founded a theological college at Cobourg in 1842. A diocesan church society was organized with branches in every parish to bring together all the varied aims and operations of older church-affiliated groups. Finally, Strachan's favourite educational child, King's College, began teaching in 1843, seventeen years after being chartered, with three professors imported from England and twenty-six students.

At his first visitation in 1841 Strachan's hour-and-a-half charge called on all his clergy to work so that "every obstacle [may be] removed which in any way hinders our Catholic and Apostolic Church from receiving into her bosom the vast majority of our growing population."[1] The proportion of Anglicans in the provincial population was indeed rising and perhaps to Strachan his long-cherished dream of an Anglican colony seemed closer to realization than ever before. His charge, however, also touched on his favourite theme of churchmanship, "evangelical truth and apostolic order," which he loved to cite as the distinctive mark of the Church of England. Strachan's conception of his church as an autonomous, eternal branch of the universal church, independent of both pope and king, had attracted him to the writings of Dr. E. B. Pusey, J. H. Newman and the other Tractarians of England, collectively called the Oxford Movement. These "few devout and learned men" had "manfully and heroically come forward to stem the torrent [of Erastianism],"[2] the same torrent that had just despoiled the church of its sacred patrimony, the Clergy Reserves. When Tractarianism assumed the garb of ritualism Strachan was still tolerant, perhaps even sympathetic, but when first Newman and then other Anglican clergy joined the Church of Rome, Strachan could neither excuse nor understand such "insidious proceedings" which were to him "a sort of insanity." "We are well rid of such men . . . . I cannot conceive it possible for a man of sense to become a Roman Catholic."[3] Strachan's churchmanship was fundamentally opposed to the evangelicalism of the Low Church but he would never allow either party to disturb the unity of his diocese.

Strachan had hoped in 1841 that the Clergy Reserves settlement would promote "the permanent welfare and tranquility of the province,"[4] but old problems soon returned to interrupt his busy schedule of diocesan activities.

This time it was not the principle but the practice that was at stake, for new government regulations formulated late in 1841 seemed to be directed more towards promoting settlement than ensuring the cash returns on which the church counted for support.[5] Strachan's complaints against these "destructive" regulations brought speedy intervention by the Colonial Office, but Strachan was now apprehensive and watchful for any mismanagement of the remaining endowment. The decline in immigration after the rebellions was reflected in sales of the reserves which dropped steadily until they reached a mere 569 acres in 1844. At the same time the income shrank by a third between 1841 and 1843, yet the cost of administering the reserves rose to unprecedented heights. Bureaucratic waste and inefficiency seemed to be responsible for this unsatisfactory state of affairs and the solution proposed by the Church of England was to transfer control of the Anglican share of the lands to the Church Society of the Diocese of Toronto. Canadian parliamentary committees considered the plan during two sessions but no action was taken and the Church of Scotland did not respond to Strachan's appeal for a united front. Suddenly in 1846 a political crisis was precipitated by the government's decision to suspend reserves sales and revalue the lands. Immediately certain Anglican Conservatives in the assembly proposed a division of the actual lands among all interested denominations. Opposition rose from all sides from the fear that such denominational control would establish an Irish-type tenant system in Canada at the expense of the independent farmers. The Church of England failed in this bid to obtain the reserves lands but could console itself with the knowledge that revaluation had raised the selling price of individual lots as much as 125 per cent, from which the church was bound to profit.

THE DIVIDED VOICE OF PROTESTANTISM

The dissolution of the Wesleyan Methodists' union in 1840 by the English Conference, because of differing attitudes towards church establishment, reproduced in that body the deep strains felt in similar circumstances just after the War of 1812. Several of the Canadians involved in the mission work among the Indians felt obliged to stay with the English party although their close friends supported the Canadian position. Over twelve hundred members left the Canadian Conference but seventeen thousand remained.[6] The Canadian Conference suffered another upheaval when Egerton Ryerson publicly defended Sir Charles Metcalfe during that governor general's clash with Baldwin, Lafontaine and the Reformers. Membership fell by over two thousand in 1844, and a dissident group founded their own newspaper to combat Ryerson's "political meddling." Other forces were, however, leading the rival bodies towards reunion. Competition had disrupted their work and caused financial hardship but both were equally concerned about the inroads on membership made by Millerism, a short-lived adventist movement, and by Tractarianism within the Church of England. Thanks to a more conciliatory attitude on the part of the English missionaries, reunion was achieved in 1846 and the government then began the delayed payments from the Clergy Reserves funds which permitted a rapid extension of mission fields.

Where the Wesleyans and their *Guardian* continued to avoid political involvement, the four smaller Methodist bodies—Episcopal, Bible Christian, New Connexion and Primitive—were undeniably active in their support of the Reform party, particularly on religious issues such as the Clergy Reserves. Together they about equalled the Wesleyans in numbers, but leadership came primarily from the Methodist Episcopals who had preserved the early Upper Canadian traditions of militant evangelism, circuit-rider democracy and lay participation in church management long after the Wesleyans assumed a conservative social respectability. The *Canada Christian Advocate*, founded in 1845 and taken over officially by the Methodist Episcopal Church two years later, was loud, bellicose and radical, parroting most of the Reform ideas of George Brown's *Globe* and always in the forefront of any battle that involved religious equality in the slightest degree. The *Advocate* reflected the unity of outlook shared by the non-Wesleyan Methodists and perpetuated the fighting voluntarism that the *Guardian* had represented before the union of the Canadas.

The union brought no change in the numerically inferior position of the Canadian Baptists who continued nevertheless to be the most militant and vocal voluntarists in the province. Since most Baptists were of Scottish descent they had much in common with the Free Church after 1844, but they also shared with Congregationalists the traditions of English nonconformity. Baptist influence in the Canadas was restricted however by two internal lines of division. Churches in the south and west of Upper Canada were closely allied to American Baptists; those in Lower Canada and the Ottawa Valley were usually missions organized from the "old country." These roughly national divisions were intersected by the issue of open *versus* closed communion, although the east tended to be open and the west closed. A weak union of Upper Canadian Baptist churches was formed in 1843 but collapsed six years later over the question of closed communion. Despite these divisions the Baptist fellowship was unanimous in its support of the voluntarist principle as were the small number of Congregationalists in the province.

Congregational organization in the Canadas had barely been started by Henry Wilkes before the union, although it grew during the next generation to include more than sixty churches. Most of these churches were concentrated in the towns of western Upper Canada because Congregationalism found its greatest strength in the urban middle class. Congregationalists laid particular emphasis on popular education and their most famous Canadian clergyman, Adam Lillie, was not only active in a variety of educational schemes but had an international reputation as a scientific writer. Canadian Congregationalism had few ties with the strong American Congregational tradition—rather it was closely associated with England and with the Colonial Missionary Society which provided much financial assistance and most of its preachers until the mid-1860s. Although home missions were placed under Canadian control in 1853, two thirds of the churches still depended on outside help and the habit of dependence was reflected in bitter comments about desertion by the mother country when the Colonial Missionary Society decided to reduce its support in 1861. Congregationalism was slow to identify with Canadianism, perhaps because its members were recent immigrants, and as late as Confederation less than 1 per cent of the population were reported as members of Congregational churches.[7]

One of the few religious by-products of the political union of the Canadas had been the union of the Church of Scotland and the United Secession Church in 1840, brought about by their common desire to share in the Clergy Reserves and by pressure from Lord Sydenham. Within this union the strong Presbyterian traditions of individualism, anticlericalism and antisacerdotalism soon appeared in a conflict between laity and clergy over control of their share of the Clergy Reserves income, and also in 1841 in a clash over the composition of the Board of Trustees of their new college, Queen's, at Kingston. A third and more serious incident which rocked the church involved the attempt by some ministers to manage church properties by a temporalities bill which evoked a major revolt by laymen against clerical grabs for power.

The same subterranean tension also played a part in the creation of the Free Church or Presbyterian Church of Canada in 1844. Scottish immigrants had followed attentively the controversy in the Kirk at home over "intrusion"—the practice of using civil courts to impose unwanted ministers on congregations. When Thomas Chalmers led a large party out of the Kirk in the famous Disruption of 1843, many sympathetic Church of Scotland members in Canada were eager to follow suit, even though the intrusion question was not relevant to the situation in the colonies. The arrival of a deputation from the Free Church in 1844 seeking support for their cause provided the needed catalyst in the Canadian scene, and one-quarter of the Canadian Synod's clergy withdrew in protest against having any connection with the Church in Scotland. The deputation's tour in Upper Canada became a triumphal procession, and when it reached Kingston, six of Queen's seven theological students quit the college to join the Free Church banner.

The strongest support for the Free Church in Upper Canada came from the recently settled western portion of the province—seventeen of the twenty-three ministers who formed the Free Church Synod resided west of

Kingston. Isaac Buchanan, a wealthy Toronto merchant who offered £50 to any congregation which separated from the Kirk, expressed the layman's independent attitude when he wrote, "Scotchmen when they dont [*sic*] like or differ with their Ministers will now have an alternative beside going to the Episcopalians & losing all his moral weight or to sects who are in too many cases little more than political dissenters."[8] Although only a minority of the Canadian Church of Scotland members seceded in 1844, within seven years the Free Church surpassed the Kirk in size—the Kirk attracted so few new members that it did not recoup its numerical losses until the eve of Confederation.

Both clergy and laity of the Canadian Free Church were distressed to discover that they could not continue to share in the Clergy Reserves (the continuing Church of Scotland clergy now got larger incomes because the number of claimants was reduced), and this may have been a factor in the Free Church's acceptance of the voluntary principle within five years of the Disruption. The Scottish Free Church was not voluntarist—it opposed state interference but not state support—but its Canadian branch, influenced by George Brown and his father Peter who pubilshed its unofficial paper, the *Banner*, quickly took as its own the ideal of separation of church and state and assumed the mantle of voluntarist leadership which the Wesleyan Methodists had abandoned in the mid-thirties. Another factor in this change of outlook was undoubtedly the movement for union between the Canadian Free Church and the smaller United Presbyterian Church, which was more Irish and American in its composition and adamantly voluntarist. Overtures for union came from both sides as early as 1844 but not until 1861 did the seventy United Presbyterian ministers join the one hundred and sixty-three clergy of the (Free) Presbyterian Church of Canada which had already absorbed the small remnants of the Independent Presbytery of Niagara and the Presbytery of Stamford a decade earlier.

SURVIVANCE AND CATHOLIC RENEWAL

The Roman Catholic Church, defender of the language, customs and faith of French Canada, had failed to block the union of the Canadas, but against the avowed intention to Anglicize the French Canadians the church would obviously fight with all the means at its command. Education was the key to *survivance*, and to frustrate Durham's plan for "neutral schools" as embodied in the school bill of 1841, the bishops organized the politicians of Lower Canada with considerable success. By 1845 their victory was complete as a new school act removed the objectionable clauses of the 1841 law and again placed the schools under denominational control within the traditional parish structure of the province.[9]

Much of this success was due to the influence of Bishop Bourget's newspaper, *Les Mélanges Religieux*. From its first appearance in 1841 the paper attacked nonsectarian education as destructive of faith and morality, but more importantly it promoted the spirit of renewal in the church by printing articles by and about leading French ultramontanists. The Canadian church was caught up in a wave of religious enthusiasm and a sense of national mission evidenced by the arrival in Canada of several orders—the Oblates, the Jesuits, the *Dames du Sacré-Coeur* and Sisters of the Good Shepherd among the earliest—and epitomized in the great revivalistic mission preached in Lower Canada throughout 1841 by the forceful Count de Forbin-Janson, Bishop of Nancy. Behind all these developments was Bourget, organizer of great public processions, ardent collector of holy relics during five visits to France and Rome, and the founder of two Canadian religious congregations. Although he owed much of his inspiration to his mentor Lartigue, Bourget was identified for more than a quarter century as the embodiment of the ideals and practices of ultramontanism in Canada.[10]

By the mid-forties ultramontanism in Lower Canada began to take on a political hue which it never acquired elsewhere in Canada. Churchmen and politicians in the province were being drawn together unwittingly by their common desire for French-Canadian *survivance*. Lafontaine and other Reformers, whom the church had suspected since 1837 of being anticlerical liberals, had coalesced with Baldwin's Upper Canadian Reform party because they were now convinced that responsible government could be used to defeat the Anglicizing purpose of the Union. Personal friendships were being forged between influential clerics and leading French-Canadian Reformers who were proving to be good Catholics and conservatives at heart. It was the political Conservatives now who offended the church by denying that it was autonomous with respect to the state. By 1846 this alliance of Reform politician and ultramontane churchman was firmly established in Lower Canada, was cemented by the open clerical support given to the Reformers in the election of December 1847 and became an operative force in Canadian life thereafter, thanks to the conjunction of ultramontane and French-Canadian national ambitions.

The story of the Catholic church in Upper Canada during the 1840s was a sharp contrast to the experience in Lower Canada. The church there had grown rapidly during the 1830s in its number of priests, congregations and members, until Irish elements predominated over Scottish. In 1840 seventy-seven-year-old Bishop Macdonell died during a visit to his native Scotland; his successor was Remi Gaulin, a bilingual French Canadian who as Macdonell's assistant during the War of 1812 had learned to preach in Gaelic, and who had become coadjutor of Kingston in 1833 through Lartigue's influence. Within a matter of months, however, Gaulin showed signs of the mental illness that required his removal in 1843. Irish-born Patrick Phelan then acted as coadjutor of his diocese until 1857 when he finally became its bishop just four weeks before his death. Bourget, intent like Lartigue on extending the influence of the French-Canadian church, was responsible for sending teaching and nursing orders of nuns to Kingston in 1845, but Phelan's presence gradually reduced the resentment of some of his clergy against Bourget's interference.

The time was ripe at Macdonell's death for a division of the Upper Canadian diocese and, at the suggestion of Gaulin, Lord Sydenham had encouraged the creation of a new bishopric covering the western portion of the province to which the Nova Scotian Michael Power was consecrated in 1842 as first Roman Catholic Bishop of Toronto. John Strachan had the same misgivings that Jacob Mountain had felt about two bishops using the same title, "a glaring infringement of primitive and Catholic order," but "thought it wiser to forbear"[11] and soon became like most Upper Canadians an admirer of the sensible and pious Power. Power was anxious to have his diocese share in the renewal of church life, and the first clergy retreat that he held was preached by a French Jesuit. The bishop hoped also that the Society of Jesus would return to the Indian mission work where its members had gained martyrdom two centuries earlier, but only modest progress was made in all these directions during his six-year episcopate.

Late in 1841 Power had approached the Colonial Office privately seeking the establishment of an ecclesiastical province for British North America. Quite independently Bourget was reviving Lartigue's plan for the same purpose and through his intervention the Propaganda repeated the approach to the British government in 1842. When the results were inconclusive Bourget recommended unilateral action by the church without waiting for approval from the government which he believed was "afraid of displeasing their [Anglican] clergy."[12] After considering the constitutional implications of the idea, the British Law Officers finally advised that the crown could not legally sanction such action in colonies which had been colonized rather than conquered by Britain. As Sydenham had noted earlier, there was no archbishop of the established Church of England in British North America, and lacking such a precedent the Colonial Office decided to do nothing. In any case Bishop Signay of Quebec was known to be lukewarm at best towards the project.

Impatient of such delays, Bourget forced the issue in 1843 by having seven fellow bishops sign a request to Rome for the creation of a province—only Newfoundland failed to support the appeal. When approached once more by the Propaganda the British government replied that it "had no intention of opposing the projected measure, but on the other hand it could not approve it directly"[13] because of popular reaction against the supposed Romanizing tendencies of the Tractarians in the Church of England. With a fine sensitivity for British political considerations, the papacy agreed in 1844 to the erection of the ecclesiastical province of Canada, composed of the dioceses of Quebec, Montreal, Kingston and Toronto, in the councils of which the bishops of Chatham, New Brunswick and Halifax could participate until a province was created for the Maritime colonies.

Signay thus became the first archbishop, a quarter-century after that premature elevation-on-paper of Plessis, but civil recognition of his office was complicated by the absence of any Anglican archbishop in Canada. A decision regarding recognition was forced on the government by a bill concerning parish organization. Would the statute refer to Signay by his old or his new title? In April 1846 W. E. Gladstone, then colonial secretary, cut the Gordian knot that had bound the Catholic church to the Protestant empire since 1763 by advising that "the principle of non-intervention" by the state in the internal affairs of the church be acknowledged in law—Signay should henceforth be addressed officially as "Roman Catholic Archbishop of Quebec."[14]

RELIGION AND EDUCATION

In opening the first session of the first parliament of the United Canadas Lord Sydenham reminded members of the state's duty to make "due provision for the Education of the People."[15] In Lower Canada education had from the first days of settlement been the preserve of the churches, but in religiously pluralistic Upper Canada the churches had been unable to provide facilities and the inhabitants had been unable to agree on the structure of any educational system.[16] The aim of the common school bill presented in the parliament of 1841 was to establish a system of secular elementary education for both Canadas which would promote national unification and Anglicization. Opposition to its lack of religious provisions came from Bishop Strachan and from the Roman Catholic bishops of Kingston and Quebec, but there were also numerous petitions requesting the mandatory use of the Bible in schools. The response to these criticisms was a blanket amendment permitting the establishment of minority confessional schools wherever desired.

Within two years this ideal of a national school system was abandoned and separate educational legislation was passed for both sections of the united province. Lower Canada retained the denominational basis for its schools but Upper Canada permitted dissentient schools, Roman Catholic or Protestant, only where the common school teacher belonged to the other major Christian group. The provision that no child need read any religious book or join in any religious exercise objected to by the parents underlined the assumption that if religious minorities were protected from insult confessional schools would soon disappear. This commonly held ideal was repeated by Egerton Ryerson, appointed Superintendent of Education for Canada West in 1844, in his famous report on a "System of Elementary Education." The principles of "Christianity . . . should be the basis of a

Provincial System of Education . . ." and ". . . may be carried into effect, without any compromise of principle in any party concerned. . . ." "Sectarian teaching may, as it has done, raise up an army of pugilists and persecutors, but it is not the way to create a community of Christians." "All that is essential to the moral interests of youth may be taught in what are termed Mixed Schools."[17]

Ryerson's plan of Christian schools for a Christian nation was implemented in the School Act of 1846 despite Strachan's repeated demands for separate Anglican schools. The religious clauses of the 1843 Act were included verbatim and clergy and laity of six denominations were made members of the Board of Education of which Bishop Power was elected chairman. The new system worked well at least as far as its religious aspects were concerned. Power promised to enlist the support of his clergy for the common, or mixed, schools and Ryerson reported in 1848, "I am not aware of a single complaint on this subject [of religious exercises and instruction]."[18]

In the parliamentary session of 1850, however, High Church Anglicans took advantage of a Roman Catholic request for more rural separate schools to seek their own confessional schools. The Reform Government scotched this Anglican move by offering a compromise to the Roman Catholics—separate schools within the provincial system for "Protestants, Roman Catholics or Coloured People" would be created on the request of twelve heads of families. For the first time, however, public opposition to special Roman Catholic educational privileges had been voiced in Canada West. To many the existence of confessional schools contradicted the nationalistic move towards separation of church and state which now seemed nearing success, and the *Globe* commented, "The principle thus admitted [of separate confessional schools] strikes at the root of our whole system of national education."[19] The unity of the system did not seem at that time in danger from separate schools because the number of such institutions was actually declining—only forty-six out of more than three thousand common schools in 1850—and was unlikely to increase because separate school supporters must provide and equip a schoolhouse while still paying taxes to the local common school. Up to this date opposition to the religious provisions of Ryerson's common school system had come exclusively from Anglicans, but the death of Power in October 1847 had introduced a new force to the Upper Canadian educational scene in the person of Armand de Charbonnel, French nobleman, second Roman Catholic Bishop of Toronto and a strong ultramontane proponent of his church's rights.

More troublesome during the 1840s than the relation of religion and education at the elementary level was the question of public aid to denominational universities. Continuing *de facto* Anglican control of King's College had caused the Wesleyan Methodists to convert Upper Canada Academy into Victoria College in 1842, just a few months after the Church of Scotland opened Queen's College in Kingston. Unlike Victoria, which was a literary institution, Queen's was intended to train clergy and its charter was more exclusively denominational than that of King's, but it was the financial difficulties of these two colleges that led to the first proposals for university amalgamation. The initiative came from Queen's principal, Thomas Liddell, who proposed to Egerton Ryerson, principal of Victoria, that King's College and its endowment should be secularized and that each denomination should provide a satellite seminary and residence at Toronto. At first the Methodists were reluctant to abandon their handsome although debt-ridden buildings at Cobourg, but in the best interests of the province they were prepared to support Robert Baldwin's bill for a university along the lines suggested by Liddell. Strachan's defence of King's was immediate and violent—these "senseless and unjust clamours" would degrade the crown, disgrace the province, jeopardize property and "place all forms of error on an equality with truth."[20] The arguments on both sides were wasted however, for the Lafontaine-Baldwin government resigned from office in November 1843 while the university bill was still being debated.

Before the university question was taken up again by the politicians the Church of Scotland in Canada was shattered by the Disruption, and Queen's lost nineteen of its thirty students to the Free Church which quickly created Knox College as a theological appendage to King's. The conservative government of William Henry Draper offered a new bill in 1845 that was an attempt to compromise between national and denominational interests by making King's the teaching college of a University of Upper Canada and offering more generous grants to Queen's and Victoria than Baldwin's bill had. Opposition to Draper's bill came from the Church of England which defended its stake in King's, but also from the Free Church, Baptists, Congregationalists and smaller Methodist denominations, all of whom objected to the giving of public money to any denominational institution.

Draper's cabinet was divided on the bill and so the issue was dropped in 1845, raised again in 1846 and dropped even more hastily. The war of words between the educational secularists and nationalists on one side and the defenders of denominational colleges on the other went on, but no legislative action occurred until John A. Macdonald produced a radically new proposal in 1847 for the sharing of King's College endowment. Macdonald proposed to vest the endowment in a board representing the colleges which would pay stipulated sums to King's, Queen's, Victoria, and Regiopolis (Macdonell's Roman Catholic seminary that had not yet attained college status). These colleges would remain independent and scattered across the province rather than amalgamated at Toronto, but they would have an assured income. The reaction of the voluntarist denominations to this scheme was predictable—the endowment belonged to all Upper Canadians, not to a few preferred churches or "paltry institutions." Macdonald's bill was condemned as "utterly base and worthless" and over sixty Baptist congregations denounced the whole scheme as "unjust."[21]

Macdonald withdrew his university bill from the assembly but unlike Draper (who had by now quit politics in disgust) Macdonald had the chance to test public opinion at a general election late in 1847 when the university question attracted more attention than Baldwin's "responsible government" theme. The results proved only that Canada West was evenly divided on the university question since the Reform victory at the polls was due to Lafontaine's French-Canadian majority in Lower Canada. After a year spent on planning new policies, Baldwin, himself an Anglican of Low Church sympathies, introduced a bill to secularize King's College more completely than even his ill-fated bill in 1843 had intended. The fact that religion was to be excluded from higher education brought charges that the plan was "impious," "infidel" and "subversive."[22] Strachan was particularly bitter that the "National Church" should be despoiled of its university charter while Queen's and Victoria retained theirs, albeit without any hope of public financial aid. All protests against the proposed "godless institution" were vain—Baldwin and his Reformers had the political strength that Draper and Macdonald had lacked to impose their philosophy on higher education. The secularization of King's and the financial death warrants for Queen's and Victoria were among the first fruits of mid-Victorian liberal nationalism in the Canadas.

"BLACK FORTY-SEVEN" AND THE CHURCHES

During the colonial era the relations between the Christian denominations were more frequently characterized by contempt than by charity. Although they faced similar problems in a shared environment, occasions of interdenominational association were few. Some Protestants might meet on the common ground of temperance or anti-Clergy Reserves groups, but the antipathy of one denomination towards another, or of Protestant towards Catholic and vice versa, was only thinly veiled by a façade of good manners. Typical of the attitude of many churches was the warning of John Strachan that Anglicans should not join in Bible societies' activities because they would thus come into contact with dissenters. Apparently only national tragedies could produce any joint effort approaching Christian cooperation, and one such calamity was the terrible typhus epidemic carried to North America's shores in 1847 by Irish peasants fleeing the "Great Hunger" of the potato famine.

Ireland's potato famine, in which an estimated seven hundred thousand died of starvation, induced two hundred thousand to migrate to the new world in 1847, and about half of that number came to British North America in the overcrowded, unventilated, pestilent holds of timber ships that offered cheap passage as they returned to Canada without other cargo.[23] After 1832, when immigrants had carried the cholera to the St. Lawrence and over seven thousand persons died in the Canadas as a result, a quarantine station was erected on Grosse Isle near Quebec with an Anglican chaplain periodically in residence. The first flush of the Irish famine migration occurred in 1846 when thirty-two thousand passed through Grosse Isle. Before the full tide of 1847 word reached Canada of the outbreak of typhus fever in Ireland and some precautionary measures were taken. By June, however, over 10 per cent of the first ten thousand arrivals were in hospital, and another ninety thousand were en route to Canada. Over five thousand died at sea; another thirty-five hundred were buried at Grosse Isle. To comfort the dying and bereaved, to bury the dead and care for the helpless and orphaned, fifteen Anglican clergy acted as volunteer chaplains, of whom three died, while of forty-four Roman Catholic priests assisting at Grosse Isle, five succumbed to the fever. Of his visit amidst the fetid atmosphere of the tents and sheds where bodies dead and alive lay on bare boards, Bishop Mountain wrote simply, "We witnessed most deplorable scenes . . . . I had nothing all day after breakfast but a glass of water and a crust of bread in one ship, and a cup of tea with no milk and a mouthful of toast in another."[24] Criticizing the rosy report of a Grand Jury on the condition of one Quebec hospital, another Anglican clergyman said, "If the noses of the Grand Jurors had to come as close to the sheds and the beds of the patients . . . if . . . they had to squeeze their way to the bedsides of individuals . . . and afterwards to pick from their garments the crawling things brushed on by that operation, they would hesitate how they call those places 'clean' or 'adequately spacious'."[25]

The fever was not, however, confined to the charnel house of Grosse Isle. Seemingly healthy immigrants were released who carried the disease to Quebec City, to Montreal, to Kingston, Toronto, Ottawa and smaller centres to the west. At Quebec and Montreal forty-six hundred immigrants, one Anglican and eight Roman Catholic priests, and seventeen nuns died. Further inland the stream of immigrants was more dispersed and advance warning made preventative measures possible. Nevertheless fourteen hundred unfortunates died in Kingston, two hundred in Ottawa, and nearly one thousand of the forty thousand who reached Toronto. One Presbyterian minister at Ottawa fell a victim, and one Catholic priest and a nun in Kingston, but the chief casualty at Toronto was Bishop Michael Power. Egerton Ryerson was "astounded and deeply affected" by the death of this "exceedingly agreeable and amiable man" who had chaired the Board of Education with fairness . . . zeal and intelligence" and a "scrupulous regard . . . for the views and rights and wishes of Protestants."[26] Clergy of most denominations had shared in the burdens and dangers of the plague, but those of the Churches of England and Rome suffered the heaviest losses.

The epidemic returned in 1848 and again in 1849 but with far less fatal results. The Canadian government was legally unable to stop the flow of immigrants, yet it had to assume the heavy costs of coping with the sick and dying, not to mention caring for the survivors for a longer period. Lord Elgin protested to the British government the inhumanity of Irish landlords who promoted this emigration from their overpopulated estates, and Bishop Signay warned the Irish bishops against the "dismal fate" of these "victims of speculation."[27] In the absence of adequate government machinery to cope with this crisis Christian benevolence generously supplied the money, clothing and food needed by the sufferers. Of some fifteen hundred penniless orphans in Lower Canada, six hundred were adopted by French-Canadian families—two hundred of them on one Sunday afternoon—while the rest were placed in the church's orphanages. "Black Forty-seven" as the Irish called the tragic episode, evoked, if only temporarily, among Canadians a spirit of charity and brotherhood of the highest order.

NOTES TO CHAPTER ELEVEN

1. J. L. H. Henderson, ed., *John Strachan: Documents and Opinions*, Carleton Library No. 44 (Toronto: McClelland and Stewart, 1969), p. 236.
2. *Ibid*., p. 234.
3. John S. Moir, "The Correspondence of Bishop Strachan and John Henry Newman," *CJT*, III (4) (October 1957), p. 225; see also John Kenyon, "The Influence of the Oxford Movement upon the Church of England in Upper Canada," *OH*, LI (2) (Spring 1959), pp. 79-94.
4. Henderson, *op. cit*., p. 232.
5. John S. Moir, *Church and State in Canada West: Three Studies in the Relation of Denominationalism and Nationalism, 1841-1867* (Toronto: University of Toronto Press, 1959), pp. 42-43.
6. John Carroll, *Case and His Cotemporaries* (5 vols.; Toronto: Rose, 1867-1877), Vol. IV, pp. 325-27.
7. John S. Moir, "The Canadianization of the Protestant Churches," *CHAR*, 1966, pp. 67-68.
8. QUA, Morris Papers, Isaac Buchanan to William Morris, 5 July 1844.
9. Jacques Monet, *The Last Cannon Shot: A Study of French Canadian Nationalism 1837-1850* (Toronto: University of Toronto Press, 1969), p. 209.
10. Jacques Monet, "French-Canadian Nationalism and the Challenge of Ultramontanism," *CHAR*, 1966, p. 66.
11. Henderson, *op. cit*., p. 209.
12. Lucien Lemieux, *L'Etablissement de la Première Province Ecclésiastique au Canada 1783-1844* (Montreal: Fides, 1968), pp. 497-98.
13. *Ibid*., pp. 509-10.
14. *Ibid*., p. 518.
15. J. G. Hodgins, ed., *Documentary History of Education in Upper Canada* (28 vols; Toronto: Queen's Printer, 1894-1910), Vol. IV, p. 4.
16. G. W. Spragge, "Elementary Education in Upper Canada, 1820-1840," *OH*, XLIII (3) (July 1951), pp. 107-22.
17. Hodgins, *op. cit*., Vol. VI, pp. 147 *ff*.
18. *Ibid*., Vol. VII, p. 165.
19. *Globe*, 9 July 1850.

20. Hodgins, *op. cit.*, Vol. V, pp. 27-31.
21. *Globe*, 17 July 1847; Hodgins, *op. cit.*, Vol. VII, pp. 13-21, 6-9.
22. *Church*, 17 May 1849; *Christian Guardian*, 18 and 25 April 1849.
23. For a most readable study of the potato famine and its results see Cecil Woodham-Smith, *The Great Hunger, Ireland 1845-1849* (New York: Harper & Row, 1962).
24. T. R. Millman, "The Church's Ministry to Sufferers from Typhus Fever in 1847," *CJT*, VIII (2) (April 1962), p. 132.
25. *Ibid.*, p. 133.
26. Quoted in C. B. Sissons, *Egerton Ryerson, His Life and Letters* (2 vols.; Toronto: Clarke, Irwin, 1937, 1947), Vol. II, p. 149.
27. John A. Gallagher, "The Irish Emigration of 1847 and Its Canadian Consequences," *CCHAR*, 1935-6, p. 49.

TWELVE

The Clash of Many Loyalties

As the province of Canada entered the second half of the nineteenth century it also entered a revolutionary age which brought about drastic and disturbing changes in the habits of everyday life and thinking. The coming of the railways, telegraph, daily newspapers, steam-powered factories, improved agricultural practices and farm machinery introduced Canada to the industrial age and all of its attendant problems. Even more unsettling were the new ideological forces of nationalism and materialism, introduced from Britain and Europe by the press and by a new wave of educated, articulate and politically active immigrants, which created profound tensions and deeply divided loyalties in the colony.

Canada's institutional reformation, based on modern concepts of efficient, democratic and secular government and inaugurated by the "Great Ministry" of Lafontaine and Baldwin, first touched matters of religion with the secularization of King's College in 1849—but there the reformation stopped. To many rank and file Reformers who had waited so long in the wilderness of opposition for the opportunity to complete the separation of church and state the government's policies seemed timid in the extreme. Those long-standing irritants, the Clergy Reserves and rectories, appeared to be forgotten by the Reform leaders. Disillusionment led to dissatisfaction that found its voice in the Clear Grit movement—a compound of old-line pre-Rebellion Reformism, liberal democracy and grass-roots fear of too much and too impersonal government.

To this basically voluntarist drive against all vestiges of church-state establishment was added almost immediately one of the most serious religious controversies in Canadian history, the so-called "papal aggression" issue which, although entirely external in origin, aroused hostility between Protestants and Catholics. A series of tragic and violent events during the 1850s and the successful demand of the Catholic Church for confessional schools, embittered every aspect of life in the united Canadas and played a major part in promoting confederation as an alternative to the political union that was foundering on the rocks of irreconcilable religious, linguistic and sectional clashes of loyalties.

PAPAL AGGRESSION AND PROTESTANT CRUSADE

The secularization of King's College by the Reform government in 1849 was a harbinger of conflicting loyalties and bitter religious controversies that were to come during the 1850s, yet it cast only a pale shadow at the moment —no one in the united Canadas could have foreseen or believed the depths of emotional and physical violence that would be awakened during the next decade and a half by events both external and internal to the province. The "fiery fifties" witnessed a triple polarization of forces within Canada—denominationalism opposing the new secular creed of liberal nationalism, Protestant opposing Catholic, and English opposing French. In part these tensions reflected the inherent ambiguity of the union—two "races," two ways of life, and two main branches of the Christian Church had been forced to reside together in a single state because of Durham's recommendations. Such a general characterization is admittedly a simplification of the complex interaction of many social, economic, political and religious forces, for neither English nor French, Protestant nor Catholic, nor even particular denominations, thought, acted, reacted or voted *en bloc*. Nevertheless the picture of a community wracked by confrontations in virtually every aspect of life remains a valid one. It also explains the basis of the Confederation movement—a desire to escape from the imposed and largely artificial union.

The incident which marked the outburst of religious antagonism in the Canadas really started in England when the papacy reconstituted a Roman Catholic hierarchy for that country in 1850, three centuries after the Henrican "reformation" nationalized the Christian church there and excluded all papal authority. The so-called "papal aggression" controversy, in which the national state and national church inveighed against this intrusion by a "foreign prince" into their jurisdiction, spread to Canada (where it had little relevance to the historic church-state relation) after George Brown took up the challenge of a Catholic politician to reprint in the *Globe* a defence of the pope's action.[1] Brown, however, added his own complaints of French and Catholic political interference in the union, and when these remarks evoked a Catholic rejoinder, a battle of words was joined in which both sides found themselves pushed step by step into extremes of position and language. Sober minds on both sides warned that no one could gain from such emotion-charged arguments, but it was apparent before the election of 1851 that many ridings would be won or lost because of the "papal aggression" controversy which had aroused the latent mutual hostility of Protestant and Catholic.

The political scene was further complicated by the revolt of the Clear Grit radical Reformers who preached the doctrines of nationalism, secularism and democracy. Although three years would pass before the Grits joined forces with Brown, the champion of "Protestant ascendancy," already they agreed that the successors of Lafontaine and Baldwin were trying to buy denominational support by their policies. Another body, which shared Brown's fear of French papist domination but which Brown could never lead, was the Orange Order. At union the Orangemen in Upper Canada numbered twenty thousand; a decade later they were forty-five thousand strong and by 1860 they were estimated at one hundred thousand.[2] Despite its religious bias the Orange Order in Canada did remain primarily a Conservative political machine rather than a religious party.

The ferment over "papal aggression" had barely begun to abate when the ex-priest Alessandro Gavazzi visited Canada in 1853 to speak in favour of the Italian nationalist movement and against the reactionary policies of the papacy. At Quebec City Gavazzi's lecture was halted by a riot in which his secretary was seriously injured, and in Montreal regular troops being used as police unaccountably fired into the crowd dispersing after the lecture, killing almost a score.[3] Human error, transplanted Irish nationalism and religious hatred caused a bloody tragedy, but Protestants viewed the two episodes as a Catholic denial of free speech and conscience. The *Christian Guardian* claimed that the Gavazzi riots had been "instigated by wicked and bigoted priests"—the Catholic press retorted that Protestant editors were a "yelping pack of curs."[4] Religious antagonism in Canada reached new depths after the brutal murder of Robert Corrigan, a convert to Protestantism, at St-Sylvestre, Canada East, in 1855. First aroused by the government's apparent apathy towards this crime, Protestant papers were then infuriated when the culprits were acquitted by a partisan judge and a Catholic jury. "The Pope rules Canada," remarked one Upper Canadian newspaper, "and why not St. Sylvester?" "A murder of a Protestant with impunity . . . will pave the way to other butcheries."[5]

Butcheries did indeed follow but they were confined to Canada West and resulted from bloody riots between Orangemen and Irish Catholics. Each side had its martyrs and each in turn raised the cry of "no justice" and the accusation of jury-packing. Through 1856 to 1859 such incidents recurred particularly on St. Patrick's Day and the Twelfth of July, and the seeming inability of the government to cope with the crises brought demands in some quarters for the formation of Catholic and Protestant political parties.[6] Although the succeeding five years were marked by continuing tension without serious clashes, the turbulent climate of the whole period was a reflection of the deep forces of sectionalism, language and religion that were tearing apart the province of Canada. Durham's plan to drive the "two nations" in the double-harness of a "single state" was an obvious failure and concerned

Canadians were looking for some political mechanism to release them from the deadlock of legislative union.

Before that escape was found in Confederation, however, religious hatred was awakened once more by the activities of the Fenian Brotherhood, an American-supported national liberation movement aimed at freeing Ireland from the English yoke by any means, including terrorism in the British colonies. Late in 1864 an Orange newspaper announced its discovery of a Fenian plot to murder all Protestants and days later the Irish brotherhood wrecked an Orange hall in Toronto, desecrating the Bible, the flag and Queen Victoria's picture.[7] The *Canadian Freeman*, self-appointed voice of Irish Catholicism, first denied that Catholics were necessarily Fenians, then abused Protestants, and finally in 1866 denounced Fenianism after the Brotherhood's American members invaded Canada at Fort Erie. Protestant reaction to these events was typified by militia volunteers shouting "To Hell with the Pope" as they marched past Bishop Lynch's palace in Toronto. No such incidents occurred in Canada East, probably because Protestants were a much smaller minority there than Catholics were in Canada West, but whatever the causes these controversies which rocked Canada in the 1850s and early sixties abated on the eve of Confederation as the two Canadas accepted renewed separation as the price of religious and national progress.

THE END OF THE CLERGY RESERVES— THE SURVIVAL OF THE RECTORIES

Five days after the Reformers won the election of 1848 an announcement in the *Canada Gazette* invited churches to apply for a share of the £1,800 surplus of Clergy Reserves funds. In due course the Wesleyan Methodists, Roman Catholics and a few Lutherans and Moravians did make requests, but the voluntarist laity of the Free Church forced that body to reject the offer while the Baptists and the United Presbyterians (a small group organized in Upper Canada in 1834 by Scottish secessionists) resolved once more that the Clergy Reserves should be used "in support of Education, to be enjoyed alike by all the people."[8] The 1840 settlement had been an imposed compromise and Reformers had waited long to obtain the power to end the reserves once and for all. When more than a year passed without any announcement of the government's intentions, many Reform newspapers began to express their dissatisfaction. In the spring of 1850 the Clear Grits won a crucial by-election from the government by advocating an end to both the reserves and the rectories, and in Toronto, where parliament would meet next, clergy of the Congregationalists, Methodist Episcopals, New Connexion, Baptists, Free Church and United Presbyterians assisted in forming the Anti-Clergy Reserves Association. These developments were followed with concern by the Churches of England and Scotland, but the Wesleyan Methodists, champions of religious equality in the 1830s, remained silent, culpably silent in the opinion of all voluntarists.

At last, in 1850, J. H. Price, Commissioner of Crown Lands, introduced to the assembly thirty-one resolutions on the Clergy Reserves.[9] The first twenty-seven rehearsed the tangled history of the reserves; the remaining four called for repeal of the 1840 Act and the empowering of the Canadian parliament to dispose of the funds "as in its wisdom it may think proper." The only reservation suggested was that without acknowledging any vested denominational rights to the reserves present recipients of monies should be treated liberally. After a surprisingly calm debate Price's resolutions passed by large majorities with one exception. That exception, the resolution denying the existence of any vested denominational rights, was approved by a margin of only two votes. Lord Elgin forwarded to the crown the address based on the resolutions with his private admonition, "I must candidly say I very much doubt whether you will be able to preserve this Colony if you retain [the Act of 1840] on the Statute Book."[10]

In March 1851, the imperial government replied that it would recommend to the Mother of Parliaments a bill giving the Canadian legislature authority to settle the reserves question in any way "provided that existing rights are respected." With the supposed "final settlement" of 1840 thus jeopardized, the Churches of Scotland and England moved quickly to defend their common interests. William Morris, who had lobbied for the Kirk in 1837, now hastened to England to defend, not demand, its share of the reserves, while the Anglican bishops of Toronto, Quebec and Montreal protested to the Queen against the proposed spoliation of that "remnant and pittance" of endowment which the national church still had. Strachan, however, played his political trump card in a *Letter on the Clergy Reserves Question*, addressed to Lord John Russell but intended for consumption in Roman Catholic Canada East.[11] It was public knowledge that French-Canadian Reformers and their ultramontane clergy friends feared that the secularization of the Protestant Reserves might invite attack on Roman Catholic endowments—the large number of votes opposing Price's resolution against vested rights reflected their concern—and Strachan played heavily on the theme that Roman Catholic endowments were ten times as large as those of the Church of England. He conveniently ignored the fact that since the Conquest Catholic properties had come from private bequests, not government grants.

The hopes of the Churches of England and Scotland in Canada seemed bleak enough as many of their laity were at best apathetic, at worst openly hostile, to the preservation of this symbol of church-statism. Help, when it did come, arrived unexpectedly from the imperial parliament where Russell's Whig government postponed the promised bill until 1852 and then resigned before any action was taken. The new Tory administration of Lord Derby announced at once that it would not sponsor any Clergy Reserves bill, because the Act of 1840 left no ground "for reasonable complaint of undue favour to particular religious denominations," because a general election had occurred in Canada since Price's resolutions were passed, and because no "Accidental Majority of the Colonial Legislature, however small," would be permitted to divert the Clergy Reserves from their original and sacred purpose.[12]

By now Baldwin, Lafontaine and Price had quit political life and the capable but unpopular prime minister, Francis Hincks, arrived in London on railway business just as the Derby government made its Clergy Reserves pronouncement. Hincks immediately reminded the Derby cabinet that Canadians had been promised legislation to let them settle this Canadian question in the Canadian parliament. A denial of this right was "likely to lead to collision" with the imperial government, and as for majorities in the Canadian legislature they were no more accidental than those at Westminster.[13] The Derby government, however, chose to ignore these arguments and Hincks returned to Canada to face a rebellion in the Reform party against this and other failures of his government. This frustration of voluntarist hopes proved to be only temporary, for the Derby government was out of office by the end of 1852 and a new Liberal ministry promised quick action on the reserves. Petitions by the S.P.G. and the Church of England in Canada and another pamphlet by Strachan rehearsing his church's claims to the reserves, for the benefit of the House of Lords, did not prevent the passing of the enabling act in the spring of 1853. Strachan's faith in British justice and the Church of England was shaken "when nine Bishops out of nineteen voted for the total confiscation of the Church property in Canada."[14]

The Clergy Reserves question was now a purely Canadian matter, but for a full year, amidst growing confusion and agitation which coincided with the anti-Catholic feeling engendered by the Gavazzi riots, Hincks' government kept silent about its intentions. Cabinet members were divided on the timing of a measure to nationalize the reserves, and Lord Elgin privately suggested a general election to obtain a new mandate. That election in the summer of 1854 shattered the old Reform party and produced John A. Macdonald's new coalition of Liberal-Conservatives, pledged to complete the Reformers' plan for secularization. True to its word the new ministry introduced legislation which turned the Clergy Reserves money into municipal loan funds but guaranteed for life the payments made under the 1840 Act.

The intention of this last provision, to ensure that the payments for religion would eventually disappear, was nullified by a clause permitting the clergy individuals to commute their shares for a lump sum from which their church would provide their salary. Thus the Clergy Reserves funds in an attenuated form continued forever, "the very injustice, against which we have desired to guard," complained George Brown's *Globe*.[15] Twenty-five thousand persons petitioned against the "treachery" of this commutation scheme but public opinion was so weary of the Clergy Reserves question that any reasonable settlement seemed acceptable. The four religious bodies who had vested rights under the 1840 Act received as commutation over £380,000—the Church of England £245,000 (64 per cent), the Church of Scotland £105,000 (28 per cent), the Wesleyan Methodists nearly £10,000 (2.6 per cent) and the Roman Catholics £21,000 (5.4 per cent) from the Protestant Reserves.

The Clergy Reserves Act claimed, in its own words, to have removed "all semblance of connexion between Church and State" in Canada[16] but, in addition to the commuted funds in the hands of the four preferred denominations, another "semblance" survived in Colborne's forty-four rectories. Voluntarists had assumed that the nationalization of the reserves would involve dissolution of the rectories and in 1851 the Reform government did begin legal proceedings to test the validity of the rectory patents. The test case was not closed until 1856 when the Chancery Court decided that, however "objectionable" the rectories might be to public opinion, the patents were "not void in law."[17] To this day the forty-four Anglican rectories of Upper Canada survive as the last and anachronistic relic of that age of church establishment in Canada.

DENOMINATIONALISM *VERSUS* NATIONALISM IN EDUCATION

With the legal transformation of King's College into the completely secularized University of Toronto in 1849, religious tests and the chair of theology were abolished, no clergyman could become its president or chancellor, and the provincial university endowment was put under a government-appointed board. Queen's and Victoria were given the choice of becoming affiliated divinity halls at Toronto or remaining at Kingston and Cobourg with no hope of receiving public aid. Voluntarist denominations were overjoyed at the prospect of a single provincial university, but the Church of Scotland and the Wesleyan Methodists determined to maintain their existing colleges. For his part Strachan immediately began to collect funds for an Anglican institution to replace the lost King's and when he obtained a charter for Trinity College in 1852 Canada West had not one but four universities.

This development in turn produced two further changes in higher education. In 1853 Baldwin's successor, Francis Hincks, transformed the "godless" institution at Toronto into a teaching body, University College, and an examining University of Toronto to which denominational colleges could affiliate and from which they would receive a share of the provincial endowment. The second change was the founding of nine more denominational colleges in Canada West before 1860—five Roman Catholic and one each by the Methodist Episcopals, Congregationalists, Baptists and Free Church Presbyterians—in reaction against Baldwin's policy of centralization. Five of these became affiliates of the University of Toronto, but Trinity was not one of them.

Because of the vague arrangement for financial aid to these affiliates, the endowment was still monopolized by the University College. Complaints against the lavish expenditures of $300,000 for buildings and scholarships at Toronto became demands for sharing the endowment when economic depression in the late fifties hampered the denominational affiliates. A concerted campaign by the Wesleyan Methodists and the Church of Scotland in 1859 to force the University to live up to the spirit of the Act of 1853 again divided the forces of the denominationalists and secularists. Extended hearings before a parliamentary committee in 1860 hardened the attitudes on each side but produced no action by John A. Macdonald's government, which had only a bare majority in parliament. When the committee failed to agree on a report the *Christian Guardian* announced a series of public meetings whose object was, "not Parliamentary inquiry, but *Parliamentary legislation*."[18]

Taking advantage of this demand for equal rights to all colleges, Macdonald called an election, offering a royal commission in return for support from the denominations who wanted university reform. He won the election by a slim margin and paid his debt by appointing a three-man commission representing Victoria, Queen's and the University of Toronto. Before a report could be submitted, however, his cabinet resigned and its Reform successor shelved the commission report which favoured equal aid for degree-granting colleges within a single provincial university. Time and more pressing problems combined to forestall any accommodation between the forces of voluntarism and of religion in higher education until after Confederation.

Of far greater immediate consequence than the university question was the campaign of the Catholic Church in Canada West for total segregation of its confessional schools from the provincial educational system. Ryerson blamed foreign and ultramontane influences for Bishop de Charbonnel's demands of 1852 for a larger share of the provincial educational grant and "the full management of our Schools, as well as Protestants in Lower Canada."[19] Ryerson noted that Catholic separate schools were getting their legal share of the grant, and that these demands were opposed to the policies of the late Bishop Power. De Charbonnel's arguments had been ill-informed but he ended the exchange on an ominous note: "I hope that by making use of all constitutional means in order to obtain our right, I will not upset the Government of Canada nor its institutions."[20]

Under political pressure from the bishops and politicians of Canada East the government did pass a supplementary school Act in 1853, relieving separate school supporters from paying common school taxes. Brown and the Grits had tried vainly to end "all recognition of any portion of the community in a sectarian capacity" and to stop these "priestly encroachments" which were undermining Canada's national and secular destiny.[21] The new law was less than de Charbonnel wanted and he now threatened to use the solid bloc of French Canadians in the assembly to "unseat any ministry" that did not "meet the just requirements of Catholics."[22] When the opportunity for political action came with a general election in 1854 the separate school question did not play a decisive role, nor was it a factor in the collapse of the Reform coalition government some months later.

After the election de Charbonnel resumed his attacks on the public school system and on Ryerson personally, extending Catholic demands further by petitioning for a share of the Protestant Clergy Reserves for his schools. Ryerson answered all detailed criticism of the school system—there could be no meeting of minds on principles—and felt sure that the new government of John A. Macdonald would not support the Catholic plan for a complete dual organization of schools in Canada West. To his surprise a bill was pushed through an almost empty assembly late in the 1855 session by the votes of French-Canadian members despite opposition from all parties and most Protestant denominations of Canada West. This first separate school Act removed virtually every restriction on the creation of Roman Catholic separate schools but still provided unified provincial control over curricula and standards.

De Charbonnel thanked the government for this latest "harmless" law and his unofficial paper, the *Mirror*, hailed the act as "a complete triumph" for the church, but within a few days the bishop announced that this Act too did not go far enough.[23] When the separate school question was revived early in 1856, however, the initiative came from Upper Canadian Protestants outraged by Corrigan's murder and upset by de Charbonnel's Lenten pastoral message which stated that Roman Catholics who did not use their vote to promote separate schools committed mortal sin. One Toronto paper which had hitherto defended separate schools condemned the bishop's action as "a despotism that would crush liberty of conscience and freedom of thought . . . ."[24] From individuals and from municipal councils in Canada West sixty-five petitions were sent to the assembly demanding the repeal of all separate school legislation. The government had no intention of extending the separate school system but only the solid support of the French Canadians in the assembly saved it from defeat by a majority of Canada West who backed George Brown's resolution to remove denominationalism from elementary education in the upper province. With the Clergy Reserves gone, interdenominational Protestant feuding had been replaced by an almost united front against Catholic and French domination and only a foolhardy government would risk alienating this sectional bloc by imposing educational changes on Canada West with French-Canadian votes.

The issue of "national" schools *versus* confessional schools was still discussed spasmodically during the next few years. Although de Charbonnel retired to a French monastery in 1857 church officials still denounced public schools as "hellbegotten" while Ryerson's trenchant pen repelled all attacks on his system. After the Act of 1855 his view of the issue was essentially the same as that of Macdonald's Liberal-Conservative government, whose policy was by self-admission one of political expediency. In 1860 and again in 1861 Richard Scott, a Conservative member of the Assembly, brought in bills to alter details of the separate school law. Both were rejected after first reading, which spurred the *Canadian Freeman* to renewed effort in 1862. In conversations with the bishops Ryerson agreed to Scott's proposals, but before these were submitted to parliament Scott added clauses giving the Catholic Church control of all curricula and regulations for separate schools. The government agreed to sponsor the bill if it were amended to meet Ryerson's objections, but the defeat of Macdonald's government and its replacement by a Reform coalition delayed the bill's passage until 1863.

As the Canadian parliament prepared to debate the proposed terms of Confederation early in 1865 the Catholic press in Canada West began "a grand and final struggle"[25] to make the Upper Canadian school system identical to that of Canada East. Scott's Act of 1863 was now denounced by the Catholic Church as "a sham and a fraud," but Ryerson defended it as "a satisfactory and final settlement"[26] approved by the bishops in 1862. When no changes in the Quebec resolutions were forthcoming, advocates of extended separate school rights in Canada West took advantage of a proposed alteration of the educational law of Canada East to introduce a bill that would have created a Roman Catholic deputy superintendent, Roman Catholic normal school and Roman Catholic Council of Public Instruction, and given the church complete control over standards and curriculum. Ryerson protested to the government against this "outrageous Bill" and Upper Canadian newspapers hailed its demise on the first reading with such headlines as, "THE BISHOPS FOILED."[27]

The last pre-Confederation attempt to extend the practice of confessional schools had failed in the face of aroused public opinion in Canada West. By the same token, however, the system of separate schools had not only avoided destruction by advocates of a "national" nondenominational system but was protected by the educational clauses of the British North America Act which froze the school rights of religious minorities as they existed in 1866. The compromise between denominationalism and nationalism in the united Canadas was a legacy to the new provinces of Ontario and Quebec, but it was a legacy embittered by the memory of harsh words, opinionated viewpoints and shattered dreams both for unity and separateness.

SLAVERY, SABBATARIANISM AND TEMPERANCE

In the new age of railways, telegraphs and factories the Christian churches in Canada showed renewed concern with old social questions and a new awareness of problems created by the changing technology. Slavery had already disappeared in British North America long before it was formally abolished by the imperial parliament in 1833, and the fact that few slaves had ever been present in these northern colonies made it easy for Canadians to condemn America's "peculiar institution" and to offer moral and material support to the anti-slavery crusade.

Before the passing in 1852 of the American Fugitive Slave law which drove countless numbers of slaves to seek asylum in British territory, Canadian assistance to the refugees had been organized on denominational lines. The appearance of *Uncle Tom's Cabin* led to the formation of a nondenominational Anti-Slavery Society of Canada at Toronto in 1851, even though the book itself was not published in Canada until a full year later.[28]

The Canadian churches were never divided internally as the American churches were by the slavery issue, but it did disrupt relations between some Canadian churches and their American counterparts. In 1845 the newly organized Free Church in Canada had scolded the American Old School Presbyterian Church for its "sinful apathy" towards slavery; in 1851, 1853 and 1857 it again officially condemned American slavery while disclaiming "any design of officious intermeddling";[29] and in 1856 Synod resolved to examine its own candidates for the ministry on their attitude towards slavery. During its meetings of 1859 the same synod questioned minutely a fraternal delegate from the American New School Presbyterian Church on the topic and when the American body was found wanting, no reciprocal delegate was appointed from Canada. An additional reason for this decision was the discovery that the New School Presbyterian Church was doctrinally unsound—in other words it was theologically liberal and so at variance with the traditions of Presbyterianism in Canada.

Canadian Baptists had condemned slavery as early as 1838; Congregationalists and Anglicans later expressed the same sentiments and a few denominations went so far as to reject fellowship with pro-slavery American churches. Among the Canadian Protestant churches only the Wesleyan Methodists refused to make any pronouncement solely because of close and sympathetic ties with the American Methodist Episcopal Church. During the 1850s most of the Canadian bodies were zealously engaged in promoting anti-slavery activities, including the resettlement of escaped slaves. Of the four pre-Confederation Negro settlements in Canada West, the earliest, the Wilberforce experiment begun in 1829, remained small and weak. The Dawn colony, founded in 1842 with Congregationalist help, was short-lived and troubled and is remembered most for its famous resident, Josiah Henson, supposed to have been Harriet Beecher Stowe's inspiration for Uncle Tom. The most successful was the Elgin settlement which included the Buxton mission started in 1849 by the Free Church minister, William King. Incorporated as a joint stock company, Elgin's relatively peaceful development owed much to King's policy of encouraging religious pluralism in every aspect of its organization—two of the stockholders were Jewish.[30]

Religion, so central a force in the life of the slaves, continued to be a vital factor after they obtained their freedom. No Negro church as such was ever established but Negro congregations emerged in connection with several denominations and frequently separated from the larger body in search of a Negro identity in Canada. Until about 1840 Negroes joined unsegregated congregations but the reluctance of white-dominated churches to give Negroes equal opportunity for advancement led to the mutually agreed conclusion that separate congregations would be preferable. "As a result, the first organized Negro institution in a Canadian community usually was a church, followed by a temperance society and a school."[31] Because American Baptists were the most active supporters of anti-slavery movements the Baptist fellowship attracted the largest number of Negroes in British North America too. The earliest Negro Baptist churches (Toronto's was founded in 1829) were initially interracial but by the 1840s most were restricting membership to Negroes. At this time Negro Baptists organized the Amherstburg Association which for several years refused to cooperate with the parallel local white Long Point Baptist Association. Although the Baptist faith predominated among Canadian Negroes, other denominations—the Methodists and to a lesser extent Presbyterians, Anglicans and even Mormons—gained but failed to hold Negro members who separated and divided into a bewildering variety of sectarian groups. The first Negro Catholic bishop in the United States, however, was a graduate of the Sulpician seminary in Montreal.

The complaints of pioneer clergy in Upper Canada that the Sabbath was not properly "kept," that settlers violated the Lord's Day with such worldly and sinful pursuits as dancing, gambling and horse racing, were heard less frequently after churches and chapels appeared in most areas and the habit of Sunday church-going and Sunday rest became almost a universal practice. The coming of the railways, however, caused renewed agitation against "Sabbath profanation." That trains ran on Sunday, and that canals and post offices were also open, was doubly offensive to many because these operations were conducted by a government which was supposedly Christian. The same concern for sabbatarianism—the strict observance of the Lord's Day—was also evident in the maritime provinces, and all the British North American colonies were deeply influenced on this issue by similar contemporary movements in Britain and the United States.

In 1853 over twenty thousand Canadians petitioned the provincial parliament for the Sunday closing of all public works and offices. In the legislature George Brown presented bills for this purpose almost every year but was never able to muster a majority for his cause. Opposition to Upper Canadian sabbatarianism came from three main sources—from churchmen like John Strachan who believed Sunday should be holy but not "blue," from legalists who charged that sabbath legislation would contravene the principle of separation of church and state, and most importantly from Roman Catholics who, holding a more liberal tradition of Sunday observance, derided the Protestants' emotional and literal interpretation of the Third Commandment as a hobbyhorse inherited from the Scottish Reformation.

A third social issue which also had British and American connections was the problem of intemperance. The temperance movement had sprung up simultaneously in all the British American colonies in the late 1820s in response to the excesses caused by a plentiful and cheap supply of liquor, and from its beginning the movement was supported by all the Christian churches. The temperance cause seemed to attract increased public attention after the passing of the famous Maine Law of 1846 and its revision in 1851 which imposed total prohibition in that state. Voluntary teetotalism had long been encouraged by temperance societies but in the 1850s popular opinion in Canada West supported a campaign for legal prohibition, encouraged by the adoption of the Maine Law in thirteen American states. Moderates objected to the idea of compulsory sobriety which they denounced as a form of socialism, but the Methodists and Baptists especially threatened at each election to turn temperance into a political issue. The close connection between religious and political reformism in this period is reflected in the contemporary comment, "Almost all men who are right on the liquor law question are also right on the Clergy Reserves question."[32]

In the 1860s a new force, the Sons of Temperance, made its appearance as a powerful organization with its own newspaper, the *Good Templar*. This society did not suggest support for any particular political party but it did arrange its temperance temples into districts corresponding exactly with electoral divisions. The Sons of Temperance assumed much of the educational work previously carried on by the churches, but all their agitation for legislative action during the pre-Confederation years failed to produce any laws to deal with the temperance problem.

CANADIANIZATION AND CHURCH SELF-GOVERNMENT

The reaction of Canadian loyalism to the War of 1812 had forced the Methodist Episcopal Church to sever its American connections. With this jurisdictional naturalization came the emphasis on a native ministry and a nationalist viewpoint which some historians have considered to be the hallmark of Canadian Methodism. This development of a psychological Canadianism was no doubt advanced by the flexible system of circuit riders which brought parsons into immediate contact with the problems and aspirations of a pioneer people, a process more difficult to achieve in those churches closely bound to and by the European tradition of the static parish organization. Other denominations, particularly the Churches of England and Scotland, were also inhibited in this process of Canadianization because their mission status involved such strong physical, financial and ideological dependence on their mother churches that the umbilical cord seemed almost to be made of iron. Protestant bodies that could think, act and organize "Canadian" had more freedom of spirit and structure to Canadianize than the established-church missions. All churches, however, whatever their degree of Canadianization, continued to face a problem common throughout Canada's history—how to absorb the recurrent waves of immigrants into a life, both religious and secular, that was different from the immigrants' heritage and experience.

By the 1850s the connection of most Christian churches to their transatlantic mother churches had become largely nominal, symbolic and sentimental. In 1844 defenders of the connection with the Church of Scotland had argued that the Disruption was irrelevant in Canada because the authority of the Kirk did not extend beyond "the quay of Greenock."[33] Such overseas ties could admittedly lead to direct interference by the higher religious body in Britain, as the Canadian Methodists had found to their regret in their union of the 1830s, but it also carried advantages such as access to government, as in the case of the Clergy Reserves interests of the Churches of England and Scotland. By midcentury, however, British churches, like the Colonial Office, had accepted the anti-imperialist doctrine of free trade—they had little interest in colonial branches that should be self-supporting and little desire to interfere with their religious life.

The nationalization of the Clergy Reserves removed a major obstacle to cooperation by Protestant churches—perhaps it also consolidated their latent anti-Romanism so recently awakened by the papal aggression controversy. Since the other major Protestant groups—Methodist, Free Presbyterian, Baptist and Congregational—were officially autonomous and Canadian, the change of intellectual climate caused by the ending of the reserves most obviously affected the status and attitude of the Church of England and to a lesser degree the Church of Scotland. Their preferred positions in the colony had depended on an imperial concept of the church and as long as benefits—financial and other—flowed from the imperial connection their loyalty to the mother churches and the empire was understandable. Now, however, disestablishment—the religious counterpart of free trade and responsible government—began the Canadianization of those two churches.

Presbyterian bodies other than the Kirk had early felt the need for Canadianization. "We are too Scotch," commented one Secessionist church missionary in 1846, "—our habits, our brogue, our mode of sermonizing are all too Scotch. The Thistle is everywhere seen . . . our mission is a foreign affair. And so it will be until we employ the country born, divest it of its Scotch character, and make it Canadian . . . ."[34] A decade later the Free Church's *Canadian Presbyter* warned against following "in a slavish spirit the forms and customs of older churches." "Our Church must open her doors and bid all Canadians enter . . . ."[35] The Church of Scotland was anxious to follow this trend—"Let us as British North Americans feel that this is our country, that our interests are here, that its institutions are our institutions"[36]—yet in 1867 only twenty-two of its one hundred and twenty-five ministers were Canadian-born, and during a quarter-century Queen's had graduated only fifteen students in theology.

Although the results of nationalizing the Clergy Reserves were not as painful for the Church of Scotland as for the Church of England, it was the latter church that made the more rapid advance towards Canadianization. As early as 1832 Strachan had proposed the creation of a diocesan synod as the best means of influencing public opinion but his fellow clergy opposed lay participation in church government until the reopening of the Clergy Reserves question in 1849. Now it was hoped that involvement of the laity might still preserve the Anglican share of the reserves and save the church from "the capriciousness and risk of the voluntary system."[37] Strachan invited laymen to his visitation in 1851, and if their presence failed to save the reserves, it did begin the practice of lay participation in most phases of Anglican church government. This unofficial "synod" petitioned the Queen to legalize its existence and Strachan explained to the Archbishop of Canterbury that because the ecclesiastical law of England did not extend to the colonies there was no local power to govern the church.[38]

Later the same year five of the seven Anglican bishops in British North America meeting at Quebec proposed that synods be created for each diocese and that an ecclesiastical province be established with a "Metropolitan" who could hold councils of bishops, clergy and laity. After the separation of church and state by the Clergy Reserves Act of 1854 the Colonial Office invited the Canadian legislature to give self-government to the Church of England. Accordingly a law permitting the creation of diocesan synods was passed and, after a decision by the imperial Law Officers that the royal supremacy was not thereby impaired, was legally finalized in 1857, one year after Strachan convened the first official synod ever to meet in the British empire.

The new structure of the self-governing Church of England in Canada was completed in 1860 with the royal appointment of Bishop Francis Fulford of Montreal as metropolitan, but only for the colony of the united Canadas. Before this date, however, the seventy-six-year-old Strachan took the first step towards dividing his diocese—which now held one hundred and fifty clergy and two hundred thousand members—by inaugurating an endowment for a new bishopric, Huron, covering the western part of Upper Canada. The election of a bishop by the diocesan synod—the first such election in the history of the Church of England—took place in 1857 and did not augur well for the future peace of the church. The Low Church Irish element, so prevalent in the western region, organized a bitter campaign and got majority clerical and lay support for Dr. Benjamin Cronyn of London, Canada West, a man in Strachan's opinion "not qualified for the office and whose low views are calculated to lower the church."[39] The defeated candidate was Strachan's confidant and former student, A. N. Bethune. A second division of the Toronto diocese occurred in 1861 when the eastern portion became the diocese of Ontario. Bethune was again a candidate and again he was defeated by a graduate of Trinity College, Dublin, J. T. Lewis, after a campaign that involved interference by provincial politicians.

These unseemly races for the mitres of Huron and Ontario so disgusted George Whitaker, High Churchman and Provost of Trinity College, Toronto, that he and many leading clergy and laity suggested allowing the church in England to exercise the electoral authority of colonial diocesan synods. Despite Strachan's disappointment at the double rejection of his favourite Bethune, he would not hear of any return to colonial status for the Church of England in Canada. He advised Whitaker that his proposal ignored "the claims of the whole Canadian Clergy and neutralizes the very powers of self-government which the Church in the colonies has been so anxious to possess . . . ."[40] Strachan's ambitions for his Canadianized church and for Canadian-born Bethune were finally realized in 1866 with the latter's election as Bishop of Niagara and coadjutor-successor for Strachan in the diocese of Toronto.

Self-government of the church in Canada had already moved another step forward in 1861 with Fulford's calling of a provincial synod before the status of the church in the colonies was again called into question in 1864. Bishop Colenso of Natal, who had been condemned for heresy by the Bishop of Capetown, appealed to the Judicial Committee of the Privy Council in England and that body decided that the crown could not control the Church of England in any colony where responsible government had been granted. The church in such colonies was now a voluntary association, unconnected to the crown. The last step in self-government was therefore a Canadian statute of 1866 allowing the provincial synod to alter its own constitution.

Disturbed by the suddenness with which this unsought independence had been thrust upon the church in the colonies, the provincial synod of Canada urged the Archbishop of Canterbury in 1865 to call a general council of all branches of the Anglican communion. Although this request was rejected, the Canadian initiative was instrumental in bringing about the less formal first Lambeth Council in 1867, which created an Anglican ecclesiastical commonwealth, embracing also churches outside the political Commonwealth in spiritual loyalty to the See of Canterbury and the traditions and principles of Anglicanism.

CONFEDERATION AND THE CHURCHES

British North American confederation was the work of politicians, but the Christian churches were naturally interested in the project because of its implications for the life of a Christian nation. Officially the churches had almost nothing to say about Confederation, but the religious press was particularly vocal and, with few exceptions, unreservedly in favour of the idea. For the Protestants of Canada West Confederation was of course the means of escaping from the uncomfortable union with French and Catholic Canada East, although Baptists, Congregationalists and Presbyterians publicly expressed regrets that the perpetuation of denominational schools would be assured by the British North America Act. A more positive note of Canadianism and loyalty was frequently sounded. The *Christian Guardian* prayed that Confederation would ensure the British connection, while the *Canadian Baptist* suggested that independence might be more desirable if the imperial tie failed to provide protection from external dangers. Religious editors often expressed their approval of Confederation in terms of opportunities for Christian mission and national destiny. "Never was there a finer field than the New Dominion for the Pulpit, the Press and the Schoolmaster," commented the *Presbyterian Witness* on June 29, 1867.

For the churches this "finer field" also presented an organizational challenge. "With the coalescing of our divided provinces it is not unnatural to connect the coalescing of our divided churches." "There never was a time when [Presbyterian union] could more appropriately be brought forward than at present," wrote one observer.[41] "Why should [Methodists] not have some sort of free and godly agreement, by which they may be known as one family from Newfoundland to Vancouver's Island?" asked the *Christian Guardian*.[42] Within the next generation the example of Confederation was in fact the stimulus for unification on a nation-wide scale of all the branches of Presbyterianism in British North America and of all the branches of Methodism.

Since the Roman Catholic church in Canada East had since the Conquest viewed itself not merely as a religious organization but as the embodiment of French-Canadian cultural identity and the means divinely appointed to ensure *survivance*, the attitude of that church as expressed by its bishops was an important factor in the Confederation movement. Officially the Quebec bishops played a relatively passive role during the movement, although they were unanimous and outspoken in denouncing through their pastoral letters and circulars the Fenian threat to the valued imperial connection. Leadership for the bishops and hence for the Canadian church ordinarily came not from the archbishop but from the two forceful advocates of ultramontanism, Bourget of Montreal and L.-F. Laflèche, coadjutor of the relatively new diocese of Trois-Rivières. Laflèche's creative mind and his interest in law and nineteenth-century science gave him a broader perspective of the Confederation proposals than the more conservative Bourget seemed to acquire.

Laflèche saw in "this project of such great importance to our future" a remedy for the political paralysis created by the balanced sectional representation in the united parliament, a paralysis which he feared might lead either to civil war or domination by Canada West if Confederation was not accepted as "a platform of salvation."[43] Systematic self-isolation by French Canadians behind a wall of linguistic nationalism would be "an Evil" for both French and English "whom God has called to live under one sky as brothers." In contrast to this clarion call by Laflèche for support to the Confederation scheme, Bourget kept silent, to the dismay of some of his fellow bishops who felt his refusal to be identified either for or against the movement was being used by politicians to do "incalculable harm" to the church. Not until the British North America Act was passed into law did Bourget express his acceptance of Confederation, although the archbishop and three of his other suffragan bishops had spoken clearly and decisively in its favour long before.

As the nucleus of the future Dominion emerged in 1867 members of all denominations in all of the colonies accepted as self-evident that the new political structure was a Christian state. Over the century that lay between the Conquest and Confederation church establishment had been displaced by voluntarism and religious pluralism. To Canadians this was sufficient proof that a prime task of the central government would be "to maintain . . . Christianity throughout the land." It was therefore entirely natural to the age and to the circumstances that some Father of Confederation, perhaps Leonard Tilley of New Brunswick,[44] proposed and all Canada accepted as the motto of the new nation the text from Psalm 72, "He shall have dominion also from sea to sea and from the river unto the ends of the earth."

NOTES TO CHAPTER TWELVE

1. For Brown's involvement in the "papal aggression" controversy see J. M. S. Careless, *Brown of the Globe* (2 vols.; Toronto: Macmillan, 1959, 1963), Vol. I, pp. 125 *ff.*
2. J. S. Moir, *Church and State in Canada West: Three Studies in the Relation of Denominationalism and Nationalism 1841-1867* (Toronto: University of Toronto Press, 1959), p. 17.
3. A masterly account of this tragic episode is given in Robert Sylvain, *Alessandro Gavazzi, Clerc, Garibaldien, Prédicant des Deux Mondes* (2 vols.; Quebec, Le Centre Pédagogique, 1962), chaps. 19 and 20.
4. *Christian Guardian*, 15 June 1853; *Catholic Citizen*, 4 May 1854.
5. *Bowmanville Statesman*, 12 February 1857; *News of the Week*, 1 March 1856.
6. Moir, *op. cit.*, p. 19 *ff.*

7. *Ibid.*, pp. 23-24.
8. *Journals of the Legislative Assembly*, 1849, Appendix JJJJ.
9. J. S. Moir, *Church and State in Canada, 1627-1867: Basic Documents*, Carleton Library No. 33 (Toronto: McClelland and Stewart, 1967), pp. 217-23.
10. A. G. Doughty, ed., *The Elgin-Grey Papers 1846-1852* (4 vols.; Ottawa: King's Printer, 1937), p. 697.
11. J. L. H. Henderson, *John Strachan: Documents and Opinions*, Carleton Library No. 44 (Toronto: McClelland and Stewart, 1969), pp. 201-13.
12. Moir, *Church and State in Canada, 1627-1867: Basic Documents*, pp. 229-30.
13. *Ibid.*, pp. 231-33.
14. OA, Strachan Papers, Letter Book 1854-62, p. 141, J. Strachan to Bishop Skinner, 5 July 1856.
15. *Globe*, 18 October 1854.
16. Moir, *Church and State in Canada, 1627-1867: Basic Documents*, p. 244.
17. *Ibid.*, pp. 251-52.
18. *Christian Guardian*, 14 November 1860.
19. *Copies of Correspondence between the Roman Catholic Bishop of Toronto and the Chief Superintendent of Schools on the Subject of Separate Common Schools, in Upper Canada . . .* (Toronto, 1853), p. 10.
20. *Ibid.*, p. 27.
21. J. G. Hodgins, ed., *Documentary History of Education in Upper Canada* (28 vols.; Toronto: Queen's Printer, 1894-1910), Vol. X, p. 111; *Globe*, 2 and 5 April 1853.
22. *Catholic Citizen*, 4 May 1854.
23. Hodgins, *op. cit.*, Vol. XII, p. 40.
24. *News of the Week*, 2 February 1856.
25. *Canadian Freeman*, 5 January 1865.
26. Hodgins, *op. cit.*, Vol. XVIII, p. 314.
27. St. Catharines *Constitutional*, 9 August 1866.
28. Fred Landon, "When *Uncle Tom's Cabin* came to Canada," *OH*, XLIV (1), (January 1952), pp. 1-5.
29. J. S. Moir, "American Influences on Canadian Protestant Churches before Confederation," *Church History*, XXXVI (4) (December 1867), p. 454.
30. See Robin W. Winks, *The Blacks in Canada: A History* (Montreal: McGill-Queen's University Press, 1971), pp. 156-62, 179 *ff*, 208 *ff*.
31. *Ibid.*, p. 339.
32. Quoted in Moir, *Church and State in Canada West*, p. xv; on temperance see also *ibid.*, pp. 25-26.
33. *Draft of an Answer to the Dissent and Protest of certain Ministers and Elders who have seceded . . . .* (Kingston, 1844).
34. Knox College, Proudfoot Papers, William Proudfoot to David Anderson, 13 July 1846.
35. *Canadian Presbyter*, July 1857, April 1858.
36. *Presbyterian*, May 1860.
37. A. N. Bethune, *A Charge Delivered at the Visitation of Clergy and Churchwardens of the Archdeaconry of York . . . , 1852* (Toronto, 1852), p. 19.
38. Moir, *Church and State in Canada, 1627-1867: Basic Documents*, pp. 254-57.
39. Quoted in J. L. H. Henderson, *John Strachan* (Toronto: University of Toronto Press, 1969), p. 94.
40. OA, Strachan Papers, John Strachan to George Whitaker *et al*, 9 September 1864; see also J. L. H. Henderson, "Episcopal Elections and the Memorialists of 1864," *JCCHS*, September 1950, pp. 2-4.
41. Quoted in J. W. Grant, "Canadian Confederation and the Protestant Churches," *Church History*, XXXVIII (3) (September 1969), pp. 327-37.
42. *Christian Guardian*, 4 July 1866.
43. Quoted in Walter Ullmann, "The Quebec Bishops and Confederation," *CHR*, XLIV (3) (September 1963), 213-34.
44. D. G. Creighton, *The Road to Confederation* (Toronto: Macmillan, 1964), p. 423.

THIRTEEN

From Sea to Sea

In the vast hinterland of the Maritime and St. Lawrence regions the Christian Church was first represented by Robert Wolfall, Martin Frobisher's chaplain aboard the *Anne Francis,* who performed divine service in 1578 on Baffin Island. Almost a century passed before the next visitor, Father Charles Albanel, travelled overland from Quebec to the shores of Hudson Bay in 1671, becoming the first white man on record to reach that inland ocean by a southerly route. But no missionaries followed Albanel's northward track. Instead the first genuine missionary thrust of the church came through the well-established pattern of connection with the fur trade. After the Hudson Bay basin was ceded to Britain in 1713, French interest in exploration, trade and conversion was redirected westward. La Vérendrye, the explorer of the prairies, was accompanied in 1731 by a Jesuit, Charles Michel Mesaiger, the first priest to see the Lake of the Woods, and despite the murder of one missionary by Sioux Indians at Lake La Croix in 1736, two other Jesuits worked in La Vérendrye's post at Portage la Prairie between 1743 and 1756. After the British conquest of New France the fur trade pushed westward across the prairies and over the Rockies to the Pacific Ocean, and northward to the shores of the Arctic, but the cross did not follow the flag into the Canadian Northwest again until 1816.

RELIGION AND THE RED RIVER COLONY

The continuous religious history of the Canadian West begins with the settlement of Lord Selkirk's colony on the Red River. Selkirk, a Scotch philanthropist who sought to improve the lot of depressed and landless crofters through emigration, had bought a large interest in the Hudson's Bay Company, proprietor of all lands in Hudson Bay basin. He planned an agricultural settlement on the Red River, an area already occupied in fact but illegally by the North West fur company, and by the Métis—Scotch- and French-Indian halfbreeds—employed by the trading rival of the Hudson's Bay Company. Selkirk purchased some one hundred and ten thousand square miles (about half in present United States territory) along the Assiniboine, Red and Winnipeg Rivers, and despatched an advance party of seventy workmen via York Factory who reached the southern part of Red River in 1812. Thereafter groups of immigrants, mostly Scotch, arrived each summer at the little settlement of Kildonan on the Red River.

By 1814 Selkirk's settlers numbered two hundred, but the "Nor'westers," who considered any settlement a threat to the fur trade, convinced almost three-quarters of the immigrants to accept free passage to Upper Canada. Against the diehard remnant on the Red River the Montreal-based traders opened a campaign of intimidation that was ended only by the tragic massacre of twenty-one settlers at Seven Oaks in 1816. Selkirk answered these attacks on his colony by employing Swiss mercenaries disbanded in Canada after the War of 1812-14 to protect a new settlement built on the present site of Winnipeg, while he personally spent most of his few remaining years at Montreal in futile legal proceedings against the North West Company.

Selkirk had promised his Scotch settlers a Presbyterian minister but the only one appointed never came to the Red River. The layman James Sutherland performed baptisms and marriages for the residents of the Kildonan settlement, as an elder, from 1815 until his removal by the Nor'westers to Upper Canada in 1818. In 1819 the Presbyterian settlers asked Miles Macdonell, Selkirk's Roman Catholic agent, to seek a minister, but none was obtained. The Hudson's Bay Company first denied any knowledge of Selkirk's promise and, when documentary proof was produced, the company repudiated responsibility for Selkirk's commitments. One hundred and ten discouraged settlers left for the United States in 1835, and more followed in 1837. Despite this loss the Presbyterian community at Kildonan still grew (natural increase rather than immigration accounted for virtually all the population growth in the West before Confederation) and in 1843 the Presbyterians estimated their own numbers generously at two thousand six hundred, the Roman Catholics at three thousand two hundred, and the Anglicans, whose three churches the Presbyterians had helped to build and fill, at only two hundred. The church lot and glebe donated by Selkirk in 1817 for Presbyterian use had previously been sold to the Anglican Church Missionary Society.

While Selkirk was at Montreal in 1815 he had urged Bishop Plessis to provide missionaries for Roman Catholics in the Red River Valley, particularly for the French Canadians and his Swiss mercenaries. Plessis saw this as an opportunity to spread Catholicism "over the immense western region"[1] between Lake Superior and Hudson Bay, and in May 1816 he sent Pierre Antoine Tabeau to visit the West, on the clear understanding that Tabeau would not be dragged into the conflict of the Hudson's Bay Company with the Nor'westers. Plessis directed Tabeau to be "an angel of peace useful to everyone and taking neither side,"[2] and requested William McGillivray, the leading Nor'wester, to instruct all his agents to welcome Tabeau and permit him to minister at their posts. When Tabeau reached Rainy Lake and learned of the Seven Oaks massacre, he decided to return at once to Montreal.

By 1818 the Red River Catholics were asking for a permanent mission and, as it seemed useless to wait for peace between the rival fur companies before dispatching missionaries, Plessis sent Joseph Norbert Provencher, S. J. N. Dumoulin and a seminary student to the Red River that August. As a result of further discussions with Selkirk, Plessis was now anxious to get title to the ten thousand acres at the Red which Selkirk had promised to the church in 1817.[3] Already he was thinking of a bishop for the West, subordinate to the diocese of Quebec, but the mission was in financial trouble. Popular interest in the project had waned and Lower Canada's new governor, the Duke of Richmond, was unlikely to give any government aid. Plessis therefore opened a public subscription and asked Selkirk to approach prominent Roman Catholics in England for assistance.[4] Simultaneously a second problem arose as a result of the 1818 agreement between Britain and the United States which established the forty-ninth parallel as the international boundary in the West, and so put the mission at Pembina into American territory.

THE EXPANSION OF PROVENCHER'S MISSION

The Red River mission expanded rapidly when five young volunteers from Kamouraska, Provencher's old parish, joined him in the summer of 1819. Plessis advised his missionaries to suppress drunkenness and superstition among the Indians, but not to enter the native villages. The officers of the Hudson's Bay Company in London had expressed to Plessis their appreciation of the civilizing influence exerted by the missionaries and, as a result of Plessis' trip to Europe in 1819, Provencher was made an auxiliary to the Bishop of Quebec.

Provencher spent the winter of 1820-21 in the east, not intending to return to the mission for another year. The merger of the two great fur companies in 1821, however, made him anxious to return to the mission field. Still he waited, gathering resources for his work, until the spring of 1822 when he was consecrated Bishop of Juliopolis in great haste so that he could leave immediately with the fur brigade. The following spring Dumoulin's Pembina mission and school, with four hundred and sixty students, was abandoned because it was now outside British territory. In any case Dumoulin had lost heart in mission work and was allowed to leave the same year. This was to be the sad but recurrent experience of Provencher's first twenty years in the West—priests who came with high ambitions departed tired and discouraged within a short time. Plessis encouraged Provencher to pursue his educational efforts among the natives with a view to training Indian priests, since Quebec had no clergy to spare for the western mission.

After Provencher's return to the West his fellow bishops kept him fully informed of developments in the East, but there was seldom any interference with his work by his superior. On his side Provencher kept up a correspondence with his associates in Lower Canada, sending regular reports of the mission work, but his relations with the Hudson's Bay Company officers at the Red River were not always amicable—apparently he was less of a diplomat than Plessis.[5] At first Provencher had used part of his house at the "Forks" of the Red and Assiniboine for religious services but after 1822 he completed a wooden church, named St. Boniface in deference to the German-speaking Swiss. Around St. Boniface there grew up schools and an Indian agricultural settlement.[6]

A new venture within the mission field began in 1832 when Georges-Antoine Belcourt established the first exclusively Indian mission at St. Paul's, on the Assiniboine, thirty miles west of the Forks. During the next decade new missionaries arrived from the East to work exclusively with the natives, and by 1840 a string of mission stations stretched from Rainy Lake to Lake Winnipegosis, English River and the Assiniboine. Despite this heartening expansion of the missions Provencher faced persistent and seemingly insurmountable difficulties because of the very nature of the work. The nomadic life of the Indians forced the missionaries to travel and live under the most uncomfortable conditions, plagued by insects and dirt, often without proper food and always subject to the whims of their hosts on whom their very existence depended. Obviously the natives could contribute little to the expenses of the missionaries, so the work inevitably depended on gifts from the settled church in the East. Above all, the missionaries were prey to loneliness as they passed long months without seeing other Europeans, let alone a brother priest, among people whose ways were strange and whose language presented obstacles to everyday living, not to mention catechizing, preaching and instruction in the subtle theology of Christianity.

The western missions could offer none of the amenities of a parish in the East—comforts such as warm houses, dry clothes, good food and fellowship—and it is not to be wondered at that many missionaries of all the Christian churches who arrived there filled with enthusiasm and high hopes for the evangelization of the natives soon found the burden unbearable. Those who did conquer these myriad difficulties were men possessed of exceptional physical and moral strength. In 1842 J.-B. Thibault reached Fort Edmonton and remained there for a decade, but an attempt to form a permanent post at The Pas in 1844 was stopped by the death of the missionary at the hands of disgruntled natives.[7] Belcourt, the pioneer missionary to the Indians, was temporarily banished from Hudson's Bay Company territory in 1848 by the autocratic governor Sir George Simpson for supporting a protest of the Métis against oppressive Company rule in the West.

Bishop Provencher's biggest problem was keeping missionaries in the field. As late as 1844 he had only four priests to serve twenty-eight hundred Catholics scattered throughout the vast mission. A quarter-century of labour by a few priests had achieved very little, but a new era was dawning as help arrived from an unexpected source. In 1845 the first of the French order of Oblates of Mary Immaculate, whom Provencher had met in Montreal, came as the vanguard of the second stage of missionary enterprise among the Indians. "This diocese," Provencher had told Turgeon, "must fall into the hands of the Oblates, it could not otherwise get recruits for its clergy."[8] With that first Oblate came a Canadian novice, Alexandre-Antonin Taché, so youthful in appearance that Provencher complained about sending a boy to do a man's job.[9] Taché and the Oblate father formed a permanent mission in 1846 at Ile-à-la-Crosse in northern Saskatchewan. Three years later Taché started a further mission on Lake Athabaska, unaware that Provencher, impressed by Taché's qualities, had already requested his appointment as coadjutor.

Taché was not yet thirty when in 1853 he succeeded Provencher to a diocese covering two million square miles, and containing four secular priests and seven Oblates. He now pressed forward Provencher's expansionist plans with renewed vigour. In quick succession new missions were opened at Lac la Biche, Lake Athabaska and Nipigon while ten Oblates and three Christian Brethren were received in the diocese. In 1855 the robust young bishop had toured all the northern missions and, seized with a dream of northward expansion, had sent one missionary exploring deep into the Peace River country.

This rapid development of his diocese proved too much for Taché to handle alone, and in 1859 he obtained the scholarly Vital J. Grandin as his coadjutor. Thibault was now the only secular priest still in the diocese: everywhere the Oblates had assumed charge of the diocesan work. The Oblates' "obsession" with the North—and rivalry with Anglican missionaries—carried Father Henri Grollier as far as the Mackenzie Delta in 1859/60, where he brought peace between the Eskimo and their enemies, the Loucheux Indians.[10] Three more missions were opened in 1861—a second post near Edmonton, one on Lake Manitoba and one on Lake Caribou. Despite his frail constitution Grandin undertook a tour of the northern missions that lasted from 1861 to 1864. But the remoteness of these posts required more immediate supervision than the distant see of St. Boniface could provide, and French-born Henry Faraud, who had worked in the Athabaska region since 1846, was appointed vicar apostolic of Athabaska-Mackenzie in 1862. By 1867 the Roman Catholic missions had followed the water highways of the West to the shores of the Pacific and Arctic Oceans.

In the first three decades after Provencher's arrival the work had been discouragingly slow, but the score of years preceding Confederation had witnessed unprecedented expansion in terms of both personnel and geographic extent. In that second period the Roman Catholic church in the West had received the indelible imprint of the boundless enthusiasm and energy of the Oblate fathers from old France, under the guidance of Taché, a son of New France. As the "great lone land" of the Canadian West was about to pass from the rule of the Hudson's Bay Company into the new Dominion of Canada, the workers in the vineyard included four bishops, five secular priests, thirty-two Oblates, a score of lay brothers and seven institutions under the care of the Grey Nuns.

THE ANGLICAN CHURCH IN THE WEST

The death of Lord Selkirk may have produced, as Plessis believed, a new religious policy for the Red River Settlement on the part of the Hudson's Bay Company. Officially the company supported the Church of England throughout its territories, and, although Roman Catholics and Presbyterians comprised most of the Christians at the Red River settlement, the Reverend John West was sent there in 1820 as company chaplain with a hundred pound grant from the Church Missionary Society towards the establishment of Indian schools.[11]

In the settlement John West found no Protestant place of worship, so he occupied Selkirk's abandoned farm about three miles from Fort Douglas. A school was established among the Scotch settlers with West's companion, George Harbidge, as master. West himself, like the Roman Catholic missionaries, was busy conducting Sunday services, marrying white residents to their Indian or halfbreed mates, and baptizing their offspring, the *bois-brûlés*. In his capacity as company chaplain West visited the posts at Brandon and Qu'Appelle during the winter of 1821 before making a brief trip to Pembina. That spring he planned a modest building to serve as combined church and school, but St. John's, as it was later named, was still incomplete when he opened it in the summer of 1822.

Despite Lord Selkirk's hope that the Anglican presence would not cause a clash with the Catholics, Provencher was critical of West and of his ample financial resources. "God grant that his doctrine may not take root in the hearts of the Indian!"[12] Dumoulin characterized the Anglican as a "fanatic," and his projected Bible Society as a "heretical undertaking." West's active measures to promote elementary education were also disturbing some of the local company officials who saw in all missionary efforts a threat to the fur economy and to their own autocratic control over the West. The best hope for converting and educating the natives seemed to lie in developing settled communities, yet every Indian who abandoned the nomadic life of a hunter was a loss to the fur trade, while the dissolute habits which the fur trade seemed to encourage strained the relations of all the churches with the Hudson's Bay Company at one time or another.

John West returned to England late in 1823, making an arduous one-hundred-mile side trip on foot from York to Churchill to conduct the first church service for the Eskimos. He never fulfilled his intention of returning to the Red River, but he was followed in 1823 by David Thomas Jones, aged twenty-four, who had already been designated as West's associate in the field.[13] Under Jones a second school was opened down river from St. John's in 1824, and St. Paul's church was built at the site in 1825.

After visiting England in 1828/9 Jones launched into several new missionary ventures. The first was his ministry to the Scotch settlers who still had no clergyman of their own. To meet their religious sensitivities Jones dispensed with such parts of the Anglican liturgy as might give offense, and soon acquired a Scotch audience that appreciated his preaching ability. His next successful undertaking was the founding of the Red River Academy in 1833 (with money from the Hudson's Bay Company) and the hiring of an assistant, John Macallum, who later succeeded him as principal. Jones also supervised the replacement in 1835 of West's wooden church, St. John's, with a larger stone building, the first completed in western Canada. By the time he left the colony in 1838 his achievements were indeed considerable.

Jones had been joined in 1825 by a second Anglican clergyman, William Cockran, who, as early as 1828, regularly visited the Grand Rapids where he opened a school in 1831 and the Lower Church (or St. Andrew's) the following year.[14] Cockran also took an interest in the Crees living at Cook's Creek, still further down the Red, and opened a school there in 1834 and a church, St. Peter's, two years later. The earlier churches and schools along the Red had served the Indians only incidentally, but St. Peter's was the first Anglican step in reaching out to the western Indians in their own settlements. After Jones's departure Cockran had to look after three churches—St. John's, St. Paul's and St. Andrew's—as well as the Indian settlement singlehandedly. Thanks to the perseverance of West, Jones and Cockran, the Anglican church was now solidly rooted in the Red River Valley, but clergy were sadly lacking for parish work, to say nothing of mission extension to the Indians.

Cockran's health suffered from his unselfish devotion and by 1840 he was asking his church superiors for tangible recognition of a generation's work on the Red in the form of more assistants and a visit by a bishop. Another missionary came in 1841, and in 1844 John Macallum, the teacher, was ordained and given the Upper Church, St. John's. The Reverend James Hunter became missionary at The Pas while a native catechist was despatched to Lac la Ronge, two hundred miles north of The Pas, in 1845. By 1850 the

Church of England had determined to copy the example of the Methodists and Roman Catholics by pushing their missions westward from the Red River Valley and again it was Cockran who reconnoitred the ground and chose Portage la Prairie, to which many Red River settlers were moving, as a desirable site. St. Mary's Church was built there in 1855 and two years later Cockran himself took charge and remained there until his death in 1865. As settlement continued to press westward Anglican churches were also built at High Bluff and Poplar Point.

Cockran's second request, for an episcopal visit, was answered not by England but by the Anglican Bishop of Quebec, G. J. Mountain who spent three busy weeks of 1844 inspecting, advising, confirming and dedicating. Impressed by the great physical and spiritual progress in the region, Mountain recommended the formation of a bishopric in the West.[15] As a centre of missionary activities the Red River Settlement urgently needed diocesan organization and supervision. A ten-thousand-pound endowment for such a bishopric had been made in 1835 by a Hudson's Bay Company factor, but for years the funds were tied up in litigation. As soon as the money did become available, David Anderson, a thirty-five-year-old widower, was consecrated Bishop of Rupert's Land, and reached the Red River in October, 1849.

Anderson, a quiet scholar of delicate constitution, seemed a poor choice for a frontier diocese of such great extent and rugged climate, but he soon proved himself possessed of qualities of character that compensated for any physical or psychological disabilities.[16] Patient and kind in his personal relations, an Evangelical challenged by the opportunity to help the Indians, Anderson quickly showed that he could travel and organize. He chose St. John's for his cathedral and created two archdeaconries in 1853. A third district was formed around James Bay, where John Horden, future bishop of Moosonee, had been sent in 1851 by the Church Missionary Society in response to requests from Anderson and the Hudson's Bay Company. Anderson visited Moose Factory and ordained Horden in 1852 during a twelve-hundred-mile tour of the diocese.[17]

The death of Macallum on the day Anderson arrived meant that St. John's church and its related Academy required the bishop's immediate personal care. The Academy became St. John's College, nucleus of the future University of Manitoba, but it demanded so much of his time that when he left for a visit to England in 1856 the work declined seriously for a decade. Anderson resigned his bishopric soon after returning to England, to be succeeded by Robert Machray, a scholarly and diplomatic thirty-three-year-old Scot whose career as second Bishop of Rupert's Land spanned the whole of that great developmental period in the Canadian West—from Confederation to the creation of Saskatchewan and Alberta in 1905.

THE METHODISTS ENTER THE WEST

At the union of the British Wesleyan Methodists and the Upper Canadian Methodists in 1834, supervision of the well-established Upper Canadian Indian mission was transferred to the senior conference in England and it remained there even during their seven years of separation that followed the Rebellion. Early in 1840, at the invitation of the Hudson's Bay Company, the English Conference prepared to send its first missionaries to the West.[18] Four men were chosen, William Mason, George Barnley, Robert Terrill Rundle, and James Evans who was already in Canada. Rundle and Mason went west with the spring fur brigade—Mason to Rainy River and Rundle to Edmonton House, nine hundred miles further west. Barnley travelled from England by ship to Moose Factory on James Bay, while Evans and his wife, accompanied by Henry B. Steinhauer, an Indian assistant, followed the first two westward at a more leisurely pace to their destination, Norway House at the outlet of Lake Winnipeg. Thus, in a single dramatic move, the Methodists occupied four of the most strategic locations in the Hudson's Bay Company territories where they could meet and convert the Indians.

James Evans was twenty-seven years old when he was appointed to teach in the Canadian Methodist Indian school at Rice Lake, Upper Canada. Two years later he entered the Methodist ministry and spent most of the next decade on Indian missions.[19] Evans shared the contemporary Methodist conviction that the printed word was God's modern means of conversion and, while still at Rice Lake, he developed a system of phonetic writing of Indian languages to enable the natives to read religious texts in their own tongue. Now at Norway House Evans displayed his inventive genius by adapting his syllabic alphabet to the Cree language, by casting type with lead salvaged from tea-chest linings, mixing soot and sturgeon oil for ink, and printing scripture verses and hymns in syllabics on birch bark by using a fur baler as a press. This printing was a monumental achievement in itself, but more important was his syllabic system which could be mastered by illiterate natives in a few days and was so adaptable that Roman Catholic and Anglican missionaries could later modify it easily for use in other Indian languages and dialects.

Even before Evans began experimenting with his homemade printing press, however, he made a round trip of eleven hundred miles to York Factory to assess the possibilities of a mission there. Although he became a close friend of Donald Ross, the Hudson's Bay Company factor at Norway House, within a year he moved his mission two miles away to a site he named Rossville. There a complex of mission buildings—chapel, school and houses—soon developed as the Methodist mission centre in the West, with several hundred Indians in residence.[20] Although each missionary was pledged by the company not to interfere with the fur trade, Evans was soon in difficulties for warning the Indians against alcohol and Sunday labour, two economic essentials of the trade in the company's opinion. For the company to have opposed Evans's influence openly would have been to put itself clearly on the side of Satan. Instead, Evans was charged with immorality by his own assistant, William Mason, who had relatives in the company. Recalled to England in 1846, Evans was cleared of every charge by a church court but died a broken-hearted man within two months.

Mason, who may have been a willing tool in a plot against Evans, remained at Norway House until 1854 when he became an Anglican priest. During his years on that mission he vaccinated many Indians and at Governor Simpson's suggestion tried to introduce the manufacture of caviar. The Rainy River mission was left under Peter Jacobs, an ordained Indian, who stayed there until 1854 despite the mission's declining importance. At Moose Factory Barnley made little progress and when he left after eight years the Methodists abandoned the mission, though it was subsequently reopened by the Church of England. Far to the west the bachelor Rundle ranged constantly through the foothills of the Rockies for eight lonely years until an accident forced his return to England. Rundle's only attempt to form a mission settlement—at Pigeon Lake, with the aid of a halfbreed preacher—was frustrated by tribal warfare.[21]

It was Rundle's presence at Fort Edmonton that had motivated Bishop Provencher to send J. B. Thibault to contend for the souls of the local Indians. Thibault's activities reveal one basic difference between the missionary philosophies of the Roman Catholic Church and other denominations working with the natives. Whereas Thibault baptized over three hundred and fifty Indians during his first visit in the summer of 1842, Methodist and Anglican missionaries received few into church membership because they held that baptism should be the last, not the first, step in the civilizing of the Indians.

Of the first band of Methodist missionaries in the West and North only Henry Steinhauer, twenty years of age when he travelled with Evans, was still in the field in 1855, having served at Rainy River, Norway House, Oxford House, and finally at White Fish Lake northeast of Edmonton, where he stayed for thirty years. This first age of Methodist Indian missions in the West fell far short of its original high purposes, but the work of Evans on the Cree syllabic alphabet remained as a contribution of major importance to the education and conversion of Canada's native peoples in succeeding generations.

THE NEW ERA OF PROTESTANT MISSIONS

Beginning in the early 1850s Protestant missions in the West underwent a similar if less spectacular growth to that of the Roman Catholics. In some degree this whole development reflected a more permissive, if not helpful, attitude on the part of the Hudson's Bay Company on whose cooperation the missionaries were ultimately dependent. The loss of the Oregon territory in 1846, the necessity of permitting free trade in furs at the Red River after 1849, the rapid increase in the Métis population and growing unrest in the Red River area, all seemed to sap the energy of the company and its aging and autocratic governor, Sir George Simpson, and to encourage renewed missionary zeal on the part of the Christian churches. This change of tone was reflected in Simpson's orders for York Factory in 1849, anticipating Bishop Anderson's arrival. "Pray take care that there be no drunken scenes at York at any time, more especially when the bishop passes or during the visits of missionaries or strangers, and do not let brigades start on Sunday."[22]

From the days of John West the work of the Church of England in the Northwest had been closely connected with and dependent upon the mother church in the mother country. Except for Bishop Mountain's visit there had been no contact with the Church of England in eastern British North America. This overseas orientation continued to be a dominant factor in the West long after Anglicanism had identified itself with Canadianism in the East. A second characteristic of Anglican missionary development in the West was its closer association with sedentary Indian groups, for unlike the Roman Catholics, or even the Methodists, who ranged more widely among the nomadic tribes of the plains and tundra, Anglican missionaries continued to work primarily in settled communities, with all the attendant advantages in terms of educational and religious development as reflected in the early emergence of a native Anglican ministry.

John Horden, the Anglican missionary at Moose Factory, obtained printing equipment from England and, using Evans's syllabic system, produced prayer books and catechisms in three local dialects. In 1855, the first winter his press operated, Horden produced sixteen hundred books. Previously the Church of England had used English exclusively in its Indian missions, employing former Hudson's Bay Company interpreters, but Horden's work proved itself so effective that it opened a new era in Anglican native missions. William Mason (who had left the Methodists to accept Anglican ordination in 1854) was sent to England in 1858 to supervise the printing of the whole Bible in Cree syllabics, a monumental task completed in 1861.[23]

Although most of the Anglican missionaries in the North and West came from England, a first step towards creating an indigenous ministry was taken in 1850 when Anderson ordained Henry Budd, senior, an Indian whom John West had baptized in 1822. Other ordinations of local whites and Indians followed, and when Anderson left Rupert's Land in 1864 about a third of the twenty-two priests in the diocese had been born or raised there, a remarkable achievement for such a young and pioneering area.

Under Anderson's supervision the Anglican missionary effort was also directed into the Mackenzie River basin. In 1858 Archdeacon Hunter descended the Mackenzie River as far as Fort Good Hope, and the same year

William West Kirkby established a mission at Fort Simpson. Another missionary, Robert McDonald, began ministering to the Loucheux tribe at Fort Yukon where he spent the next forty-two years. Anglican missionary work among the Indians, and particularly the efforts of Hunter, were viewed with alarm by the Oblates who tried to establish posts at every point occupied or visited by the Anglicans. This rivalry of the missionaries was marked by bitter personal antagonism between Hunter and Grollier, each of whom was so anxious to prevent the other's gaining any advantage with the natives that the company had to arrange for their simultaneous departure from the Mackenzie River area when they both received orders to move to other missions.

In 1852 the Canadian Wesleyan Methodist Church accepted control of Western missions from the English Conference and began active supervision by sending John Ryerson to London in 1853 to obtain permission from the Hudson's Bay Company for an inspection tour the following year.[24] Ryerson's published account of his tour, *Hudson's Bay* (1855) attracted Eastern attention to this virtually unknown region. Thomas Hurlburt, a Canadian of Loyalist stock who, like James Evans, had spent his early preaching years on Indian missions,[25] and Robert Brooking, an English Methodist with experience in West Africa, went respectively to Norway House and Oxford House in 1854 to revive the nearly deserted Methodist missions.

A third missionary, Thomas Woolsey went to Rundle's "parish," the area just east of the Rockies, vacant since Rundle's departure in 1848. When Woolsey reached Edmonton in 1855, he discovered that Rundle's influence on the Indians was still alive, so he undertook to reach those who had waited so long for the return of "the herald of salvation" and to re-establish the mission at Pigeon Lake. With the approval of George McDougall, superintendent in the West and Brooking's successor at the central mission of Norway House, Woolsey also began a new station at Victoria on the North Saskatchewan River. When he left in 1863, McDougall made Victoria the western headquarters in his drive to reinvigorate the Methodist missions. From there McDougall travelled west to re-establish contact with the tribes Rundle had known a generation before. McDougall's forceful leadership was inaugurating a dynamic era in the Methodist western missions at the very moment the West was entering Canada's future.[26]

Although Selkirk had promised his Scottish settlers a clergyman of their own persuasion, thirty years later no minister had come to the patient Presbyterian settlers on the Red River and no Presbyterian missionaries had entered the West. After two generations of waiting for a Church of Scotland clergyman they were prepared to support any Presbyterian minister they could get. Their latest appeal to the Free Church of Scotland in 1846 had fallen on deaf ears—no volunteer could be found among the clergy. The General Assembly, however, did refer their petition to the Free Church in Canada where their plight aroused the interest of the indomitable Robert Burns of Knox College.[27] Burns was instrumental in getting a recent graduate, John Black, then secretary to the French-Canadian Missionary Society, as minister to the Red River. Black reached Kildonan in 1851, "the first standard bearer of the Cross" in the Northwest, as *The Ecclesiastical and Missionary Record* of August 1851 described him with uncharitable silence towards other denominations in the West.

John Black was hardly a willing standard bearer. On the night of his ordination he wrote to his brother, "I have been forced into it against my will."[28] "Nobody else would go, and so I am called on to go." Once in the settlement, however, Black's self-sacrifice brought an immediate reaction from the grateful settlers. After his first sermon given in the Anglican church, three hundred persons left to join in future services at his manse. Although he spoke no Gaelic, Black had won the unstinting support of the settlement's Scotch community. In less than two years a stone church seating five hundred was completed and debt-free, like the manse.

The church that had forced Black to bear its standard to the West seemed disinclined, however, to give him any aid. Black complained that all the synod's talk of sending an assistant ended in talk. Bibles for the Kildonan Presbyterians were obtained only through the good offices of Bishop Anderson.[29] Black, who was also concerned about the spiritual destitution of the Western Indians and about the problem of drunkenness in the settlement, took an active part in the local interdenominational temperance movement.[30] Although the Red River was only three weeks distant from Canada, the Canadian Free Church remained indifferent to Western needs.

A change in Presbyterian attitudes came only after the gold rush in British Columbia had awakened interest in the West. The same year, 1862, that the first Canadian Presbyterian missionary was despatched to the Pacific Coast, James Nisbet was sent to join Black. In his reports to the Foreign Missionary Committee, which had just adopted the West as a field of operations, Nisbet urged the immediate extension of Presbyterian missions, especially to the Indians.[31] Black, who with Nisbet now served three stations as well as Kildonan, supported this interest with a challenge to the Canadian church. "Let this be the distinction of the Synod of 1864. Let it begin the work of heathen missions and first of all let it acknowledge the claims of the heathen of our own country, of British North America."[32] The synod took up Black's challenge two years later by appointing Nisbet missionary to the Crees at Prince Albert, replacing him at the Red River by Alexander Matheson who had been born there and largely educated by Black. However belatedly, the Presbyterian Church in Canada had finally entered the western vineyard where it would reap a rich harvest during the years after Confederation.

MISSIONS BEYOND THE ROCKIES

From 1825 when the Hudson's Bay Company established Fort Vancouver in Oregon on the lower Columbia River the company tried to supply the handful of officials at the post with Anglican chaplains, but the first chaplain arrived only in 1836 and departed three years later. No replacement came until 1849 when the company shifted its headquarters to Vancouver Island because the Treaty of 1846 had given the United States control of the Oregon territory. In the intervening years the Roman Catholic Church entered the Pacific Coast area. In 1843 Jean-Baptiste Bolduc, a missionary in the Oregon territory, came to the future site of Victoria. A Belgian Jesuit, Pierre-Jean de Smet, was already working alone in the interior around Okanagan and Kamloops until 1842, when Modeste Demers, one of the pioneer priests at the Red River, joined him after a trip through the lower Fraser valley the previous year. A second Jesuit, John Nobili, followed Demers's route through the Fraser valley in 1845, while de Smet was making a two-thousand-mile circuit up the Kootenay, across to Edmonton and back down the Columbia.[33]

These early missionary travels in the vast region of the Rockies and beyond were primarily exploratory—too few priests were involved to make more than a temporary impact on the thousands of Indians they encountered. The great opportunity for evangelism among the west coast tribes could not be neglected, however, and in 1847 Demers was consecrated Bishop of Vancouver Island, suffragan to his former companion, Norbert F. Blanchet, now Bishop of Oregon City.[34] Still no fixed mission was established outside Victoria until 1858 when Oblates from Oregon settled at Esquimalt. One year later four Sisters of Ste. Anne founded a school at Victoria and the mission to the interior was reopened by two priests on Lake Okanagan.

Fort Victoria on the Island became the Hudson's Bay Company's western headquarters in 1849 but only a handful of settlers had arrived in the region before the discovery of gold on the Fraser and Cariboo rivers attracted a tidal wave of gold-seekers. To cope with the problems of law and order in the unruly mining camps, the mainland was made the separate colony of British Columbia in 1858 under Sir James Douglas who was also governor of Vancouver Island. Now the mainland area suddenly assumed a new importance for the churches and, as in the Red River valley two generations earlier, they were confronted with the double task of ministering to the new arrivals while trying to carry on their mission to the natives.

The gold rush was responsible for the appointment of George Hills as Anglican Bishop of British Columbia in 1859, and for the opening of churches at Hope, Douglas and Barkerville for the use of the miners. Similarly it forced the expansion of Roman Catholic missions to serve the miners, and Presbyterians, Methodists and Congregationalists also entered this new field of endeavour where the absence of religious influences was obvious on every hand. Describing the riotous conditions in the Cariboo, one missionary reported, "The services of public worship were conducted in a bar-room and a billiard-saloon. . . . Profane language is almost universal, and is employed with diabolical ingenuity. The names of 'Jesus Christ' and the 'Almighty' are introduced in most blasphemous connections. Going to church is known as 'the religious dodge' . . . ."[35]

Although news of the gold strike had early aroused Presbyterian missionary interest,[36] Presbyterianism was unrepresented west of the Rockies until after the union of the Free Church and United Presbyterian Synods of Canada in 1861. Inspired by the new wave of missionary activity then sweeping the whole Presbyterian communion (and undoubtedly influenced by the public interest in the West fostered by that leading Presbyterian and journalist, George Brown), the Canada Presbyterian Church despatched the Reverend Robert Jamieson to British Columbia in 1862. The Canadians were not aware that the Irish Presbyterian Church had sent the Reverend John Hall to Victoria the previous year. Finding Hall already settled there Jamieson decided to proceed to New Westminster on the mainland where he established a church. Another Canadian, Daniel Duff, joined Jamieson in 1864, but no presbytery was formed on the coast until after Confederation.[37]

The Canadian Wesleyan Methodist Church, which had taken over the western missions from the British Missionary Society in 1854, responded quickly to the challenge of the settlements on the Pacific mainland. In 1858 Enoch Wood, Superintendent of Missions, wrote the Wesleyan Missionary Society in London regarding the need for missionaries and the society replied with a grant of £500. More than a dozen Canadian preachers volunteered for service in British Columbia and four were selected in 1859.[38] Ephraim Evans, brother of the unfortunate James, reported in 1861 that their work was not progressing too well. At Fort Yale R. A. Browning had almost finished a church with the aid of all denominations, even of Confucians, but only one Methodist had contributed. For lack of a promised assistant, Evans had to remain at Victoria, while Ebenezer Robson was working with the Nanaimo Indians. Robson, the best known of the group, later made Hope his headquarters and itinerated through the scattered settlements along the Fraser until 1865.[39]

Early in 1859 the Colonial Missionary Society of the Congregational Union in England proposed to establish a mission at Victoria, and the Reverend William F. Clarke, a Canadian active in anti-slavery work in Wisconsin was chosen for the post. From the three thousand residents of the tiny capital he mustered a congregation of over one hundred, but soon he was embroiled by the "colorphobia" of some of his flock.[40] White members, mostly Americans, insisted that the numerous blacks who had come from California be isolated in a "Negro corner" of the rented church room. Within a few weeks

Clarke's congregation had become predominantly Negro as whites deserted to a second Congregational missionary, Matthew Macfie, who had arrived direct from England and established a rival and segregated congregation. Although there was a Negro preacher in Victoria, the Negroes refused to organize a Negro congregation because such a step would perpetuate the prejudice they had sought to escape by leaving the United States. Clarke, the "black man's preacher," was strongly supported by Canadian Congregationalists, but the Colonial Missionary Society saw the trouble in Victoria simply as a clash of personalities, not of principles. Despite moral support from clergymen of other denominations Clarke abandoned his mission in 1860 rather than accept segregation. Later he was vindicated by the Colonial Missionary Society which ordered Macfie to end segregation, but in any case Macfie's work collapsed in 1862 for lack of funds and Congregationalism disappeared from British Columbia until after Confederation.

While the Protestant churches concentrated mainly on the areas of white settlement during the decade of the gold rush, Roman Catholic missions, largely under Oblate auspices, were directed towards the native tribes. Other Oblate mission posts soon followed the original one on Lake Okanagan—St. Charles at New Westminster in 1860, St. Mary's, thirty miles further up the Fraser River in 1861 (where a native industrial school was opened in 1865), and St. Michael's near Fort Rupert in 1863. In the latter year, French-born Louis-Joseph d'Herbomez was made vicar apostolic on the coastal mainland, and St. Louis College was opened in Victoria. The last of the pre-Confederation Roman Catholic Indian missions was begun at Williams Lake in 1867. A controversial Anglican mission project began in 1862 when William Duncan, the Anglican Church Missionary Society lay worker at Fort Simpson, moved his Christian Tsimshians to Metlakatla to save them from the demoralizing contacts with European civilization. His educational experiments attracted much attention but his success depended largely on his personal and almost dictatorial influence over his Indian followers.[41]

By 1867 the gold rush that had fostered the missionary effort on the British Pacific coast was coming to an end. European settlement was now firmly established in southern Vancouver Island and the valley of the Fraser River. The two Pacific colonies were reunited in 1866 to assist their search for a new economic basis. For this new colony of British Columbia, for the vast Northwest stretching from the Rockies to the Great Lakes, and for the Christian churches labouring across that half of the continent, the years ahead offered the bright prospects of sharing in the transcontinental destiny of the young Dominion of Canada.

In retrospect this half-century of Christian mission in the West and North had been an era of great activity by several of the churches. Except, however, for the missions among European settlers in such places as the Red River, Victoria and the gold fields of the Fraser, where the work was essentially a prelude to the recreation of all the physical and spiritual aspects of Canada's transatlantic heritage, the achievements were spectacular for quantity rather than quality. In the process of Christianizing the scattered indigenous population, brave and devoted men had explored half a continent in the face of hardships and danger. They had converted thousands who with their descendants remained true to the new faith. But it was beyond the ability of the missionaries or the society of that era to make much improvement in the quality of life of these nomadic stone-age people. Evans's syllabic writing could open new vistas both spiritual and secular, and Mason could experiment among them with vaccinations, yet these remained isolated examples of material progress. Not until after Confederation, when West was joined to East in a dominion from sea to sea, when the transcontinental railway brought the full tide of European settlement and a link to the technological civilization of modern western Europe, would the churches be in a position to offer the native peoples much more than the promise of salvation.

NOTES TO CHAPTER THIRTEEN

1. G. L. Nute, ed., *Documents Relating to Northwest Missions 1815-1827* (St. Paul, Minnesota, Historical Society, 1942), p. 8, J.-O. Plessis to Lord Selkirk, 8 April 1816.
2. *RAPQ*, 1928-9, p. 90, J.-O. Plessis to Miles Macdonell, 8 April 1816.
3. *Ibid.*, p. 117, J.-O. Plessis to J.-H. Roux, 21 June 1818.
4. *Ibid.*, p. 126, J.-O. Plessis to Lord Selkirk, 26 January 1819.
5. Antoine d'Eshambaut, "La Compagnie de la Baie d'Hudson et l'effort missionaire," *RSCHEC*, 1944-5, pp. 89-99.
6. Alfred Bernier, "Les Pionniers du Collège de Saint-Boniface," *RSCHEC*, 1948-9, pp. 71-80.
7. Alfred A. Sinnott, "Jean Edouard Darveau, 1816-1844, First Martyr Priest among the Missionaries to the Indians in Western Canada," *CCHAR*, 1960, pp. 13-20.
8. Quoted in A. G. Morice, *History of the Catholic Church in Western Canada* (2 vols.; Toronto: Musson, 1910), Vol. I, p. 225.
9. Quoted in J.-E. Champage, *Les Missions Catholiques dans L'Ouest Canadien (1818-1875)* (Ottawa: Editions des Etudes Oblates, 1949), p. 72.
10. Lionel Groulx, "La Conquête missionaire de l'Arctique," *RSCHEC*, pp. 27-35.
11. John West, *The Substance of a Journal during a Residence at the Red River Colony* (London, 1824).
12. Nute, *op. cit.*, p. 381, J.-N. Provencher to J.-O. Plessis, 29 November 1822; *ibid*, p. 342, S. Dumoulin to J.-O. Plessis, 20 March 1822.
13. T. C. B. Boon, *The Anglican Church from the Bay to the Rockies* (Toronto: Ryerson Press, 1962), pp. 22 ff.
14. *Ibid.*, pp. 35 ff.
15. W. B. Heeney, *Leaders of the Canadian Church* (3rd Series; Toronto: Ryerson, 1943), p. 10.
16. Boon, *op. cit.*, pp. 63 ff.
17. Anderson recorded the events of his epic tour in his book, *The Net in the Bay* (London, 1854).
18. J. H. Riddell, *Methodism in the Middle West* (Toronto: Ryerson, 1946), pp. 7 ff.
19. *Wesleyan Repository*, May 1861. See also Fred Landon, "Some Letters of James Evans," *The Bulletin*, UCA, 1952, pp. 5-10, and E. R. Young, *The Apostle of the North, Rev. James Evans* (Toronto: Briggs, 1900).
20. UCA, Donald Ross Letters, various dates.

21. Riddell, *op. cit.*, pp. 24-31; Gerald Hutchison, "Early Wesleyan Missions," *The Bulletin*, UCA, 1959, pp. 32-40.
22. Quoted in George Bryce, *Mackenzie, Selkirk, Simpson* (The Makers of Canada Series) (Toronto: Oxford University Press, 1926), p. 316.
23. T. C. B. Boon, "The Use of Catechisms and Syllabics by the Early Missionaries of Rupert's Land," *The Bulletin*, UCA, 1960, pp. 8-17, and "The Centenary of the Syllabic Cree Bible, 1962-1962," *ibid.*, 1964, pp. 27-34; Norah Story, "Printing in Syllabics at Moose," *ibid.*, 1958, pp. 5-7.
24. Riddell, *op. cit.*, pp. 40-41; *Minutes of . . . Annual Conferences of the Wesleyan Methodist Church in Canada* (Toronto: Green, 1863), Vol. II, p. 212.
25. *Wesleyan Repository*, May 1861.
26. Hutchison, *op. cit.*; John Maclean, *McDougall of Alberta* (Toronto: Ryerson, 1927), pp. 14-36.
27. Burns aroused Presbyterian interest in the West with a historical account of the Free Church mission to the Red River published in *Canadian Presbyterian Magazine*, October 1851.
28. UCA, John Black Letters, John Black to James Black, 31 July 1851.
29. *Ibid.*, same to same, 9 April 1857.
30. *Ibid.*, same to same, 3 April 1861.
31. *Home and Foreign Record*, November 1862.
32. Quoted in C. W. Gordon, *The Life of James Robertson* (Toronto: Westminster, 1908), p. 88.
33. R. J. McGuiness, "The Missionary Journey of Father DeSmet, S.J., in the Years 1845-46," *CCHAR*, 1941-2, pp. 35-46; J. M. Hill, "The Most Reverend Modeste Demers, D.D., First Bishop of Vancouver Island," *ibid.*, 1953, pp. 29-35. DeSmet's account of his work can be read in his autobiographical *Life, Letters and Travels . . . 1801-1873* (4 vols. in 2; New York, 1905).
34. For the story of the Oblates in the Pacific Region see Kay Cronin, *Cross in the Wilderness* (Vancouver: Mitchell, 1959).
35. Matthew Macfie, *Vancouver Island and British Columbia* (London, 1865), p. 415.
36. *Canadian Presbyter*, August, 1858.
37. Gordon, *op. cit.*, p. 80; *Home and Foreign Record*, December 1862; George King, "Presbyterianism in Western Canada," *The Bulletin*, UCA, 1956, p. 16.
38. *Wesleyan Methodist Magazine*, January, August, 1862; E. Robson, *How Methodism Came to British Columbia* (n.p., 1904).
39. Alexander Sutherland, *Methodism in Canada* (London, 1903), pp. 282-83.
40. *Canadian Independent*, January, June, December 1860, November 1861; P. H. Reid, "Segregation in British Columbia," *The Bulletin*, UCA, 1963, pp. 1-15.
41. Of several biographies of Duncan, the most readable is J. W. Arctander, *The Apostle of Alaska* (2nd ed.; Westwood, N.J.: Revell, 1909). For a critical analysis of Duncan's work see Morris Zaslow, "The Missionary as Social Reformer: The Case of William Duncan," *JCCHS*, VIII (3) (September 1966), pp. 52-69.

Abbreviations

ARCHIVES

DOA — Archives of the Anglican Diocese of Ontario (Kingston)
OA — Ontario Department of Public Records and Archives
PAC — Public Archives of Canada
QUA — Queen's University Archives
UCA — United Church Archives (Toronto)

PUBLICATIONS

CCHAR — *Canadian Catholic Historical Association Report*
CHAR — *Canadian Historical Association Report*
CHR — *Canadian Historical Review*
CJT — *Canadian Journal of Theology*
JCCHS — *Journal of the Canadian Church History Society*
OH — *Ontario History* (continuing *Papers and Records of the Ontario Historical Society*)
RAPQ — *Rapport de l'archiviste de la Province de Québec*
RSCHEC — *Rapport de la Société Canadienne d'Histoire de l'Eglise Catholique*

A Select Bibliography

This bibliography is not intended to be definitive in any sense, but merely to serve as a guide for the general reader to books in print, or reasonably accessible, and for the student to the major primary sources of church history available in Canada. The range of materials, both manuscript and printed, primary and secondary, relating to the theme and period of this volume is so extensive that only the most important items can be included here.

GUIDES TO MATERIALS

No bibliography of Canadian religious history exists but the following are useful finding aids. *A Current Bibliography of Canadian Church History* has been printed in *CCHAR* annually since 1964. *A Catalogue of the Maritime Baptist Historical Collection in the Library of Acadia University* (Kentville, 1955) covers both manuscript and printed materials in that repository. *The Bulletin*, published annually since 1948 by the Committee on Archives of the United Church of Canada, contains reports on both the central and regional archives of that church, as well as the guides to specific collections of papers and to materials on particular topics: Presbyterianism (1957), (1958), Methodist Episcopal Church (1964), Church of England Missionary Societies (1958), smaller denominations (1959), Foreign Missionary Committee of the Presbyterian Church (1955), Church union (1950). Finding aids, both published and unpublished, for the PAC are listed in *Guide to Calendars, Registers and Descriptive Lists of Series and Collections in the Public Archives*, Report of the Public Archives, 1949.

PRIMARY SOURCES

Manuscript

Most manuscript sources for Canadian religious history are in denominational archives but important collections also exist in some government archives. The largest repository for Protestant records is the central Archives of the United Church of Canada, currently housed in Victoria University, Toronto. Additional material relating to Presbyterianism may be consulted in the Archives of the Presbyterian Church at Knox College, Toronto, and in the Queen's University Archives. Records of the Baptist communion for the Atlantic region are kept at Acadia University, those for the rest of Canada are in the Baptist Historical Collection, McMaster University, Hamilton. The Archives of the General Synod of the Anglican Church in Toronto contain important but not extensive materials, while Anglican diocesan archives are of limited value except for Ontario Diocese (Kingston) which holds the papers of John Stuart. Roman Catholic records of dioceses and archdioceses are not as well organized or accessible as those of Protestant churches except for the individual papers of the bishops of Quebec that are stored in the Archives de la Province de Québec and which have been extensively calendared in the *RAPQ* over a number of years.

The Archives de la Province de Québec also house records of the Anglican Diocese of Quebec and many private papers relating to religious history. The Department of Public Records and Archives of Ontario contains numerous collections of religious interest including transcripts of Bishop Macdonell's papers, and most of Bishop Strachan's papers, the balance of which are in Trinity College, Toronto, and the Toronto (Public) Reference Library. Other provincial archives individually hold less important items and groups of papers concerning the Canadian churches. Except for an extensive collection of parish registers most church-related papers in the Public Archives of Canada are to be found within essentially private and political collections or in government records series.

Printed

Collections of source materials relating to Canadian religious history are rare and the following are the only ones specifically concerned with the period of this volume: Henri Têtu, ed., *Mandements, Lettres Pastorales et Circulaires des évêques de Québec* (Quebec, 1888), vols. II, III, IV; J. L. H. Henderson, ed., *John Strachan: Documents and Opinions*, Carleton Library No. 44 (Toronto: McClelland and Stewart, 1969); J. S. Moir, ed., *Church and State in Canada 1627-1867: Basic Documents*, Carleton Library No. 33 (Toronto: McClelland and Stewart, 1967); and J. S. Moir, ed., *The Cross in Canada* (Toronto: Ryerson, 1966), which reprints selections from primary and secondary sources.

Most denominational periodicals, which are such an important primary source for this period, are listed in "Canadian Denominational Periodicals in Victoria University Library," *The Bulletin*, UCA, 1953, and T. R. Millman, "Canadian Anglican Journalism in the Nineteenth Century," *JCCHS*, III, No. 5. Two books dealing with the development of the religious press are

Lorne Pierce, *The House of Ryerson, 1829-1954* (Toronto: Ryerson, 1954) and H. U. Trinier, *A Century of Service: Story of the Canadian Baptist 1854-1954* (Toronto: Board of Publication, Baptist Convention of Ontario and Quebec, 1955).

SECONDARY SOURCES

Few comprehensive histories of Canada's religious development have been written. One of the earliest was E. H. Oliver, *The Winning of the Frontier* (Toronto: Ryerson, 1930), an attempt to apply Frederick Jackson Turner's thesis of the influence of the North American frontier on Canadian religious history. H. H. Walsh's *The Christian Church in Canada* (Toronto: Ryerson, 1956) was in the author's words "a first attempt to give an over-all picture of Canadian church development" and served as the inspiration for undertaking this three-volume study. D. J. Wilson's *The Church Grows in Canada* (Toronto: Canadian Council of Churches, 1966), written for the Centennial celebrations of 1967, is lively in style but concerned primarily with the larger Protestant denominations. John W. Grant, ed., *The Churches and the Canadian Experience* (Toronto: Ryerson, 1963) is a useful collection of essays on the traditions of various denominations in Canada.

Very few denominational histories have appeared and most are now out of date. No history of the Roman Catholics or the Congregationalists exists. Philip Carrington, *The Anglican Church in Canada, a History* (Toronto: Collins, 1963), is a general treatment of its subject, as is E. R. Fitch's older volume, *The Baptists of Canada: A History of Their Progress and Achievements* (Toronto: Standard, 1911). Presbyterian history for this period is covered by William Gregg's two volumes, *History of the Presbyterian Church in the Dominion of Canada* (Toronto: Presbyterian, 1885) which stops at 1834 and *Short History of the Presbyterian Church in the Dominion of Canada* (Toronto: Poole, 1900) which covers the story to 1875. Two more readable small volumes that embody recent scholarship are N. G. Smith, A. L. Farris and H. K. Markell, *A Short History of the Presbyterian Church in Canada* (Toronto: Presbyterian, 1965) and *Enkindled by the Word: Essays on Presbyterianism in Canada* (Toronto: Presbyterian, 1966), a series of biographical studies. *Centennial of Canadian Methodism* (Toronto: Briggs, 1891) contains chapters on the various branches of Methodism that operated in this country. Dominic of Saint-Denis, *The Catholic Church in Canada: Historical and Statistical Summary* (6th ed.; Montreal: Thou, 1956) is a mine of detailed information useful for reference purposes. A. G. Dorland, *A History of the Society of Friends [Quakers] in Canada* (Toronto: Macmillan, 1927) is a serious study of that denomination; C. R. Cronmiller, *History of the Lutheran Church in Canada* (n.p., Evangelical Lutheran Synod of Canada, 1961) is a popularly written survey of its subject.

The secular history of this period is available in numerous one-volume histories of Canada, but the fullest studies, which contain excellent bibliographies, are in the Canadian Centenary Series being published by McClelland and Stewart, for which six of seven relevant volumes have been issued to date: Hilda Neatby, *Quebec, 1760-1791* (1966), G. M. Craig, *Upper Canada, 1784-1791* (1963), W. S. MacNutt, *The Atlantic Provinces, 1712-1857* (1965), J. M. S. Careless, *Canada, 1841-1857* (1967), E. E. Rich, *The North, 1670-1857* (1967) and W. L. Morton, *The Critical Years, 1857-73* (1964).

SCHOLARLY JOURNALS

It is impossible to list individual articles but the following journals and annuals deserve special note. *JCCHS* (1959-) is a quarterly magazine of Canadian Anglican history, with an index of volumes 1-10 in December 1968. *CCHAR* and *RSCHEC* have been published annually as a single volume on Catholic history since 1934. *CJT* (1955-1970) printed articles on church history in nearly every issue, as did the older *Canadian Journal of Religious Thought* (1924-1932). Neither of these periodicals has been indexed. Papers on religious topics have appeared occasionally in the quarterly *CHR* and the annual *CHAR* for which partial indexes are available. *CHR* provides in each issue a bibliography of recent publications which includes a section on religious history. *OH* contains many articles on church history but the only finding aid is a mimeographed Table of Contents available from the Ontario Historical Society. Other provincial historical journals that have carried religious history are *Bulletin des recherches historiques* (1895-) which was fully indexed, *Collections of the Nova Scotia Historical Society*, and *Saskatchewan History*. The Canadian Society of Church History, a nondenominational organization, has published its papers annually since 1967 in a mimeographed form distributed to its members. A few articles relating to Canadian church history have also from time to time been carried by various journals in the United States, the most important of which is *Church History*.

REGIONAL DENOMINATIONAL HISTORIES AND BIOGRAPHIES

Atlantic Provinces

On the "Planter" period see I. F. Mackinnon, *Settlement and Churches in Nova Scotia 1749-1776* (Montreal: Walker, 1930), W. P. Bell, *The "Foreign Protestants" and the Settlement of Nova Scotia* (Toronto: University of Toronto Press, 1961), M. W. Armstrong, "Neutrality and Religion in Revolutionary Nova Scotia" in *Historical Essays on the Atlantic Provinces*, edited by G. A. Rawlyk, Carleton Library No. 35 (Toronto: McClelland and Stewart, 1967), and J. M. Bumsted, *Henry Alline* (Toronto: University of Toronto Press, 1971). About one-half of Goldwin French's excellent study, *Parsons &*

Politics (Toronto: Ryerson, 1962) is concerned with Methodism in the Maritimes, but see also the older volumes of T. W. Smith, *History of Methodism in Eastern British America* (2 vols.; Halifax: Methodist Book Room, 1877, 1890), its sequel, D. W. Johnson, *History of Methodism in Eastern British America* (Sackville: Tribune, n.d.), and William Wilson, *Newfoundland and its Missionaries* (Cambridge, Mass., 1866). R. V. Harris, *Charles Inglis, Missionary, Loyalist, Bishop* (Toronto: General Board of Religious Education, 1937) describes the early period of Anglicanism, and William McCulloch, *Life of Thomas McCulloch D.D. Pictou* (Truro, 1920) provides background on Presbyterianism. Of the several histories of the Baptists, the most useful and most recent is G. E. Levy, *The Baptists of the Maritime Provinces 1753-1946* (Saint John: Barnes-Hopkins, 1946). A. A. Johnston, *A History of the Catholic Church in Eastern Nova Scotia*, Vol. I, 1611-1827 (Antigonish: St. Francis Xavier University Press, 1960) is a detailed history of a wider territory than the title indicates. The only extensive account of religion in Newfoundland is found in D. W. Prowse's old but compendious *History of Newfoundland* (London: Macmillan, 1895) and its supplementary chapter, "A History of the Churches in Newfoundland."

Quebec

A large number of books and articles are available on the religious history of Quebec from 1760 to 1867, but most of the writing is in French. The basic study of the Roman Catholic Church is still Auguste Gosselin's monumental *L'Eglise du Canada après la Conquête, Première Partie 1760-1775* (Quebec: Laflamme, 1916), *Deuxième Partie 1775-1789* (Quebec: Laflamme, 1917), but it should be supplemented by such modern works as Marcel Trudel, *L'Eglise canadienne sous le Régime militaire, 1759-1764* (2 vols.; Montreal, 1956; Quebec: Les Presses Universitaires Laval, 1957) and for the nineteenth century by Lucien Lemieux, *L'Etablissement de la Première Province Ecclésiastique au Canada 1783-1844* (Montreal: Fides, 1968), Léon Pouliot, *Monseigneur Bourget* (2 vols.; Montreal: Beauchemin, 1955, 1956), and Jacquet Monet, *The Last Cannon Shot: A Study of French-Canadian Nationalism 1837-1850* (Toronto: University of Toronto Press, 1969) which discusses the relationship between nationalism and ultramontanism. R. C. Dalton, *The Jesuits' Estates Question 1760-1888* (Toronto: University of Toronto Press, 1968) is a scholarly study of that long-standing land problem. Gaston Carrière, *Les Missions catholiques dans l'Est du Canada et l'honorable Compagnie de la Baie d'Hudson (1844-1900)* (Ottawa: Université d'Ottawa, 1957) and Edouard Lecompte, *Les Jésuites du Canada au XIXe siècle*, Tome Premier 1842-1872 (Montreal: Messager, 1920) are studies of two other aspects of this period.

Books on Protestant church history in Quebec are limited to the two excellent biographies by T. R. Millman, *Jacob Mountain, First Lord Bishop of Quebec* (Toronto: University of Toronto Press, 1947) and *The Life of the Right Reverend, the Honourable Charles James Stewart* (London, Ont.: Huron College, 1953), to relevant parts of S. Ivison and F. Rosser, *The Baptists in Upper and Lower Canada before 1820* (Toronto: University of Toronto Press, 1956) and W. S. Reid, *The Church of Scotland in Lower Canada, Its Struggle for Establishment* (Toronto: Presbyterian, 1936). Important background history to the religious development of the province is to be found in A. L. Burt, *The Old Province of Quebec*, Carleton Library, Nos. 37, 38 (2 vols.; Toronto: McClelland and Stewart, 1968) and H. T. Manning, *The Revolt of French Canada 1800-1835* (Toronto: Macmillan, 1962). Robert Sylvain, *Alessandro Gavazzi (1809-1889)* (2 vols.; Quebec, Centre Pédagogique, 1962) contains a masterly account of the famous Gavazzi riots.

Upper Canada

Although a wealth of material has been published on the religious history of Upper Canada, most of the standard works are now quite old and scarce. The story of Wesleyan Methodism in the province is recorded in John Carroll, *Case and His Cotemporaries* (5 vols.; Toronto: Rose, 1867-1877) while two other branches of Methodism are covered by Thomas Webster, *History of the Methodist Episcopal Church in Canada* (Hamilton: Canada Christian Advocate, 1870) and R. P. Hopper, *Old-Time Primitive Methodism in Canada* (Toronto: Briggs, 1904). Goldwin French, *Parsons & Politics* (Toronto: Ryerson, 1962) is a comparative study of Wesleyan Methodism in Upper Canada and the Maritimes. *Salvation! O the Joyful Sound*, a selection of John Carroll's writings edited by John W. Grant (Toronto: Oxford University Press, 1967) makes lively reading about the early Methodists, and C. B. Sissons, *Egerton Ryerson, His Life and Letters* (2 vols.; Toronto: Clarke, Irwin, 1937, 1947) is essential to virtually every aspect of the history of the period. Clara Thomas, *Ryerson of Upper Canada* (Toronto: Ryerson, 1969) is a briefer, popular work emphasizing Ryerson's education role. The only book approaching a regional history of the Anglican Church is W. P. Bull, *From Strachan to Owen* (Toronto: Perkins Bull Foundation, 1938) but J. L. H. Henderson, *John Strachan 1778-1867* (Toronto: University of Toronto Press, 1969) is a stimulating pen-portrait of the most famous Canadian Anglican of that time, and Anne Wilkinson, *Lions in the Way* (Toronto: Macmillan, 1956) portrays the life of the Oslers, a typical rural Anglican clergyman's family. Histories of the Roman Catholic Church in the Province are scarce, and the only generally accessible and useful volumes are W. P. Bull, *From Macdonell to McGuigan* (Toronto: Perkins Bull Foundation, 1939) and Brother Alfred (Dooner), *Catholic Pioneers in Upper Canada* (Toronto: Macmillan, 1947).

Among the histories of smaller denominations are E. E. Gray's beautifully written *Wilderness Christians: The Moravian Mission to the Delaware Indians* (Toronto: Macmillan, 1956), L. J. Burkholder, *A Brief History of the Mennonites in Ontario* (Toronto: Livingstone, 1935), and the relevant parts of S. Ivison and F. Rosser, *The Baptists in Upper and Lower Canada before 1820* (Toronto: University of Toronto Press, 1956) and Reuben Butchart, *The Disciples of Christ since 1830* (Toronto: Churches of Christ, 1949).

Fred Landon, *Western Ontario and the American Frontier*, Carleton Library No. 34 (Toronto: McClelland and Stewart, 1967) has excellent descriptions of pioneer religious life, while the following deal with aspects of the church-state issue in Upper Canada; J. S. Moir, *Church and State in Canada West* (Toronto: University of Toronto Press, 1959), F. A. Walker, *Catholic Education and Politics in Upper Canada* (Toronto: Dent, 1955), Alan Wilson, *The Clergy Reserves of Upper Canada, a Canadian Mortmain* (Toronto: University of Toronto Press, 1968) and by the same author a brief and popular version, *The Clergy Reserves of Upper Canada* (Canadian Historical Association, Historical Booklet No. 23, 1969), and finally J. L. H. Henderson, "The Abominable Incubus: The Church as by Law Established," *JCCHS*, X (September 1969), pp. 58-66. Background to the religious conflicts in Upper Canada is provided by Aileen Dunham, *Political Unrest in Upper Canada 1815-1836*, Carleton Library No. 10 (Toronto: McClelland and Stewart, 1963).

The West

Recent and good histories of this region include T. C. B. Boon, *The Anglican Church from the Bay to the Rockies* (Toronto: Ryerson, 1962), F. A. Peake, *The Anglican Church in British Columbia* (Vancouver: Mitchell, 1959) and J. H. Riddell, *Methodism in the Middle West* (Toronto: Ryerson, 1946). C. C. McLaurin, *Pioneering in Canada: a story of the Baptists* (Calgary, the author, 1939) contains good material on the early period before the Baptists entered the West. A. G. Morice, *History of the Catholic Church in Western Canada* (2 vols.; Toronto: Musson, 1910) is a storehouse of information but displays strong denominational bias. J. E. Champagne, *Les Missions catholiques dans l'Ouest canadien (1818-1875)* (Ottawa: Editions des Etudes Oblates, 1949) is a good account of the work of the Oblates, and Kay Cronin, *The Cross in the Wilderness* (Vancouver: Mitchell, 1959) describes the Oblates' missions in British Columbia.

The only book dealing with Presbyterian history in the West before Confederation is the popularly written *John Black of Old Kildonan* (Toronto: Ryerson, 1958) by Olive Knox, while the most recent biography of James Evans, *The James Evans Story* (Toronto: Ryerson, 1966) by Nan Shipley, is interesting reading but its conclusions are debatable.

STUDIES ON SPECIAL ASPECTS

In addition to the books on church-state relations cited above, see E. R. Norman, *The Conscience of the State in North America* (Cambridge: Cambridge University Press, 1968), a comparative study of the problem in Canada, Britain and the United States. C. B. Sissons, *Church and State in Canadian Education* (Toronto: Ryerson, 1959) is a province-by-province examination of that topic and the only book of its kind available. S. D. Clark, *Church and Sect in Canada* (Toronto: University of Toronto Press, 1948) is a sociological history of the role of the smaller religious groups in Canada based on most extensive reading of Canadian religious history. The moral attitudes and social beliefs of Canadians have not received much attention from historians but two items should be noted as exceptions and guideposts for future research: W. H. Elgee, *The Social Teaching of the Canadian Churches, Protestant, The Early Period, before 1850* (Toronto: Ryerson, 1964) and M. A. Garland and J. J. Talman, "Pioneer Drinking Habits and the Rise of the Temperance Agitation in Upper Canada prior to 1840," *OH*, XXVII (1931), pp. 341-364. Studies of Canadian reaction to the "Papal Aggression" controversy are J. B. Conacher, "The Politics of the 'Papal Aggression' Crisis, 1850-1851," *CCHAR*, 1959, pp. 13-28, and F. A. Walker, "Protestant Reaction in Upper Canada to the 'Popish Threat'," *ibid.*, 1951, pp. 91-107; while the North American background including some references to Canada can be found in R. A. Billington, *The Protestant Crusade, 1800-1860* (Chicago: Quadrangle, 1964).

Index